Grace Hartley's Southern Cookbook

GRACE HARTLEY'S SOUTHERN COOKBOOK

Over Forty Years of Recipes from
The Atlanta Journal

Galahad Books • New York City

Published in 1980 by
Galahad Books
95 Madison Avenue
New York, New York 10016
By arrangement with Doubleday & Company

Library of Congress Catalog Card Number: 76-6238
ISBN: 0-88365-472-5

Printed in the United States of America

IN MEMORY OF
MAMA
ALLIE BRILEY HARTLEY
A Most Remarkable Woman

Dedicated to all the good cooks who have made the book possible. And special thanks to my husband, Judson Germon, to Mary Patterson, and to Faith Brunson, who encouraged me to put these pages together.

Contents

Foreword

This book is not designed as a "know-it-all" or "do-it-all" cookbook. It is written for the pleasure of sharing recipes that have been a part of our heritage.

The recipes have come from hundreds of homes and eating places. Many of them are heirlooms passed down through several generations. I have visited in many of the homes they came from. I have personally received recipes from famous chefs and readers from far and near who have been more than generous over these forty years. They have shared their recipes not only with me but with the readers of *The Atlanta Journal* during my years as food editor.

Some of the donors claim their recipes are original. However, most of the recipes are just those people enjoy and have used for many years in their own homes. The majority are native to this area and feature many of the products grown here, such as corn and corn meal products, peas, pimiento, peanuts, pecans, sweet potatoes, chicken, and a great variety of southern vegetables. I have deliberately not attempted to make the recipes uniform, since each one reflects the personality of the sender.

The South is also noted for its breads, both quick breads and yeast breads, and most cooks take pride in serving their own homemade breads every day, whether they be biscuits, hot rolls, corn pone, or a fancy sweet bread.

Since we have people from many lands and all areas of our own country now living in the Southeast, they, too, have contributed to our vast file of recipes. These folks have also influenced the native menus and have adapted many of their regional recipes to the use of the products available here.

I grew up on a farm in middle Georgia where my family was a self-sustained unit, growing all the food we needed. A generous surplus was always available for the numerous kinfolks and friends who arrived, many times without warning.

My father was one of twelve children and my mother one of seven. This meant big family reunions several times a year, and food was a most important item!

Of course, food was a big item at any time! Cooking was a full-time job. I remember at my grandmother's house breakfast was always served just about dawn, for farmers must rise early. The table was filled with big slabs of home-grown ham, slices of bacon or sausage, eggs, plenty of generously sized biscuits, preserves, jam, jelly, and syrup—all home-grown or homemade.

As soon as breakfast was over, someone was dispatched to the garden to gather fresh vegetables for a hearty noon meal. Often, in the afternoon, there was time for a little sewing, mending, flower gardening, or perhaps visiting with a neighbor.

Supper usually consisted of the leftovers from noon with the addition of meat or rice.

Many of the practical things I know about cooking I learned while sitting on the kitchen stove wood box and keeping my eyes on Mama. The theory I learned at college, where I received my degree in home economics.

Childhood memories have filled my own kitchen as I have prepared many of Mama's wonderful dishes. Mama, who died in 1970 at age ninety-three, liked to say my cooking was better than hers!

Grace Hartley's Southern Cookbook

1

BREAD

Many a good cook's reputation rests on the wonderful breads that come from her kitchen.

Back in the early days of our country, the making of good breads was part of every young girl's training. Hot biscuits, corn pone, hoe cake, beaten biscuits, and spoon bread were only a few of the delicacies set before the family.

Women learned to make their own yeast and from this they developed a great variety of tasty breads. The use of corn meal was far-reaching and its usage was a delight in such things as hush puppies, corn meal loaf, muffins, and in combination with sweet potatoes and fruits.

The breads presented here may have been brought from many parts of the Americas or the world, but all of them have been used in homes in the South and passed along to us as favorites to be shared with others.

There is nothing quite so satisfying as the making of breads. The feel of the dough as it's mixed and kneaded, the rising of the dough as it bakes, and finally, the delight of eating. There is also nothing as tantalizing as the delightful aroma of yeast bread as it bakes.

Although we had quick breads—biscuits and corn bread—every day at our house when I was a child, only once a week or every ten days did Mama bake yeast breads. This never failed to be one of our most exciting days and we knew just exactly the time the bread would come out of the oven. Our noses told us that—and we were never too far away from the kitchen when those handsome golden loaves were ready. Mama always let us eat one loaf while it was still hot—slathered with home-churned butter!

Baked Brown Bread

1 cup seedless raisins	1 teaspoon salt
¾ cup corn meal	1 egg
¾ cup whole wheat flour	1 cup sour milk or buttermilk
1½ cups sifted all-purpose flour	¾ cup molasses
1½ teaspoons soda	2 tablespoons melted shortening
1 teaspoon baking powder	

Rinse and drain raisins. Combine with corn meal and whole wheat flour. Sift together flour, soda, baking powder, and salt, and stir into first mixture. Beat egg lightly and stir in sour milk, molasses, and shortening. Add to dry mixture and stir until all of flour is moistened. Turn into greased loaf pan, 10×5×3 inches. Bake in moderate oven, 350 degrees, about 50 minutes. Let cool about 10 minutes before slicing. 1 loaf.

Buttermilk Nut Bread

1½ cups sifted flour	2 eggs, well beaten
¾ teaspoon salt	½ cup sugar
¾ teaspoon soda	2 tablespoons butter or
1½ teaspoons baking powder	margarine, melted
¾ cup wheat germ	⅓ cup molasses
1 cup chopped walnuts	1 cup buttermilk

Sift flour, salt, soda, and baking powder together. Add wheat germ and walnuts; mix well. Stir together eggs, sugar, butter or margarine, molasses, and buttermilk. Add to dry ingredients and beat until smooth. Pour into greased 9×5×3-inch loaf pan and bake in a moderate oven, 350 degrees, for 1 to 1¼ hours. 1 loaf.

Corn Bread

1½ cups corn meal
3 tablespoons flour
1 teaspoon salt
1 teaspoon soda

2 cups buttermilk
1 egg
2 tablespoons drippings or
   butter

Sift dry ingredients together into mixing bowl. Add buttermilk and egg, stirring until combined. Melt drippings in skillet or baking pan and add to batter.

Pour batter into hot skillet or baking pan; bake at 450 degrees for 20 to 25 minutes. Cut into wedges or squares. Serve hot. Bread may also be baked in a corn-stick pan. 9 servings.

Crackling Corn Bread

Mrs. Henry Odum, Covington, Georgia

2 cups corn meal
½ cup sifted flour
3 teaspoons baking powder
2 teaspoons salt

1 egg, beaten
2 cups milk
1 cup cracklings, or more if
   desired

Sift the dry ingredients together. Add egg to milk, stirring to mix; add cracklings, chopped in small pieces, and mix well. Then pour the milk and egg into the dry mixture, beat, and bake in a greased pan in moderate oven 350 degrees for 30 to 40 minutes or until golden brown. Serve hot. 6 servings.

Soooo good! It's better than cake.

Custard Corn Bread

Mrs. C. C. Schuman, Monticello, Florida

2 eggs, beaten
¼ cup sugar
½ cup evaporated milk
½ cup water
1 cup buttermilk
1 teaspoon soda

1½ cups water-ground corn
   meal
½ cup flour
1 teaspoon salt
2 tablespoons melted butter

TOPPING:

  ½ cup evaporated milk　　　　　*½ cup water*

Combine all ingredients and pour into greased pan. Top with evaporated milk mixed with water. Do not stir. Bake at 325 degrees about 45 minutes. 6 servings.

Cranberry Bread

Mrs. James A. Lee, Atlanta, Georgia

  2 cups flour　　　　　　　　*¾ cup orange juice*
  1 cup sugar　　　　　　　　*1 tablespoon grated orange rind*
  1 teaspoon baking powder　　*1 egg, well beaten*
  ½ teaspoon soda　　　　　　*½ cup chopped nuts*
  1 teaspoon salt　　　　　　　*2 cups fresh cranberries,*
  ¼ cup shortening　　　　　　　　*coarsely chopped*

Mix and sift together flour, sugar, baking powder, soda, and salt. Cut in shortening until mixture resembles coarse corn meal. Combine orange juice and grated rind with egg. Pour all at once into dry ingredients, mixing just enough to dampen. Carefully fold in nuts and cranberries. Spoon into greased 9×5×3-inch loaf pan. Spread corners and sides slightly higher than center. Bake in a 350-degree oven for approximately 1 hour. Remove from pan. Cool. 1 loaf.

Dilly Bread

Mrs. Eugene Callaway, Rayle, Georgia

  1 package yeast　　　　　　　*1 tablespoon minced onion*
  ¼ cup lukewarm water　　　　*2 tablespoons dill seed*
  1 cup cottage cheese　　　　　*1 tablespoon butter*
  ¼ teaspoon soda　　　　　　　*1 egg, well beaten*
  2 tablespoons sugar　　　　　*2½ cups flour*
  1 teaspoon salt

Dissolve yeast in lukewarm water. Heat cottage cheese to lukewarm. In it dissolve soda, sugar, and salt. Add onion, dill seed, butter, and yeast. Add egg, and small amounts of flour at a time. This makes a soft dough. Let stand covered in buttered bowl to rise, about 1 hour. Knead well and place in greased casserole or loaf pan. Let rise again, about 1 hour. Bake at 350 degrees for 40 minutes. Brush with melted butter and sprinkle with salt and dill seed. Very good with barbecued or smoked meats. 8 servings.

Southern Hush Puppies

Mrs. Gerald Hayes, Jr., Atlanta, Georgia

1 cup corn meal	3 teaspoons baking powder
½ cup flour	1 small onion, chopped fine
1 teaspoon salt	Buttermilk
½ teaspoon soda	Fat for frying

Mix all dry ingredients. Add onion and enough buttermilk to form a soft dough or batter. The batter should be thick enough to drop from a spoon into deep, hot fat. Fry to a golden brown and drain excess fat on paper towel.

NOTE: If you have fried fish, you may use same fat to fry hush puppies. 6 servings.

Indian Bread

Mrs. P. D. (Frances) Alexander
Joy-Ja-Lan Gardens, Lithonia, Georgia

4 cups water-ground corn meal, scalded with boiling water (about 4 cups)	1 cup flour, preferably whole wheat
½ cup ribbon cane syrup	⅔ cup sour buttermilk
¼ cup blackstrap molasses	½ teaspoon soda
1 cup scalded milk	2 tablespoons melted butter
2 teaspoons salt	2 eggs, beaten

Combine first five ingredients, let stand overnight or 24 hours. Stir in remaining ingredients. Add more milk or water for thinner batter. Let sit 2 hours in warm place. Pour into greased pan, a pound-cake or deep-dish casserole or skillet. Bake in slow oven, 225 to 250 degrees, about 2 hours. When half done brush top with butter. 12 servings.

Old-fashioned Light Bread

1 package yeast	*3 cups flour*
½ cup lukewarm water	*2 tablespoons melted shortening*
2 tablespoons sugar	*2 tablespoons salt*

Dissolve yeast in lukewarm water. Dissolve sugar in yeast-luke-warm water mixture. Combine mixture and half the flour. Mix well. Let rise for about 1½ hours. Add shortening, salt, and enough flour to make a stiff dough. Turn out on a board and knead thoroughly until dough has a fine grain. Place in a greased bowl and when doubled in bulk make into two loaves and put in lightly greased 9×5×3-inch pans; brush with melted shortening. Bake about 1 hour in moderately hot 350-degree oven. 2 loaves.

Joe's first effort proved fatal—it was a huge success and he hasn't been able to stop baking since.

Pumpernickel Bread

Joe Gross, Atlanta, Georgia

¼ cup very warm water	*1 tablespoon caraway seed*
1 package active dry yeast	*2 cups rye flour*
2 cups milk, scalded and cooled	*3 cups whole wheat flour*
to lukewarm	*1 cup whole bran*
2 teaspoons salt	*2 tablespoons melted butter or*
2 tablespoons sugar	*oil*

Pour water into large bowl, add yeast, and stir to dissolve. Stir in milk, salt, sugar, and caraway seed. Mix flour and bran and add 5 cups, 1 cup at a time to milk mixture to make stiff dough.

Sprinkle bread board heavily with some of the flour and flour hands. Turn dough onto board and knead until smooth, adding flour as you go along, until all is used.

Place dough in greased bowl; brush top with butter. Cover and let rise in warm place (80 degrees) until doubled in bulk, about 1½ hours. Punch down, squeeze out air with hands. Divide in half and shape each half into loaf. Place in well-greased pans, 5¼×9¼ inches, and let rise to double, 45 minutes to 1 hour.

Bake at 375 degrees for 45 minutes (if glass pan is used, reduce time to 35 minutes). Turn out at once and cool on rack. This bread freezes well. 2 loaves.

Salt Rising Bread

PART I

4 small Irish potatoes
1 quart boiling water
1 teaspoon salt

2 tablespoons sugar
4 tablespoons corn meal

Peel and cut potatoes thin. Pour boiling water over them. Add salt, sugar, and corn meal. Put tepid water in a large container, and place the vessel containing the mixture in it. Let stand 24 hours. Bubbles will form similar to soap bubbles. The salt-rising odor will be unmistakable if yeast starter is good.

PART II

Strain first part and add 2 cups warm milk, ¼ teaspoon baking soda, and enough flour to make a stiff sponge. Let rise until light, approximately 2 hours.

PART III

Sift 4 cups flour, 1 teaspoon salt; add 4 tablespoons shortening. Mix thoroughly. Add sponge and more flour to make soft dough. Knead quickly so dough will not chill. Fill two 9×5×3-inch greased pans one-half full. Let rise until doubled in size. Bake in moderate oven 350 degrees, 45 to 60 minutes. 2 loaves.

Shortbread

½ pound butter
½ cup sugar
2 cups flour

Mix all the ingredients together with your hands until dough resembles coarse meal. The warmth of the hands softens the butter and makes the bread a bit crispy. Pat the mixture into an ungreased

9×9-inch pan. Pierce the dough every 2 inches with a fork. Bake at 300 degrees for 40 minutes or until lightly browned. Cut into small squares while warm. 6 servings.

Spoon Bread

Mrs. F. C. McElwain, Decatur, Georgia

1 cup corn meal
1 teaspoon salt
1 heaping teaspoon baking
   powder
2 eggs, beaten

2 cups milk
1 cup boiling water
1 tablespoon melted butter
1 tablespoon melted shortening

Mix corn meal, salt, and baking powder. Add eggs, milk, and enough boiling water to make a very thin batter. Then add butter and shortening. Pour into well-greased 8-inch square baking dish and bake 30 to 40 minutes at 375 degrees. 6 servings.

Sweet Potato Bread

Mrs. James E. Davis, Atlanta, Georgia

1 cup sugar
2 cups flour
1⅓ teaspoons soda
1 teaspoon salt
1 teaspoon cinnamon

1 teaspoon cloves
⅓ cup vegetable oil
1 cup mashed and sieved sweet
   potato
⅔ cup nuts and raisins

Sift together the dry ingredients. Add oil and mix thoroughly along with the sweet potato. Add nuts and raisins. Bake in well-greased 9×5×3-inch loaf pan for 1 hour at 350 degrees. 1 loaf.

Baking Powder Biscuits

2 cups sifted flour
3 teaspoons baking powder
1 teaspoon salt

¼ cup shortening
¾ cup milk

Sift the dry ingredients together and cut in the shortening. Add milk, stirring until all flour is moistened. Turn out on lightly floured board. Knead dough about 20 seconds, then roll to about ½ inch thick. Cut biscuits and place on ungreased baking sheet. Bake at 450 degrees for 8 to 10 minutes. 12 two-inch biscuits.

Beaten Biscuits

4 cups flour
1 teaspoon salt
1 teaspoon baking powder
1 tablespoon sugar

4 tablespoons chilled shortening
Equal parts chilled milk and ice
*   water (about 1 cup)*
Melted butter

Sift together the dry ingredients. Cut in shortening until the consistency of corn meal. Add the milk and water to make a stiff dough. Beat the dough with a mallet until well blistered. This is a long process, requiring ½ hour or more. When the dough is smooth and glossy, roll it to the thickness of ½ inch and cut it with a biscuit cutter. Spread the tops with melted butter. Pierce through the biscuits with a fork. Bake them at 325 degrees, for about 30 minutes. 24 biscuits.

Louisiana Calas

Mrs. Dalton F. Scott, Decatur, Georgia

½ cup raw rice
3 cups water
Salt
1 yeast package
2 tablespoons lukewarm water

3 eggs, well beaten
½ cup sugar
3 tablespoons flour
Fat for frying
Powdered sugar

Boil rice in the water, slightly salted, until very soft and mushy. When cold, add the yeast liquefied in the lukewarm water. Let rise overnight. In the morning add the eggs with the sugar and flour and beat thoroughly. The mixture should be of the consistency of a thick batter. Set aside to rise for about 15 minutes. Then drop by tablespoonfuls into deep hot fat (350 degrees). Cook to a light golden color, turning several times. Drain on soft crumpled paper. Sprinkle with powdered sugar and serve very hot. 6 servings.

Buttermilk Biscuits

Mrs. Herbert Garrison, Homer, Georgia

2 cups plain flour —
1 teaspoon salt
¼ teaspoon soda

3 teaspoons baking powder
½ cup lard
1 cup buttermilk

Sift dry ingredients together; cut in lard, then stir in buttermilk. On a floured board knead the dough about 10 times. Roll out, cut, place on ungreased baking sheet, and bake at 450 degrees for 12 to 15 minutes. 12 biscuits.

Caraway Cheese Biscuits

1½ cups sifted flour
1 teaspoon baking powder
½ teaspoon soda
1 teaspoon salt
½ cup whole bran cereal

½ cup grated sharp cheese
2 teaspoons caraway seeds
⅓ cup shortening
½ cup buttermilk or sour milk

Sift together flour, baking powder, soda, and salt. Combine with cereal, cheese, and caraway seeds. Cut in shortening until mixture resembles coarse corn meal. Add buttermilk, stirring only until combined. Turn dough out on a lightly floured board and knead gently a few times. Roll out to ½-inch thickness. Cut with floured 1¾-inch biscuit cutter. Place on ungreased baking sheet. Bake in very hot oven, 450 degrees, about 12 minutes. 1½ dozen biscuits.

Cinnamon Rolls

½ cup milk
⅓ cup sugar
1 teaspoon salt
½ cup corn oil
1 package yeast
¼ cup lukewarm water
3 eggs, well beaten

3½ cups flour
½ teaspoon cinnamon
¼ teaspoon allspice
½ cup raisins
⅓ cup citron, finely cut
1 egg white

Scald milk; remove from heat. Add sugar, salt, and corn oil. Cool to lukewarm. Sprinkle yeast over warm water in large mixing bowl.

Stir until dissolved. Add milk mixture and eggs. Add flour and spices.

Beat until batter is shiny and smooth. Stir in fruit. Scrape batter from sides of bowl. Cover and let rise in warm place, free from draft, until doubled in bulk, about 1 hour and 20 minutes. Stir down and let stand covered for 10 minutes.

Gently pour batter into well-greased 9×13×2-inch pan. With knife that has been dipped in oil, cut down and across batter to make 24 individual buns.

Cover and let rise until doubled in bulk; about 1 hour. Brush top with egg white. Bake in moderate oven, 350 degrees, about 18 minutes. 24 rolls.

FROSTING for the rolls is made by combining 1 cup of confectioners' sugar with 1½ tablespoons milk or fruit juice; blend well. Stir in 2 or 3 drops of vanilla extract. Frost rolls when they have cooled. About ½ cup.

Enriched Corn Meal Crisps

⅞ cup enriched corn meal
1 cup boiling water
2⅓ tablespoons melted butter
½ teaspoon salt

Add corn meal gradually to boiling water; when smooth, remove from heat, stir in butter and salt. Spread evenly on a buttered baking sheet to ⅛-inch thickness, using long, broad spatula.

Bake at 350 degrees until well browned. Cut in 2½-inch squares. Remove from pan, and serve at once. Crisps are good with soups and salads. 4 servings.

Corn Dodgers with Ham Hock

1 ham hock	*1 teaspoon salt*
2 cups corn meal	*1 scant tablespoon shortening*
½ cup flour	*½ teaspoon soda*
1 tablespoon sugar	*½ cup buttermilk*

Cook ham hock until well done in enough water to make plenty of broth.

In a mixing bowl combine meal, flour, sugar, and salt. Skim fat off top of ham hock broth, add to shortening. Add to meal mix and stir until hot through. Dissolve soda in buttermilk, stir into meal mixture, and add enough water so mixture can be made into balls. Drop a few at a time into hard boiling broth (they should float). When all have been added, cover. Turn heat to low and simmer until dodgers are fluffy and done. Serve with the meat from cooked ham hock, 12 dodgers.

Corn Meal Batty Cakes

1 cup corn meal   *1 egg, beaten*
½ teaspoon soda   *1¼ cups buttermilk*
½ teaspoon salt

Sift dry ingredients together. Add egg and buttermilk to dry ingredients, beating until smooth. Pour 1 tablespoon batter for each cake onto a well-greased hot skillet.

Bake until brown, turning only once. If batter gets too thick, add a little more buttermilk. Serve with butter and your favorite jam or preserves. 6 servings.

Dough Boys

Mrs. Max A. Clayton, Atlanta, Georgia

1 cup corn meal   *½ teaspoon minced onion*
1 teaspoon salt   *2 eggs, beaten*
1⅓ cups boiling water   *Flour*
1 teaspoon chopped parsley
   (optional)

Combine meal and salt and add to boiling water. Remove from heat, stir to smooth thick mush. Cool, add remaining ingredients except flour. Form into 2-inch balls, roll in flour to coat, drop into boiling ham hock liquid. Cover tightly and steam 10 minutes. 8 balls.

A very dear departed friend in whose home I spent many wonderful days.

Cream Muffins

Mrs. Willa Evans, Wadley, Georgia

4 eggs, separated	2 cups self-rising flour
2 teaspoons baking powder	½ pint heavy cream
¼ teaspoon salt	

Beat egg yolks until lemon-colored. Add baking powder, salt, and flour. Whip cream and egg whites separately and fold into mixture. Bake in slightly greased muffin tins at 350 degrees about 20 minutes. 12 to 18 muffins.

Okra Pancakes

Mrs. Opal Austin Cotton, Beaufort, South Carolina

1 cup sliced steamed okra	1 cup sifted corn meal (or
1 egg, beaten	enough to make stiff batter)
1 teaspoon diced onion	Fat for frying

Mix cooked okra, egg, and onion; then add meal until thick enough for batter. Fry in hot, deep fat until brown. Serve hot. They are delicious served with catsup, tomato sauce, or melted cheese.

Cold Grits Waffles

Mrs. Edgar Langston, St. Simons Island, Georgia

2 eggs, beaten	1 cup flour, sifted
1½ cups milk	3½ teaspoons baking powder
2 teaspoons cane syrup	5 tablespoons butter or
1 cup cold grits (leftover)	margarine

To eggs, add milk, syrup, grits, and flour to which baking powder has been added, beating until smooth. Add shortening and mix well.

NOTE: The addition of syrup gives the waffles a delicious flavor and a golden-brown color. 4 servings.

2

APPETIZERS

No words are sweeter to the hostess than, "such beautiful, delicious food." And there is no greater asset to a party than a relaxed hostess. One way to be relaxed is to plan party food that is prepared well in advance.

The recipes in this section have been served with great success in thousands of homes in our area. Many of them have been used over and over in my own home on numerous festive occasions.

If one has advance time, a host of the recipes may be prepared and frozen even several weeks prior to time of serving. Most of them may be fixed and refrigerated at least a day or so early. This leaves time for last-minute things, such as arranging and garnishing, as well as table settings.

Chutney Cream Dip

1 cup sour cream
1 to 2 drops garlic juice
¼ teaspoon grated onion

¼ cup finely chopped chutney
1 teaspoon lemon juice
Salt to taste

Combine all ingredients and blend thoroughly. Use blender if available. Chill overnight or several hours to allow flavors to blend. 1¼ cups.

A long-time favorite on the Sunday-evening buffet.

Marinated Artichoke Hearts

John J. Chalfa, Executive Steward
Herman Yursich, Executive Chef
The Cloister, Sea Island, Georgia

½ cup olive oil
¼ cup white vinegar
1 teaspoon chopped chives
1 tablespoon chopped green
  olives
1 tablespoon whole capers
1 tablespoon chopped gherkins
½ tablespoon dried leaf
  tarragon

1 hard-cooked egg, chopped
1 teaspoon onion juice
Salt and pepper to taste
4 (No. 303) cans tiny artichoke
  hearts
1 tablespoon chopped parsley

Mix together all ingredients except artichokes and parsley. Pour the mixture over the artichokes in a wooden salad bowl. Mix lightly and sprinkle parsley on top. Allow to marinate for at least 2 hours in the refrigerator. Serve cold. 8 servings.

Chilled Canapé Pie

Pastry for 2-crust pie
6 egg yolks
3 tablespoons soft butter
2 cups sour cream
3 tablespoons flour

½ teaspoon salt
¼ teaspoon garlic salt
1½ cups grated Swiss cheese
2 (4½ ounces each) cans
  deviled ham

Roll crust to fit a 12-inch round shallow pizza pie pan. Bake at 425 degrees for 10 minutes or until lightly browned. Cool. Blend eggs, butter, and sour cream in top of double boiler, then stir in flour and seasonings. Cook over boiling water until quite thick. Add Swiss cheese, blend well, and cook just until cheese is melted. Cool thoroughly. Spread deviled ham on baked shell, then spread cheese mixture evenly over top. Cover with protective film and refrigerate 2 hours or overnight. Just before serving cut into twenty-four wedges and garnish with watercress, radishes, olives, cherry tomatoes, pickled fans, or cucumbers. 24 appetizers.

Avocado Tomato Dip

2 avocados, peeled and pitted
2 tablespoons lemon juice
2 tablespoons vinegar
1 medium tomato, peeled,
    chopped, and drained
¼ cup finely chopped onion

2½ teaspoons salt
1 teaspoon Worcestershire
    sauce
½ teaspoon sugar
⅛ teaspoon pepper
4 dashes Tabasco sauce

Press avocados through a coarse sieve. Add lemon juice and vinegar immediately. Then add tomato and blend. Add onion, salt, Worcestershire sauce, sugar, pepper, and Tabasco. Mix well.

Cover closely and chill. Serve as a dip with spiced vegetables. 3 cups.

Beef Tenderloin Hors d'Oeuvres

6 to 8 bacon slices
1 whole beef tenderloin, 4 to 5
    pounds
1 (5-ounce) bottle steak sauce

½ (1 stick) butter or margarine
1 (7-ounce) can mushroom
    buttons
1 loaf French bread

Lay strips of bacon over the tenderloin. Place on rack in roasting pan and bake uncovered at 400 degrees for 15 to 25 minutes. In the meantime, heat to boiling the sauce, butter, and mushrooms with juice in chafing dish. Cut bread into bite-size pieces.

Place meat on heated platter. Slice very thin bite-size pieces; dip in sauce and place on bread. 12 to 20 servings.

Party Cheese Ball

2 (8 ounces each) packages
    cream cheese
1 (8-ounce) package sharp
    Cheddar cheese, shredded
1 tablespoon chopped pimiento
1 tablespoon chopped green
    pepper
1 teaspoon finely chopped
    onion

1 teaspoon lemon juice
2 teaspoons Worcestershire
    sauce
Dash cayenne pepper
Dash salt
Finely chopped pecans

Place the cream cheese in a bowl and cream it until soft and smooth. Add the shredded cheese and mix until well blended. Add pimiento, green pepper, onion, lemon juice, Worcestershire sauce, and seasonings and blend well. Shape into a ball. Wrap in waxed paper and chill for at least 24 hours. Roll the ball in chopped pecans. 24 appetizers.

Hot Cheese Puffs

½ cup butter
2 cups grated sharp Cheddar
  cheese

1 cup sifted flour
⅛ teaspoon salt
¼ teaspoon paprika

Cream butter and grated cheese. Add flour, salt, and paprika. Shape into 1-inch balls. Freeze on cookie sheet and store in freezer bags until ready to use.

Place on ungreased baking sheet and bake at 350 degrees for about 15 minutes or until puffed and brown. Takes longer if hard frozen and will not puff as much. 25 to 30 small puffs.

Williamsburg Cheese Straws

Mrs. George Craft

1 cup sifted all-purpose flour
½ teaspoon salt
¼ teaspoon dry mustard
⅛ teaspoon cayenne
¼ cup butter or margarine

1 cup grated sharp Cheddar
  cheese
1½ tablespoons ice water
1 teaspoon celery seed

Into medium bowl, sift flour with salt, mustard, and cayenne. With pastry blender, cut in butter and half the cheese until mixture resembles coarse crumbs. Add water, stir lightly to blend. Shape into a ball.

On lightly floured surface, roll out pastry to ⅛-inch thickness. Sprinkle with remaining cheese. Fold dough in ball, roll out to ⅛-inch thickness again. With pastry wheel or cutter, cut into desired shape. Sprinkle with celery seed. Place on an ungreased cookie sheet. Bake in a preheated 350-degree oven for 12 minutes or until pale brown. 4 to 5 dozen appetizers.

Crab Meat Canapé

Mrs. R. Tyre Jones, Canton, Georgia

2 pounds king crab meat	1 cup mayonnaise
2 large cucumbers	½ cup grapefruit juice
½ cup finely chopped green	6 tablespoons lemon juice
onion	½ cup chopped parsley

Shred crab meat and remove any membrane. Peel and seed cucumbers; chop very fine or purée in blender; retain all juice. Mix all ingredients except parsley in large bowl, including all juices, and marinate for at least 3 hours in refrigerator (overnight is better). Strain mixture and reserve juice (see Secret Soup below). Pile mixture in serving bowl, garnish with parsley, and surround with small rounds of melba toast. 20 servings.

Secret Soup

Use marinade saved from Crab Meat Canapé and chill thoroughly. Add equal amounts of either coffee cream, sour cream, or whipping cream. Serve chilled in bouillon cups. 4 servings.

Escargots Bourguignonne

Chef George Wyerman
Plantation Club, Hilton Head Island, South Carolina

1 pound butter	2 tablespoons finely sliced
2 cloves garlic	chives
2 tablespoons finely chopped	Juice of ½ lemon
shallots	½ teaspoon Worcestershire
½ cup dry white wine	sauce
2 tablespoons finely chopped	48 snails and shells
parsley	

Whip butter. Combine garlic, shallots, and wine in a blender at high speed. Whip this mixture into butter. Add seasonings and combine mixture thoroughly. Wash and drain snails according to directions. Fill snail shells three-quarters full with the butter mixture. Add snails and close opening with the butter. Place shells in snail dishes or in a flat baking dish, open end up. Broil until butter is light brown. Serve hot with toasted slices of French bread. 8 servings.

Chipped Beef and Horseradish Log

2 (3 ounces each) packages
   cream cheese
2 teaspoons horseradish
1 teaspoon prepared mustard

2 (2½ ounces each) jars dried
   chipped beef
2 tablespoons butter or
   margarine

Soften cream cheese with horseradish and mustard. Chop the dried beef until fine and sauté in butter until well frizzled. Form cheese mixture into a ball or a log, and roll in the dried beef mixture. Wrap in waxed paper or foil and chill. Cut in thin slices and serve on toasted buttery crackers. 4 dozen appetizers.

Cucumber Fish Appetizer

Chef Willi Neumann, Sheraton Biltmore Hotel, Atlanta, Georgia

½ pound fillet of sole
¼ cup soy sauce
¼ cup cider vinegar

2 teaspoons sugar
¼ teaspoon powdered ginger
3 cucumbers

Chop the fish very fine. Combine the soy sauce, vinegar, sugar, and ginger in a bowl; stir in the fish. Let stand 1 hour. Peel the cucumbers, cut lengthwise, scoop out the seeds, and slice very thin. Pour the fish mixture over them and let stand 10 minutes. Serve in a bowl with crackers as a dip. About 3 cups.

Lobster Dip

1 (5-ounce) can lobster,
   drained, cleaned, and diced
¼ cup chopped celery
2 tablespoons pickle relish

½ teaspoon lemon juice
¼ teaspoon salt
⅛ teaspoon pepper
⅓ cup mayonnaise

Combine lobster, celery, pickle relish, lemon juice, salt, and pepper. Add mayonnaise and toss until well blended. About 1 cup.

Southwestern Guacamole

2 large ripe avocados
2 medium tomatoes, peeled
1 medium onion or 2 or 3 green
    onions
1 green chili or more, to taste

1 tablespoon lemon juice
Coriander, salt, and pepper to
    taste
Dash liquid pepper sauce

Chop first four ingredients coarsely and toss with seasonings. Serve as a dip with toasted tortillas, corn chips or raw vegetables. About 2 cups.

Hoppin' John Dip

¼ pound (6 slices) bacon, cut
    into ½-inch pieces
¾ cup chopped onion
1 (10-ounce) package frozen
    blackeye peas
2 cups water

1 teaspoon salt
¼ cup raw rice
2 teaspoons vinegar
¼ teaspoon cayenne pepper
Potato chips

Cook bacon in large saucepan. Remove with slotted spoon and drain on absorbent paper; reserve. Add onion to bacon fat in saucepan; cook until tender. Add blackeye peas, water, and salt. Cover and cook over medium heat for 15 minutes. Stir in rice; cover and cook over low heat for 25 to 30 minutes, until rice is tender. Purée mixture in blender or food mill. Add vinegar and cayenne. If mixture is thick, stir in enough boiling water to make of dipping consistency. Heat. Sprinkle with crumbled bacon and serve with potato chips. About 3 cups.

Chicken Livers with Tarragon

1 pound chicken livers
½ teaspoon monosodium
    glutamate
½ teaspoon salt
⅛ teaspoon pepper
1 tablespoon minced onion

1 tablespoon minced parsley
½ teaspoon dried leaf tarragon
2 tablespoons olive or salad oil
Flour for dredging
Butter

Combine livers with monosodium glutamate, salt, pepper, onion, parsley, tarragon, and oil in a bowl. Let marinate 30 minutes. Drain. Roll livers in flour.

Cook in butter over medium heat in skillet, about 5 minutes, turning occasionally. Place on small skewers. If desired, garnish with small cocktail onions and olives. About 1½ dozen.

Pickled Mushrooms

The Cloister, Sea Island, Georgia

3 pounds mushrooms
½ cup finely chopped onions
2 cloves garlic, crushed
½ cup olive oil
1 cup dry white wine

½ cup lemon juice
6 bay leaves
1 tablespoon oregano
Salt and pepper to taste
1 tablespoon chopped parsley

Carefully remove mushroom caps from stems. Reserve stems for some other use. Sauté onions and garlic in olive oil until golden. Add mushroom caps, wine, lemon juice, bay leaves, oregano, salt, and pepper.

Cover the pot and let simmer slowly on top of range for 30 minutes. Remove from heat and pour into salad bowl. Keep in refrigerator overnight. Before serving, remove bay leaves, sprinkle with chopped parsley. Serve cold. 8 servings.

Nippy Roquefort Dip

½ pound Roquefort cheese
¼ cup mayonnaise
1 teaspoon onion juice
2 tablespoons madeira or
  muscatel wine

2 teaspoons shredded lemon
  peel
2 Delicious apples, sliced
Lemon juice

Mash the Roquefort cheese with a fork, blend in mayonnaise, onion juice, wine, and lemon peel. Chill until ready to serve. Serve with fresh apple slices which have been dipped in lemon juice. About 1 cup.

Peach of a Dip

1 (1-pound) can freestone peach slices
¼ cup finely chopped chutney
Potato chips

Drain peaches. Purée drained peaches in food mill or force through sieve; add pulp remaining in food mill to puréed mixture. Stir in chutney; chill. If desired, garnish with mango slices or with peach slices. Serve with potato chips. About 1¼ cups.

Bourbon Pâté

½ pound butter
1 small onion, chopped
1 pound chicken livers
1½ cups chicken broth
2 tablespoons sweet sherry
½ teaspoon paprika
⅛ teaspoon allspice
½ teaspoon salt
⅛ teaspoon white pepper
1 clove garlic, minced
½ cup Bourbon
1 envelope plain gelatin
1 cup chopped pecans

Melt butter; add onion and chicken livers. Cook 10 minutes, stirring occasionally. Add ¾ cup broth, sherry, paprika, allspice, salt, pepper, and garlic. Cook 5 minutes. Remove from heat, add Bourbon. Soften gelatin in remaining ¾ cup broth; cook over boiling water until dissolved. Place chicken liver mixture in blender, blend until smooth.
Stir gelatin and pecans into chicken liver mixture. Turn into 5- or 6-cup mold. Chill until firm. 24 appetizers.

Pâté Maison

¼ cup butter or margarine
1 pound chicken livers
½ cup finely chopped onion
1 teaspoon salt
¼ teaspoon each dry mustard,
    freshly ground black pepper,
    and powdered thyme
⅛ teaspoon mace
¼ cup heavy cream

Heat butter in skillet. Add chicken livers and onion. Cook over medium heat, stirring frequently, for 5 to 8 minutes or until livers are done and onion is tender but not brown. Force livers with onion through strainer or food mill.

Blend in seasonings and cream. Turn into serving container and chill. Serve with thinly sliced French bread, crackers, or toast rounds. 1⅓ cups.

Sausage Pinwheels

Prepare a short biscuit dough. Roll very thin into a rectangle about 12×18 inches. Flour needed to make this size would be about 1½ cups.

Let pork sausage meat reach spreading consistency at room temperature. Add a few drops of Tabasco sauce or shake of cayenne to the sausage to make it nippy hot. Spread over rolled dough, then roll as for jelly roll, moistening edges with water to seal.

Roll should be approximately 2 inches in diameter. Cover with transparent wrap; store in refrigerator until ready to use. Or freeze if desired.

Slice about ⅓ inch thick, place on baking sheets, and bake in 375-degree oven until light brown and done. Serve piping hot. 3 to 4 dozen pinwheels, depending on size.

Marinated Shrimp

Jekyll Island Luau, Jekyll Island, Georgia

10 pounds shrimp in shell	*¼ cup lemon juice*
4 pounds large white onions	*2 teaspoons salt*
1 quart olive oil	*2 teaspoons sugar*
1½ pints cider vinegar	*Few drops Tabasco*
1 pint capers with liquid	*2 tablespoons Worcestershire*
2 teaspoons crushed garlic or	*sauce*
garlic powder	

Cook shrimp. Peel and devein, wash and drain. Cut onions into rings. In a deep, flat pan alternate layers of shrimp and sliced onions until all are used. Combine the remaining ingredients and pour over shrimp and onions. Cover and let stand in refrigerator overnight.

Serve as appetizer or as a salad in lettuce cups. About 50 servings.

Shrimp Paste

Mrs. E. J. Filson, Savannah, Georgia

1½ pounds raw shrimp	Dash cayenne and black pepper
½ cup softened butter	Toasted bread crumbs
1 teaspoon salt	Additional butter
1½ teaspoons Worcestershire sauce	

Cook, shell, and devein shrimp; run through food chopper and mash to smooth paste. Mix in softened butter and seasonings and blend to butterlike consistency. Press into small loaf pan, top with toasted crumbs and dot with butter. Bake in very hot oven, 450 degrees, for about 15 minutes.

This may be served hot or cold. Chill, slice thin, and serve on crackers as hors d'oeuvres. 24 servings.

Turkey Cocktail Crisps

24 bite-size pieces cooked roast turkey	12 slices bacon, cut in half
12 pitted prunes or dried apricots, cut in half	Wooden food picks

For each cocktail crisp, wrap a bite-size piece of cooked turkey with a piece of prune or apricot in a half slice of bacon. Fasten with wooden pick. Bake at 400 degrees for 20 minutes or until bacon is crisp. Drain and serve immediately. 24 servings.

NOTE: The crisps may also be prepared under the broiler instead of in the oven.

Spiced Vegetables

4 raw carrots	3 cups water
4 stalks celery	½ cup vinegar
1 small head cauliflower	1 tablespoon mixed pickling spice
¼ pound fresh small mushrooms	1½ teaspoons whole dill seed
4 cloves garlic, sliced	1 teaspoon whole mustard seed
1 tablespoon salt	

Cut carrots and celery into 3-inch sticks. Separate cauliflower into flowerets. Place with mushrooms in bowl with sliced garlic and salt.

Combine water, vinegar, mixed pickling spice, dill seed, and mustard seed. Bring to boil. Pour over vegetables. Cool. Refrigerate several days before serving.

Remove vegetables from spiced brine and arrange on hors d'oeuvre dish. Serve cold with dip. 3 pints.

3

✖✖✖✖✖✖✖✖✖✖✖✖✖✖✖✖✖✖✖✖✖✖✖✖✖✖✖

SOUPS

I grew up in a family that really liked soup—just any kind of soup! I remember when we were children, my brother John dashed up to Mama one cold winter afternoon and begged for soup for supper. When Mama said, "But, honey, I don't have anything to make soup with," he quickly replied, "Oh, just make clear water soup."

So, Mama was great at making soup from just about nothing and having it come out elegantly. Vegetable soup was a favorite—and still is. Its base can be any kind of meat stock, with plenty of fresh or canned vegetables, or both, added. Soups just sort of grow as you accumulate enough leftovers.

Today in my own home, I keep homemade soup all the time. It's easy to make a huge pot at one cooking and freeze it for future use. Begin with a chuck roast and when the meat is fork tender in the cooking water, remove meat from bone and cut meat into pieces. Add vegetables and seasonings. Corn, okra, tomatoes, and onion are favorites. But use whatever you have. With corn bread this soup is a whole, satisfying meal.

Southern flavor and charm abound at A. J. Anthony's Pitty Pat's Porch in downtown Atlanta. There are rocking chairs to sit in while you enjoy your favorite beverage and a world of southern foods await in the dining room.

Hearty Beef and Vegetable Soup

2 pounds beef or stew beef or oxtails
1 large soup bone
1 tablespoon salt, plus 2 teaspoons
3½ quarts water
6 carrots, cut in half lengthwise, then in 2-inch pieces
¾ cup chopped celery
¾ cup chopped green pepper
1 (1-pound, 12-ounce) can tomatoes, undrained
½ (16-ounce) package frozen peas

½ (10-ounce) package frozen lima beans
½ (10-ounce) package frozen cut green beans
1 (12-ounce) can whole kernel corn, drained
2 tablespoons chopped parsley
1 (6-ounce) can tomato paste
2 teaspoons sugar
½ teaspoon pepper
2 potatoes, pared and cubed

Place beef, soup bone, 1 tablespoon salt, and water in large kettle. Cover; bring to boil. Skim surface and cook about 10 to 15 minutes. Add carrots, celery, green pepper, and tomatoes. Bring to boil, simmer about 30 minutes. Add remaining ingredients except potatoes; cover and simmer 2 hours. Then add potatoes and continue cooking at simmer for 1½ hours.

Remove meat and bone from kettle; discard bone. Cool meat; cut into smaller pieces and add to soup. Refrigerate several hours. Skim fat from surface. Reheat before serving. About 5½ quarts. Serve with small corn bread cakes.

White Cabbage Soup
Mrs. C. W. Haines, Morrow, Georgia

2 tablespoons fat or butter
6 cups coarsely shredded cabbage
1 tablespoon molasses or brown sugar

2 quarts pork stock or bouillon
6 whole allspice
6 white peppercorns
Salt to taste
½ pound ground beef

Melt fat in Dutch oven. Add cabbage and molasses or brown sugar and cook quickly until cabbage is slightly browned. Add stock and seasonings and bring to boil. Add tiny (size of hazelnut) meatballs made of seasoned ground beef and cook gently for 10 minutes. If richer soup is desired add small pork link sausages instead of beef. 6 to 8 servings.

Senate Bean Soup

2 pounds small navy pea beans   1 onion, chopped
4 quarts hot water   Butter
1½ pounds smoked ham hocks   Salt and pepper to taste

Wash pea beans and run through hot water until beans are white again. Put over heat in the 4 quarts hot water. Add ham hocks, boil slowly, approximately 3 hours in a covered pot. Braise onion in a little butter, and when light brown, add to bean soup. Season with salt and pepper, then serve. 8 servings.

Cream of Vegetable Soup Base

2 tablespoons butter   3 cups milk
1 tablespoon minced onion   About 1½ cups vegetable pulp
2 tablespoons flour   (cooked vegetables and
2 teaspoons salt   cooking water) or vegetable
1½ teaspoons pepper   purée

Melt butter in 2-quart saucepan or top of double boiler. Add onion and simmer until soft but not brown, about 3 minutes. Combine flour, salt, and pepper; add to butter and onion, stirring until well blended. Gradually add milk, while stirring constantly. Cook over low heat or boiling water, stirring constantly, until thickened. Gradually add vegetable pulp and liquid while stirring; blend well. Keep over heat until mixture is heated through, but do not boil. Serve piping hot. 4 servings.

Cream of Pea Soup

Add ¼ teaspoon celery salt and ¼ teaspoon dry mustard to flour and seasonings when making Cream of Vegetable Soup Base in above recipe. Use 2 cups fresh peas, or one 10-ounce package frozen peas, or one No. 2 can peas. Cook fresh peas in 1 cup boiling salted water in tightly covered saucepan until very tender; or cook frozen peas as directed on package; or heat canned peas in own liquid. Drain peas and press through sieve. Add to soup base and heat through. Garnish with croutons.

Cream of Potato Soup

Add ¼ teaspoon celery salt to flour and seasonings when making Cream of Vegetable Soup Base. Cook 2 cups diced potatoes, ¼ cup chopped onion, 1 stalk celery, diced, in 1½ cups boiling salted water in covered saucepan until tender. Press through sieve. Add the remaining potato liquid to potato pulp. Add to soup base and heat through. Garnish with chopped chives.

Cream of Tomato Soup

When making Cream of Vegetable Soup Base, increase butter to 3 tablespoons and flour to 4 tablespoons. Add 1 tablespoon chopped onion, ½ teaspoon celery salt, and 1 whole clove to one No. 2½ can tomatoes and boil gently in uncovered saucepan for 15 minutes or until reduced to 2½ cups. Press through sieve. Heat and add to cream soup base. Serve immediately. Garnish with chopped parsley or cheese popcorn.

Green Soup

4 large potatoes
8½ cups boiling salted water
1 pound spinach, washed and shredded
½ cup butter or 3 tablespoons olive oil

Cook the potatoes in the boiling salted water until tender. Press potatoes through a sieve and return them to water in which cooked. Add spinach and butter or oil. Cook uncovered over high heat 2 to 3 minutes. (It is important not to cook the soup uncovered more than a few minutes after adding spinach so it will remain a beautiful green.) 4 servings.

Georgia Gumbo

Mrs. K. K. Causey, Carrollton, Georgia

¼ cup bacon drippings	1 quart sliced okra
1 large onion	1 cup boiling water
6 fresh tomatoes, peeled and sliced	Salt and pepper to taste

Into a heavy frying pan put bacon drippings; slice onion quite thin and fry in drippings to a very light brown. Care must be taken not to burn or cook too much, for this would ruin the entire dish. Add tomatoes, okra, and water; stir often; add seasoning when half done.

Cook about 1 hour. The mixture should be thick enough to be eaten with a fork. Serve with dry rice or as a vegetable with small individual corn meal hoecakes which should be well done and crusty. 6 servings.

Half a dozen fresh mushrooms, broiled, chopped, and added, would make the dish more delicious. To rub the pan with a cut clove of garlic gives another added touch.

Louisiana Gumbo

Charles H. Kupfer, Atlanta, Georgia

1 (10-ounce) package frozen okra or ½ pound fresh	1 large green pepper
	5 celery stalks with leaves
1 bunch (6 to 8) green onions (tops included)	1 small onion

Chop vegetables very fine and brown in ½ cup margarine or butter. Add the following except for the gumbo filé powder.

1 (8-ounce) can tomato sauce	Salt to taste (1 teaspoon or less)
2 (10¾ ounces each) cans beef bouillon	1 tablespoon sugar
2 (10¾ ounces each) cans water	2 tablespoons vinegar
1 (6-ounce) can crab meat or equal amount of fresh	2 tablespoons gumbo filé powder
1 (6-ounce) can shrimp or equal amount of fresh	

Simmer on low heat for 1 hour. Remove from heat and add 2 tablespoons gumbo filé powder and stir for a minute or two. Serve over rice in a bowl. 8 servings.

NOTE: If you use okra, do not use the gumbo filé powder and vice versa. Filé powder is preferred. Do not add the powder until after removing pan from heat. Once the filé powder is added, the gumbo cannot be reheated as it will become stringy and unfit to eat.

Creamy Celery Olive Soup

½ cup (pitted) ripe olives
3 tablespoons butter or
    margarine
1 small onion, chopped
1 cup thinly sliced celery
1 teaspoon minced celery leaves

3 tablespoons flour
3 cups milk
1 teaspoon salt
⅛ teaspoon pepper
⅛ teaspoon dill weed
Paprika

Cut olives into wedges. Heat butter in saucepan. Add onion, celery, and leaves; cook until tender crisp, stirring occasionally. Stir in flour. Add half the milk and stir well. Add remaining milk with salt, pepper, dill weed, and olives. Stir while soup comes to full boil and thickens slightly. To serve, garnish with paprika. 4 to 6 servings.

French Onion Soup

1 cup thinly sliced onions
1½ tablespoons butter or
    margarine
1½ teaspoons flour
5 cups Beef Soup Stock
½ teaspoon Worcestershire
    sauce

¼ teaspoon salt
⅛ teaspoon ground white
    pepper
Toasted rolls, halved or pieces
    of toast
Grated Parmesan cheese

Sauté onions in butter or margarine until golden brown. Stir in flour and cook 1 minute. Add Beef Soup Stock and cook for 1 hour. Season with Worcestershire sauce, salt, and pepper.

Pour into flat ovenproof dishes or tureen. Arrange toast on top of soup and sprinkle with grated Parmesan cheese. Individual dishes may be placed under broiler until cheese is brown. 6 servings.

Okra Soup

1 soup bone   2 cups tomato pulp
4 cups finely cut okra   Salt and pepper to taste

Cover soup bone with cold water and allow to come to a boil.
Cook about 1 hour. Add okra and tomato pulp. Season. Simmer for
2 hours or until thick. Rice is invariably served with this soup and
sometimes corn and butter beans. 6 to 8 servings.

For variety, make Southern Gumbo from Okra Soup: add 1 onion,
chopped and browned in butter, 1 cup chopped green pepper, and ½
teaspoon celery seed. Cook all together until thick. 8 servings.

Beef Soup Stock

2 pounds soup meat and bones   ½ cup sliced carrots
1 tablespoon salt   ¾ cup diced fresh tomatoes
2 quarts cold water   ½ cup chopped green pepper
½ cup chopped onion   2 tablespoons chopped parsley
2½ cups chopped celery (stalks
    and leaves)

Simmer meat, bone, salt, and cold water for 2 hours. Add vegetables and cook for 1½ hours longer. Strain and chill soup. Remove
fat. 6 servings.

Oyster Bisque

Radium Springs Inn, near Albany, Georgia

1 slice onion   2 cups light cream
1 stalk celery, diced   Salt and white pepper to taste
2 tablespoons butter   Dash Tabasco sauce
1 quart oysters and juice   ¼ cup dry sherry

Cook onion and celery in butter until translucent, but not brown.
Chop the oysters, add juice, onion, and celery. (If you have a
blender, use it.) Put in an enameled saucepan with cream, salt,
pepper, Tabasco, and sherry. Simmer over low heat, stirring constantly. Do not allow to boil. 4 to 6 servings.

Mobile Oyster Soup

1 quart oysters and juice
1 quart rich milk
2 tablespoons butter
1 tablespoon minced parsley

Dash onion salt or 1 teaspoon
    onion juice
Salt and pepper to taste

Strain oyster liquid into saucepan; heat but do not boil. Heat milk in double boiler; stir in hot oyster broth. Add butter and seasonings and oysters. When oysters puff and are crinkled at edge, serve at once. 6 servings.

Peanuts are a major crop in our area—we use them in many good things. This is one of them.

Peanut Butter Soup

1 tablespoon butter or
    margarine
2 tablespoons flour
1 small onion, finely chopped

1 quart chicken stock or milk,
    hot
¼ cup finely chopped celery
1 cup peanut butter

Melt butter or margarine in the top of a double boiler over direct heat. Add flour and brown lightly, stirring constantly. Add onion, cooking until limp. Add chicken stock or milk, celery, and peanut butter and place over boiling water. Stir until smooth and heated through. 4 servings.

Peanut Soup Creole

½ cup chopped onion
2 teaspoons peanut oil
1 tablespoon flour
1½ teaspoons salt

½ teaspoon celery salt
½ cup peanut butter
2 cups milk
2 cups tomato juice

Sauté onion in peanut oil until tender but not browned. Add flour and seasonings. Blend in peanut butter. Add milk gradually, stirring to blend. Cook and stir until mixture comes to a boil and is thickened. Add tomato juice and bring just to a boil. Serve hot. About 5 cups.

Pork Sausage Soup

Mrs. A. C. Castleberry, Atlanta, Georgia

1 cup dried lima beans	*1 cup cubed raw potatoes*
4 cups water	*1 teaspoon salt*
1 pound pork sausage meat	*¼ teaspoon pepper*
⅓ cup chopped onion	*1 tablespoon chopped parsley*
¼ cup chopped celery	*1½ cups milk*

Soak beans overnight in water. Do not drain. Cook over low heat until tender. Shape sausage into 2-inch balls and brown in a skillet. Remove sausage from pan and pour off all but 1 tablespoon of drippings. Add onion, celery, and potatoes to drippings in pan. Stir and cook over medium heat until vegetables are tender. Add salt, pepper, and parsley to cooked beans. Stir in cooked vegetables. Add milk, stirring constantly. Add sausage balls. Cover and simmer 20 minutes. 4 to 6 servings.

Cloister Shrimp Bisque

The Cloister, Sea Island, Georgia

1½ cups butter	*4 quarts chicken broth*
2 cloves garlic	*2 cups dry sherry*
4 bay leaves	*1 quart light cream*
½ teaspoon rosemary	*¼ pound (1 stick) butter*
2 cups diced onion	*2 cups small diced shrimp*
2 cups diced celery	*Salt and pepper to taste*
2 pounds fresh shrimp, washed, cleaned, and passed through food chopper	*1 cup brandy*
	1 tablespoon monosodium glutamate
1½ cups flour	*1 pint heavy cream, whipped*
2 cups tomato paste	*Nutmeg*

Melt butter. Add garlic, bay leaves, rosemary, onion, celery. Cook 10 minutes and add the ground shrimp. Cook 10 minutes longer; add the flour. Cook for 5 minutes and add tomato paste, chicken broth, and sherry; bring to boil and add light cream. Cook for 30 minutes and strain through cheesecloth. Stir in slowly ¼ pound butter, diced shrimp, salt, pepper, brandy, and monosodium glutamate. Before serving, top each cup with a teaspoon of whipped cream, sprinkle with a little nutmeg, and place under broiler to glaze. Serve very hot. 24 servings.

She Crab Soup

Chef Manuel Filotis,
The William Hilton Inn, Hilton Head Island, South Carolina

2½ tablespoons butter	*⅛ teaspoon pepper*
1 tablespoon flour	*½ teaspoon Worcestershire*
2 quarts milk	*sauce*
2 cups white crab meat flakes	*½ teaspoon salt*
½ cup crab roe	*½ cup dry sherry*
Few drops onion juice	*½ pint heavy cream, whipped*
⅛ teaspoon mace	

Melt butter in top of double boiler and blend with flour until smooth. Add milk gradually, stirring constantly. Add the crab meat and roe and all seasonings. Simmer over hot water for 20 minutes.

To serve, place 1 tablespoon warm sherry in individual soup bowls, then add soup and top with whipped cream. 8 servings.

Split-pea Soup

Mrs. Dewey Conn, Clarkston, Georgia

2 cups green split peas	*3 tablespoons flour*
3 quarts water	*2 teaspoons salt*
1 ham bone (cracked)	*⅛ teaspoon pepper*
¼ cup chopped onion	*2 cups milk*
3 tablespoons butter	

Wash and soak peas overnight in hot water to cover. Drain, put peas in saucepan, and cover with water. Add ham bone and onion and cook until peas are soft. Remove ham bone. Press pea mixture through a sieve. Melt butter in saucepan. Blend in flour, salt, and pepper. Heat until mixture bubbles. Remove from heat.

Add milk gradually, stirring constantly. Bring rapidly to boiling, cook 1 to 2 minutes longer. Blend into sieved pea mixture. Heat thoroughly and serve hot. 12 to 14 servings.

Cumberland Fish Chowder

Mr. and Mrs. Lawrence S. Miller, Jekyll Island, Georgia

4 to 5 pounds flaky fish (mullet, bass, sheepshead)
4 cups diced potatoes
3 cups chopped onion
1 cup chopped celery
Salt to taste
½ teaspoon black pepper
½ teaspoon monosodium glutamate

2 teaspoons Italian seasoning
4 cups water, including fish stock
¼ pound butter or margarine
1 quart whole milk
½ cup dry sherry

Place fish in pot, cover with water, and cook about 1 hour or until it falls from bones. Pick and remove all bones. Save fish stock. There should be about 4 cups fish flakes and 2 to 3 cups stock.

Place potatoes, onions, celery, and seasonings in medium-size pot with fish stock and enough water to make 4 cups. Cook at low temperature for about 45 minutes or until tender.

Add butter or margarine and fish and bring to boil. Slowly stir in milk but do not allow to boil again. Heat until almost boiling, add sherry, and serve at once. Delicious with hush puppies. Makes about 4 quarts of chowder or 12 servings.

Fresh Vegetable Chowder

3 medium raw potatoes, cut in half
2 cups boiling water or soup stock
⅔ cup sliced small onions
1 cup sliced fresh carrots
1 cup diced celery

3 cups milk
¼ cup butter or margarine
½ teaspoon ground black pepper
1¾ teaspoons salt
Fresh parsley

Cook potatoes in boiling water or stock until tender, about 20 minutes, in covered saucepan. About 10 minutes before cooking time is up add onions, carrots, and celery. Cover and cook until tender. Remove potatoes, mash and return to soup pot. Potatoes thicken the soup. Add milk, butter, black pepper, and salt. Heat thoroughly. Serve in soup bowls garnished with fresh parsley. 6 servings.

Spanish Clam Chowder

Joseph B. Curtis, St. Augustine, Florida

1 pound white bacon	*½ pound white potatoes*
1 pound onions, sliced	*1 quart water*
1 large can (28 ounces)	*1 quart clams*
tomatoes (2½ cups)	*1 pint milk*
1 teaspoon each, rubbed sage,	*Salt and pepper to taste*
ground allspice, cloves, and	*1 datil pepper*
thyme	

Cut bacon in small pieces and fry. When brown, remove from pan and fry onions in fat. Put bacon back and add tomatoes, sage, allspice, cloves, and thyme. Cook until fairly thick. While sauce is cooking, cook potatoes in water until tender; mash in same water and add to sauce. Clean and chop clams; add with clam water to sauce and cook at low heat ½ hour. Just before serving add milk and salt and pepper and datil pepper. 6 servings.

Corn Chowder

4 tablespoons finely cut white	*1 teaspoon salt*
bacon	*⅛ teaspoon pepper*
4 tablespoons minced onion	*1 cup boiling water*
1 cup finely diced raw potatoes	*2 cups whole milk*
½ cup finely cut celery	*2 cups cream-style corn*
½ cup finely cut carrots	
4 tablespoons minced green	
pepper	

Cook bacon slowly in kettle until fat begins to fry out. Add onion and cook slowly until golden brown. Add potatoes, celery, carrots, green pepper, and seasonings with the water. Cook until tender but not mushy. Just before serving, add milk and corn. Heat thoroughly but do not boil. Serve with parsley and Parmesan cheese, if desired. 6 servings.

4

SALADS

Salads know no season, and without them many meals would be incomplete. They may be used as appetizers, accompaniments to the meal, as the main dish of a meal, or as a dessert. They are great for picnics, covered-dish suppers, and for carried lunches.

One of the secrets of a successful salad maker is learning to choose pleasing combinations of ingredients with contrast in color, texture, form, and flavor. Experiment with color but be sure food combinations do not clash.

Cut or tear foods into pieces that are large enough to be identified, yet small enough to handle easily in eating. Avoid cutting salad greens—tear them into pieces. Cutting greens tends to make them wilt faster.

Keep hot salads hot, not lukewarm, and cold salads icy cold.

Use the correct dressing. Don't drown salads. Too much dressing will make salads limp, soggy, and unattractive. A small amount of dressing adds just the right flavor. Add dressings at the last possible moment. If salads stand in their dressing too long, they tend to lose crispness and are unattractive.

Macaroni Beef Pimiento Salad

1 tablespoon salt
2 quarts boiling water
2 cups (8 ounces) elbow
*   macaroni*
4 tablespoons salad oil
¼ cup vinegar
1 tablespoon lemon juice
1 teaspoon salt
¼ teaspoon pepper

¼ teaspoon dry mustard
¼ teaspoon chervil
1 medium onion, chopped
1 (4-ounce) jar pimiento,
*   drained and diced*
2 cups (about ½ pound) thinly
*   sliced cooked roast beef*
1 medium cucumber, thinly
*   sliced*

Add 1 tablespoon salt to rapidly boiling water. Gradually add macaroni so that water continues to boil. Cook uncovered, stirring occasionally, until tender. Drain in colander.

In large bowl, toss macaroni with 2 tablespoons oil. In saucepan, combine vinegar, remaining 2 tablespoons oil, lemon juice, salt, pepper, mustard, chervil, onion, pimiento, and beef. Heat thoroughly and toss lightly with macaroni. Chill.

Score cucumber by running tines of fork end to end; cut into thin slices and arrange around salad before serving. 4 to 6 servings.

Chicken Mousse

2 cups chicken stock, seasoned
2 teaspoons minced parsley
¼ cup minced celery
2 tablespoons chopped pimiento
¼ cup chopped ripe olives
½ teaspoon salt
¼ teaspoon paprika

3 egg yolks, beaten
2 envelopes plain gelatin
¼ cup cold water
2½ cups diced cooked chicken
1½ cups whipped cream
1 tablespoon lemon juice
1 tablespoon horseradish

Place stock and next six ingredients in double boiler until hot. Pour in egg yolks slowly and cook 2 minutes. Add gelatin, soaked 5 minutes in cold water, and cook until partly thick. Add remaining ingredients and pour into a 6-cup mold rinsed with cold water. Chill until firm. Unmold onto chilled platter. Garnish with watercress or parsley. 8 servings.

Hearty Beef Salad

2 cups diced cooked beef
½ cup French dressing
½ cup diced cooked potatoes
½ cup cooked green beans
½ cup coarsely grated carrots

¼ cup chopped sweet pickle
2 hard-cooked eggs, diced
½ cup mayonnaise
4 to 6 lettuce cups

Pour French dressing over beef and marinate for 1 hour in refrigerator. Chill potatoes and beans. Combine beef, potatoes, beans, carrots, pickle, and egg. Moisten with mayonnaise and mix lightly. Serve in lettuce cups. 4 servings.

Chicken Salad Supper

2 cups diced cooked chicken
1 cup diced cooked carrots
1 cup cooked peas
1 cup diced celery
2 teaspoons minced onion
¾ teaspoon salt

⅛ teaspoon pepper
¾ cup mayonnaise
6 hard-cooked eggs, deviled
Sliced tomatoes
Boston lettuce

Combine chicken, carrots, peas, celery, onion, salt, and pepper with mayonnaise. Press into an 8-inch square pan lined with waxed paper. Place in refrigerator until ready to serve. Unmold on platter; garnish with deviled eggs, sliced tomatoes, and lettuce. 6 servings.

Chicken Salad in Pimiento Cups

2 (7 ounces each) cans or jars
  whole pimientos, drained
3 cups chopped cooked chicken
2 cups cold cooked rice
1 cup thinly sliced celery
1 cup drained canned pineapple
  tidbits
1 ripe avocado, diced
  (optional)

½ teaspoon curry powder
Salt to taste
½ cup French dressing
½ cup sour cream
Seasonings to taste
Salad greens

The pimientos should be well drained and all excess moisture removed with paper towels.

One way to stuff pimientos is to hold the pod cupped in the palm of your hand and carefully pack the salad mixture into it. Another way is to use greased custard cups or muffin tins (3 or 3½ inches in diameter) as follows: Open pimiento pods down one side to flatten. Press two opened pods into each cup, reserving leftover pieces for later use as garnish or ingredient. Chill pimiento cups while preparing salad.

To prepare salad, combine and toss together all ingredients except last four; chill. Blend together French dressing and sour cream; taste and adjust seasonings. Additional curry powder may be used here or a few tablespoons of very finely chopped chutney.

Combine salad mixture and creamy dressing, mixing well. Fill pimiento cups and chill until ready to serve or at least 3 hours. Serve on salad greens. 8 servings.

Regal Chicken Salad

Mrs. A. Eugene Bowers, Jonesboro, Georgia

CRANBERRY LAYER

2 tablespoons unflavored
   gelatin
½ cup cold water
¼ cup orange juice
1 (1-pound) can whole
   cranberry sauce
Dash cloves
Dash cinnamon

CHICKEN LAYER

2 tablespoons unflavored gelatin
¼ cup cold water
1 cup sour cream
¼ cup salad dressing
2 cups diced cooked chicken
¾ cup slivered almonds
½ cup minced celery
½ teaspoon salt
¼ teaspoon poultry seasoning
Salad greens

CRANBERRY LAYER

Soften gelatin in cold water. Place over low heat and stir constantly until gelatin dissolves. Add orange juice, cranberry sauce, and spices. Spoon into a 2-quart mold and chill until firm.

CHICKEN LAYER

Soften gelatin in cold water. Place over low heat and stir constantly until gelatin is dissolved. Remove from heat and blend in sour cream and salad dressing. Add other ingredients and spoon over firm cranberry layer in mold. Chill until firm. Turn out onto bed of crisp greens and garnish as desired. 8 to 10 servings.

Ham, Pea, and Celery Salad

2 (3 ounces each) packages
   celery or mixed vegetable
   salad gelatin
½ teaspoon salt
¼ teaspoon onion salt
2 cups boiling water

1½ cups cold water
2 tablespoons vinegar
1½ cups diced cooked ham
1 cup cooked peas
½ cup sliced celery
Salad greens

Dissolve gelatin and salts in boiling water. Add cold water and vinegar. Chill until very thick. Fold in ham, peas, and celery. Pour into 1½-quart ring mold. Chill until firm. Unmold on crisp greens. Garnish with mayonnaise and additional peas if desired. 8 to 10 servings.

Green Pea and Crab Salad

1 (10-ounce) package frozen
   peas, cooked and chilled
1 (8-ounce) package frozen
   crab meat, broken into chunks
½ cup sliced celery
½ cup mayonnaise or salad
   dressing
3 tablespoons lime or lemon
   juice

1 tablespoon drained capers
½ teaspoon tarragon leaves
1 tablespoon sliced green onion
1 tablespoon chopped parsley
2 ripe avocados, peeled and cut
   in half
Salad greens

Combine peas, crab meat, and celery in mixing bowl. Blend together mayonnaise or salad dressing, 2 tablespoons lime or lemon juice, capers, tarragon, onion, and parsley. Pour over pea mixture. Toss lightly to coat ingredients. Marinate in refrigerator 30 minutes to 1 hour. Drizzle remaining tablespoon of lime or lemon juice over avocado halves; fill with salad mixture. Arrange on crisp salad greens. 4 servings.

Turkey Salad

3 cups diced cold turkey
1 cup diced celery
1 tablespoon fresh lemon juice
½ teaspoon ground thyme
1½ teaspoons salt
⅛ teaspoon garlic powder
⅛ teaspoon ground black pepper
⅓ cup mayonnaise

Combine all ingredients and spoon into center of a cranberry ring. 6 to 8 servings.

Salmon Salad

6 cups diced cooked potatoes
1½ cups minced celery
1 cup diced cucumber
½ cup sliced green onion
1 (1-pound) can salmon, drained and flaked
1 tablespoon chopped fresh basil
1½ cups mayonnaise
½ cup sour cream
¼ teaspoon pepper
1 teaspoon salt
2 tablespoons lemon juice or vinegar
Parsley and tomato "roses" for garnish

Combine potatoes, celery, cucumber, onions, salmon, and basil.

Combine mayonnaise, sour cream, pepper, salt, and lemon juice or vinegar. Stir into potato-salmon mixture. Pack into a 10-cup mold and chill. When ready to serve, unmold onto cold serving platter and garnish with parsley clusters and tomato "roses." Serve with mayonnaise. 8 to 10 servings.

Shrimp Mousse

2 envelopes plain gelatin
½ cup cold water
1 cup bouillon (use 2 cubes of
   beef or chicken in 1 cup hot
   water)
¼ cup mayonnaise
1 teaspoon grated onion
1 tablespoon minced parsley
2 cups finely chopped cooked
   shrimp

½ cup heavy cream, whipped
½ cup thinly sliced cucumbers
¼ cup thinly sliced radishes
1 tablespoon lime juice
Freshly ground black pepper
   and salt to taste
Dash Worcestershire sauce
Dash Tabasco sauce

Soften gelatin in cold water 5 minutes. Heat bouillon to boiling and add gelatin. Stir until dissolved. Cook until thick and syrupy. Add rest of ingredients in order given and spoon into 4-cup mold that's been rubbed with salad oil. Bottom of mold may be covered with thin slices of cucumber and radishes for pretty final effect. Cover with waxed paper and chill until firm. Unmold on flat chilled serving plate and garnish with additional cucumbers and radishes. Serve with extra mayonnaise. 6 to 8 servings.

Shrimp Salad

2 cups water
1 bay leaf
2 teaspoons salt
2 pounds raw shrimp
2 tablespoons olive oil
¼ cup minced shallots or onions

2 cloves garlic, minced
1 cup chopped green pepper
2 tablespoons soy sauce
1 apple, peeled and grated
¼ cup chopped peanuts
1 cup Coconut Milk

Bring the water, bay leaf, and salt to a boil; cook the shrimp in the mixture 8 minutes. Drain, cool, clean, and cut each shrimp into quarters.

Heat oil in skillet; sauté the shallots and garlic 3 minutes. Cool 5 minutes and mix with the green pepper, soy sauce, apple, peanuts, and Coconut Milk. Pour over the shrimp and chill 1 hour. 6 to 8 servings.

COCONUT MILK

When fresh coconut milk is not available pour 1 cup hot milk over ½ cup flaked coconut; let stand 30 minutes, then squeeze through cheesecloth to extract milk.

Fresh Cantaloupe Shrimp Salad

3 medium-size cantaloupes
½ teaspoon powdered mustard
½ teaspoon warm water
⅔ cup mayonnaise
4 tablespoons chopped fresh
  tomatoes
1½ tablespoons fresh lemon
  juice
1 tablespoon prepared
  horseradish sauce
1 teaspoon chili powder
½ teaspoon salt
⅛ teaspoon minced fresh garlic
⅛ teaspoon cayenne pepper
18 medium-size shrimp,
  cooked, peeled, and deveined

Cut cantaloupes in half and remove seeds and stringy portion. Combine powdered mustard with warm water and let stand 10 minutes for flavor to develop, then combine with remaining ingredients except shrimp and spoon sauce into cavities of cantaloupes. Arrange 3 shrimp around sauce; serve chilled. 6 servings.

Shrimp Curry Rice Salad

Mrs. Blanton Lovin, Brunswick, Georgia

¼ cup chopped onions
1 tablespoon vinegar
2 tablespoons salad oil
½ teaspoon curry powder
1½ cups cooked rice
1 cup diced celery
¼ cup diced green pepper
2½ cups cooked shrimp
¾ cup mayonnaise
Salad greens

Combine onion, vinegar, oil, and curry powder in a bowl. Stir in rice. Chill 2 hours to blend flavors. Just before serving add celery, green pepper, and shrimp. Add mayonnaise and mix lightly. Serve on crisp salad greens. 6 servings.

Tuna and Cottage Cheese Loaf

2 envelopes unflavored gelatin
½ cup cold milk
1 cup sour cream
1 cup mayonnaise
2 cups creamed cottage cheese
2 (6½ ounces each) cans flaked tuna
1 tablespoon minced green onion
¼ cup sliced stuffed olives

1 cup finely chopped celery
2 tablespoons lemon juice
Salt and pepper to taste
3 ripe tomatoes, peeled and sliced
2 cucumbers, unpeeled and sliced
Salad greens
5 hard-cooked eggs, deviled

Soften gelatin in cold milk for 5 minutes, then dissolve over boiling water. Cool. Add cream, mayonnaise, cottage cheese, drained tuna, onion, olives, celery, and lemon juice. Season with salt and pepper and pour into a 9×5-inch metal loaf pan or individual molds. Chill until firm.

Unmold loaf on flat oblong tray or platter. Arrange overlapping slices of tomatoes and cucumbers on salad greens on each side. Garnish with deviled egg halves and serve with any desired dressing. 8 to 10 servings.

Congealed Asparagus Salad

Bill Bailey, Club Manager, Fitzgerald, Georgia, Country Club

¾ cup sugar
1½ cups water
½ cup white vinegar
2 envelopes unflavored gelatin
½ teaspoon salt
1 cup chopped celery
2 pimientos, chopped

Juice of ½ lemon (2 tablespoons)
2 teaspoons grated onion
½ cup chopped pecans
1 (10½-ounce) can cut asparagus

Combine sugar, 1 cup water, and vinegar; bring to a boil. In separate container dissolve gelatin in remaining ½ cup water; add to sugar mixture. Cool; add remaining ingredients and pour into 6-cup mold. Refrigerate to set. 8 to 10 servings.

Great with fried fish and hush puppies.

Stay Crisp Slaw

Mrs. Hosea Varnn, Thomasville, Georgia

8 cups shredded cabbage (use knife)	1 envelope unflavored gelatin
2 carrots, shredded	⅔ cup sugar
1 green pepper, cut in thin strips	⅔ cup vinegar
½ cup chopped onion	2 teaspoons celery seed
¾ cup cold water	1½ tablespoons salt
	¼ teaspoon black pepper
	⅔ cup salad oil

Mix shredded cabbage and carrots, green pepper, and onion; sprinkle with ½ cup cold water; chill. Soften gelatin in remaining ¼ cup cold water. Mix sugar, vinegar, celery seed, salt, and pepper in saucepan; bring to boil. Stir in softened gelatin. Cool until slightly thickened; beat well. Gradually beat in salad oil; drain vegetables. Pour dressing over top; mix lightly until all vegetables are coated with dressing. May be served immediately or stored in refrigerator. Stir just before serving to separate pieces. 12 servings.

Hot Slaw

1 medium head cabbage	1 teaspoon flour
¼ cup cider vinegar	1 egg
3 teaspoons sugar	1 teaspoon grated onion
⅓ teaspoon salt	1 teaspoon minced green pepper
⅓ teaspoon dry mustard	
1 tablespoon butter	1 teaspoon diced pimiento

Boil cabbage no more than 1½ minutes, barely covered with salted water. Saving the water, drain cabbage carefully, shred, and set to one side in serving bowl. Into ½ cup of the cabbage water stir vinegar, sugar, salt, and mustard. Melt butter and blend with flour, then add to vinegar mixture. Stirring continuously, boil until thick. Beat egg gently into 3 tablespoons of hot mixture, then stir into rest of mixture. Add onions and pepper. Continuing to stir, cook until slightly thick again to complete the sauce. Ladle over shredded cabbage while hot and toss. Sprinkle with pimiento. 6 servings.

Fruited Slaw

1½ quarts crisp shredded   ¼ cup mayonnaise
  cabbage   ¼ cup sour cream
3 cups sliced fresh nectarines   2 tablespoons fresh lemon juice
1 cup seedless green grapes   ½ teaspoon salt
1 cup tiny marshmallows
  (optional)

Combine all ingredients and toss well to blend. 6 to 8 servings.

Cauliflower Sour Cream Slaw

1 large head cauliflower   1½ teaspoons caraway seed
½ cup French dressing   ½ teaspoon salt
¼ cup sliced green onions   1 cup sour cream
¼ cup chopped celery leaves

Cut cauliflower into thin slices. Marinate in French dressing in a
large bowl. Chill for several hours. Meanwhile, in a small bowl,
gently fold onion, celery leaves, caraway seed, and salt into sour
cream. Drain cauliflower; toss lightly with sour cream dressing. 6
servings.

Green Green Salad

Mrs. Hansell A. Parks, Atlanta, Georgia

Chopped endive   ½ cup catsup
Lettuce and parsley   ⅓ cup mayonnaise
Chopped celery   ½ teaspoon steak sauce
Green pepper rings   2 tablespoons pickle relish
1 small onion, chopped   Dash dry mustard
2 small tomatoes, chopped   2 hard-cooked eggs, chopped
¼ cup vinegar

Toss together endive, lettuce, parsley, celery, and green pepper.
Soak onion and tomato in vinegar a few minutes. Add catsup, mayonnaise, steak sauce, relish, and mustard; mix well. Spoon dressing
over salad greens in bowl and garnish with eggs. 6 to 8 servings.

Cucumber Salad

Mrs. Bill Olsen, Cordele, Georgia

7 cups sliced cucumbers (very thin)
3 tablespoons salt

½ cup sugar
1¼ cups vinegar
½ cup water

Combine cucumbers and salt and let stand for 1 hour. Then place cucumbers in a cheesecloth bag and press water out. Combine sugar, vinegar, and water. Add cucumbers to this solution and chill until ready to serve. 10 to 12 servings.

Cucumber Beet Salad

1½ cups sliced cooked beets
2 tablespoons vinegar
1½ cups diced cucumber
½ cup sour cream

2 tablespoons minced onion
1 tablespoon chopped sweet pickle
Lettuce or spinach leaves

Let beets stand in vinegar 1 hour. Mix with next four ingredients. Serve on crisp lettuce or spinach leaves. 6 servings.

Gazpacho Salad

Mrs. George Brumley, St. Mary's, Georgia

6 large tomatoes
6 green onions
2 to 3 stalks celery
4 cucumbers

2 green peppers
Salad Dressing
Crisp lettuce cups

Chop first five ingredients into bite-size pieces. Toss and let stand. At serving time, drain, add Salad Dressing to moisten, and fill lettuce cups. 8 servings.

SALAD DRESSING

½ cup olive oil
1 cup red wine vinegar
¼ teaspoon freshly ground pepper

¼ teaspoon salt
1 clove garlic
¼ teaspoon chopped mint
¼ teaspoon oregano

Combine all ingredients in closely covered jar the night before using. Refrigerate. Remove the clove of garlic before serving. 1½ cups.

Head Lettuce with Bacon Sauce

1 large head lettuce
3 slices bacon
2 tablespoons bacon fat
2 tablespoons flour
1 cup milk
2 teaspoons finely chopped
   onion

¾ teaspoon salt
⅛ teaspoon ground black
   pepper
2 teaspoons fresh lemon juice

Cut lettuce into six wedges. Place on a rack in a large saucepan. Pour in only enough boiling water to cover bottom of saucepan. Cover and cook 5 minutes or until lettuce is tender but still crisp. (The lettuce will darken slightly.)

In the meantime, cook bacon until crisp. Drain. Reserve 2 table-spoons of the bacon fat and mix with flour until smooth in a small saucepan. Gradually add milk and onion. Cook until medium thickness, stirring constantly. Crumble bacon and add along with salt, pepper, and lemon juice. Mix well. Serve over steamed lettuce wedges. 6 servings.

Country Kitchen Potato Salad

4 cups diced cooked potatoes
2 hard-cooked eggs, chopped
½ cup chopped celery
¼ cup chopped pickle
⅔ cup mayonnaise
1 tablespoon vinegar
1 tablespoon instant minced
   onion

2 teaspoons mixed herbs
⅛ teaspoon monosodium
   glutamate
¼ teaspoon white pepper
1 teaspoon dry mustard
¼ teaspoon crushed fennel seed
   (optional)

Put potatoes, eggs, celery, and pickle in bowl. Blend together remaining ingredients and gently mix with potato mixture. Chill. 6 servings.

German Potato Salad

6 slices bacon, cut in pieces
2 medium onions, diced
2 tablespoons flour
2 tablespoons sugar
2 teaspoons salt

3 teaspoons paprika
1 cup water
1 cup cider vinegar
8 large boiled potatoes, diced
4 hard-cooked eggs, diced

Brown bacon and onion in large skillet. Mix flour with bacon fat and add seasonings and liquids. Stir and cook until smooth. Add diced potatoes and eggs. Continue cooking until heated through. 10 servings.

Herbed Hot Potato Salad

James C. Tilly, Rome, Georgia

8 medium-size potatoes, pared
and sliced ¼ inch thick
1 cup sliced celery
3 tablespoons sugar
2 teaspoons salt
¼ teaspoon pepper
1 (1-ounce) package exotic
herbs salad dressing mix

3 tablespoons cider vinegar
2 tablespoons salad oil
⅓ cup heavy cream
1 medium-size red onion,
peeled, sliced, and separated
into rings

Cook potatoes and celery in boiling salted water for 10 minutes or just until tender. Drain carefully to avoid breaking slices. Combine sugar, salt, pepper, exotic herbs, and vinegar in a cup; stir in oil and then cream. Drizzle over hot potatoes; spoon into center of serving platter. Top with onion rings. 8 servings.

Sweet Potato Salad

2 (1½ pounds each) cans sweet
potatoes or yams
4 green onions, finely cut
1 teaspoon salt
1½ cups finely cut celery

1 teaspoon lemon juice
4 hard-cooked eggs, mashed
½ cup mayonnaise
½ cup tangy mustard-flavored
dressing

Drain liquid from potatoes. Mash potatoes and combine with remaining ingredients. Cover well and refrigerate. This may be made a day in advance. 8 servings.

When Phil Campbell was Georgia's Commissioner of Agriculture, I visited with him and his wife Nan at their home in Watkinsville. Mrs. Campbell prepared this salad along with other good things. Mr. Campbell later became U. S. Undersecretary of Agriculture.

Tomato Aspic and Cottage Cheese Salad

2 envelopes unflavored gelatin
½ cup cold water
2½ cups tomato juice
¼ cup lemon juice

1 tablespoon horseradish
½ tablespoon minced onion
1 teaspoon salt

Soften gelatin in cold water. Heat tomato juice and add gelatin. Add remaining ingredients and pour into 6×10-inch loaf pan or a 4 cup round mold. Chill until firm then add the white layer. 12 servings.

1 tablespoon gelatin
¼ cup cold water
1 cup hot water

1 cup sieved cottage cheese
1 cup salad dressing
Salad greens

Soften gelatin in cold water; add hot water. Cool until syrupy. Beat until fluffy and fold in remaining ingredients. Place over tomato layer and chill until firm. Unmold on salad greens. Serve with any desired dressing.

Wilkes's Special Tossed Salad

Mrs. Roy Wilkes, Atlanta, Georgia

2 tomatoes, quartered for
  garnishing
1 cup sliced cauliflower
  flowerets
½ head lettuce, broken in small
  pieces
3 tablespoons crumbled blue
  cheese

Watercress
Parsley
½ cucumber, sliced
6 radishes, sliced
1 tablespoon capers
Salad Dressing

Put all ingredients except dressing in salad bowl and toss together. Pour Salad Dressing over this. 4 servings.

SALAD DRESSING

¼ teaspoon black pepper
½ teaspoon sugar
½ teaspoon salt
¼ teaspoon dry mustard
Paprika
Garlic salt, optional
1 cup olive oil

Juice of 1 large lemon
2 tablespoons vinegar
1 tablespoon tomato juice
1 teaspoon grated onion
Few drops Tabasco sauce,
  optional

Combine dry ingredients with oil. Mix well, then add other ingredients. Shake well in jar. Best if allowed to stand a few hours. 1½ cups.

Horseradish Ring with Vegetable Salad

1 envelope (1 tablespoon)
  plain gelatin
¼ cup cold water
½ cup boiling water
1½ cups cottage cheese
¼ to ⅓ cup prepared
  horseradish

2 tablespoons lemon juice
¼ teaspoon salt
1 to 2 teaspoons sugar or equal
  in non-caloric sweetener
¼ teaspoon paprika
Lettuce
Vegetable Salad

Soften gelatin in the cold water. Add boiling water and stir until dissolved. Combine with the cottage cheese that has been blended smooth in an electric blender or mixer, horseradish, lemon juice, salt, sugar, and paprika. Mix well and pour into a fancy 1-quart mold. Chill until firm.

Unmold on lettuce leaves and surround with the vegetables. 8 servings.

VEGETABLE SALAD

1 small head red cabbage,
  shredded
½ green pepper, cut into rings
2 tomatoes, cut in eighths

Radish roses
Cucumber slices
Lettuce
Crisp dry toast

If ring mold is used, fill center with mixed vegetables. Serve with a dressing made by blending 1 cup cottage cheese, 2 tablespoons lemon juice, dash of paprika and salt.

Serve with crisp dry toast made by rolling slices of sandwich bread with a rolling pin. Trim off crusts and cut bread into any desired shape. Place on cookie sheet in 250-degree oven for 8 to 10 minutes until toasted.

Fresh Cranberry Salad

2 envelopes unflavored gelatin
½ cup fresh orange juice
1 cup hot water
1 cup sugar
¼ teaspoon salt
¾ teaspoon ground cloves

4 cups raw cranberries
1 cup diced celery
1 teaspoon grated orange rind
¼ cup fresh lemon juice
½ cup chopped nuts
3 cups turkey salad

Soften gelatin in orange juice. Stir in hot water, sugar, salt, and cloves. Mix well. Put cranberries through a food chopper, using medium blade, and add to mixture. Stir in celery, grated orange rind, lemon juice, and nuts. Pour into a 5-cup ring mold. Chill until firm and ready to serve. Unmold and fill center with turkey salad. Serve with mayonnaise. 12 servings.

24-hour Fruit Salad

2 eggs, beaten
4 tablespoons vinegar
4 tablespoons sugar
2 tablespoons melted butter
1 cup whipping cream
2 cups drained, pitted, halved
   white cherries

2 cups drained pineapple
   chunks
3 cans mandarin oranges,
   drained
2 cups miniature marshmallows

Put eggs in top of double boiler, add vinegar and sugar, beating constantly while cooking. Cook until thick and smooth. Add butter and cool. When cool, fold in whipped cream, fruits, and marshmallows. Spoon into mold. Let stand in refrigerator for 24 hours. Serve chilled. 8 to 10 servings.

Double Apple Salad
Mrs. Albert M. Rudd, Kingston, Georgia

4 tablespoons heavy cream	1 large red apple
2 tablespoons mayonnaise	1 large carrot
2 teaspoons apple jelly	1/3 cup drained crushed
1/3 medium-size cabbage	pineapple

Mix cream, mayonnaise, and jelly in a bowl and let stand at room temperature about 20 minutes. Beat with rotary beater or mixer until smooth. Shred or chop cabbage rather fine. Chop apple and carrot, leaving red peeling on the apple. Add pineapple and toss lightly in the dressing. Serve at once. 6 servings.

Banana Apple Rose Salad

6 red apples	3 bananas, sliced
Lemon juice	1/2 cup chopped nuts
2 (3 ounces each) packages	Mayonnaise
cream cheese, at room	Lettuce
temperature	

Begin preparation at least 2 hours before serving. Without peeling, core apples. Remove one slice from top; save. Scoop out apples, leaving about a 1/2-inch wall. Save apple meat that has been scooped out to mix later with filling.

Score inside of apple with a paring knife. Brush all exposed surfaces of apple and top with lemon juice to keep from darkening and wipe outside dry.

To form petals, start at the top of apple, pressing level teaspoon of cream cheese against side of apple and then drawing spoon down with curving motion. Form two to three rows of petals. For an extra-special look, tint one package of cheese light pink, the other a deeper pink. Refrigerate roses for at least 1 hour.

Just before serving, dice apple meat which was saved from scooping out apples and combine with banana slices and nuts. Add enough mayonnaise to hold together.

Carefully spoon mixture into apple roses. Top with apple slice and additional banana slices. Serve on lettuce. 6 servings.

Marinated Olive Salad

4 cups drained, pitted, unstuffed   1 teaspoon crumbled basil
   green olives   leaves
1 large onion, thinly sliced   ½ cup wine vinegar
1 cup thinly sliced celery   ½ cup olive oil
1 teaspoon crumbled oregano   ¼ cup pimiento strips
   leaves   Lettuce

Drain olives. Cover olives with cold water and let stand in a cool place several hours. Drain olives. Mix olives with onion, celery, oregano, basil, vinegar, oil, and pimiento. Chill at least 4 hours before serving.

Line a salad bowl with crisp lettuce and add olive mixture. 6 to 8 servings.

Salad may also be served as an antipasto ingredient.

Spiced Peach Mold

1 (29-ounce) jar pickled   1 (8-ounce) package cream
   peaches   cheese
1 cup fresh orange juice   ½ cup crushed pecans
1 (3-ounce) package   Lettuce
   orange-flavored gelatin

Remove seeds from pickled peaches, tearing as little as possible. Bring peach juice and orange juice to a boil; add gelatin. Soften cream cheese with a little of the juice and add pecans. Fill peach hollows with cream cheese. Place each peach in an individual mold and fill with gelatin; allow to congeal. Garnish with slivers of orange peel and serve on lettuce. 8 to 10 servings.

Pineapple Strawberry Salad

4 slices pineapple   2 tablespoons lime juice
Watercress or endive   1 tablespoon honey
1 pint fresh strawberries   2 tablespoons salad oil

For each serving, place a pineapple slice on watercress on a salad plate. Stem all but four of the strawberries. Cut the stemmed berries into lengthwise slices and arrange them petal fashion on the pineapple slices. Garnish each portion with a whole berry. Combine lime juice, honey, and salad oil and serve over salad. 4 servings.

Summer Rainbow Salad

3 ripe avocados
Lime or lemon juice
¼ teaspoon salt
1 cup strawberries or other berries
1 large orange

1 cup melon balls
2 tablespoons mint jelly
2 tablespoons orange juice
2 tablespoons lime or lemon juice

Cut avocados lengthwise into halves; remove seeds. Cut avocado balls with melon ball cutter or ½-teaspoon measure; reserve shells. Sprinkle balls with lime juice and half the salt. Rinse and hull strawberries; cut into halves. Pare and section orange.

Arrange avocado balls, berries, orange sections, and melon balls in avocado shells; chill.

Heat together mint jelly and orange juice; cool. Add 2 tablespoons lime juice and remaining salt; spoon onto fruit. 6 servings.

Raisin Salad

Mrs. Louise Hudgins, Griffin, Georgia

½ cup water
⅔ cup raisins
½ cup boiling water
1 (3-ounce) package lime gelatin
½ cup ginger ale
5 tablespoons lemon juice

Salt
½ cup finely cut celery
½ cup shredded carrots
¼ cup chopped sweet pickle
Crisp salad greens
Mayonnaise

Boil raisins in ½ cup water 5 minutes. Let cool. Pour ½ cup boiling water over gelatin and stir until dissolved. Add ginger ale, lemon juice, and few grains of salt and stir until blended. Chill until thick but not firm. Add celery, carrots, pickle, and raisins. Pour into 4-cup mold and chill until firm. Serve unmolded on salad greens and topped with mayonnaise. 4 servings.

Swamp cabbage is the heart of our lowland swamp palm—and is elegant eating.

Swamp Cabbage Salad

Mrs. Leslie Hatchett, Lamont, Florida

> *2 cleaned heads (buds) swamp cabbage*
> *1 (No. 3) can chunk pineapple*
> *1 small (2-ounce) jar maraschino cherries, halved*
> *Mayonnaise*

Chop cabbage, drain pineapple and cherries, and add to cabbage. Combine some of the fruit juices with mayonnaise to thin somewhat. Pour over cabbage and mix. 4 to 6 servings.

5

CHEESE AND EGGS

Gathering eggs from the hen nests was one of my chores when I lived on the farm. Sometimes, when we had used an unusual number of eggs, it was necessary practically to roust the ole hen off the nest to get enough. Now that every store has a super abundance, we still use eggs in great quantity. They go into something for almost every meal of the day.

Cheese, too, played an important part in my early years. My recollection of eating at my grandmother Hartley's abundant table was a hoop of cheese always on the "side table." My grandfather would cut off a small piece for dunkin', in his mustache cup of hot coffee. I was allowed a piece of cheese without the coffee.

The Southeast produces eggs in great number and some of our best recipes for their usage have been developed by wives of men in this business. Here are some of their best recipes put together in this section. You will find many other uses for both cheese and eggs as ingredients scattered throughout the book.

Ham Rarebit

¼ cup ham fat   1 bouillon cube
¼ cup flour   ¼ cup grated Cheddar cheese
1 teaspoon dry mustard   ½ cup diced cooked ham
1½ cups milk

Melt fat, add flour and mustard. Stir in milk, add bouillon cube
and grated cheese. Heat slowly and stir until smooth. Add ham and
cook over low heat about 4 or 5 minutes longer. Serve on hot buttered toast. 4 servings.

This is one of the dishes Mrs. Yates Green served to a group of
food editors on a tour of Georgia.

Cheese Custard

Mrs. Yates Green
New Perry Hotel, Perry, Georgia

3 eggs   ½ package (12 to 15) saltine
3 cups milk   crackers
3 cups shredded sharp Cheddar   Salt and pepper to taste
    cheese

Beat eggs lightly, stir in milk and cheese. Crumble crackers and
add to mixture. Season to taste with salt and pepper. Pour into flat
2-quart casserole. Bake at 350 for 30 to 40 minutes, or until set. 8 to
10 servings.

Cheese Loaf

2 eggs   1 tablespoon melted margarine
1½ cups grated Cheddar cheese   ¾ teaspoon salt
1½ cups soft bread crumbs
2 cups evaporated milk mixed
    with 1 cup water

Beat eggs. Add remaining ingredients in order given. Pour into a
greased 1½-quart baking dish. Set in a pan of hot water and bake in
a slow oven, 325 degrees, until set, about 1 hour. 8 servings.

Cheese Soufflé with Cranberry Sauce

1 tablespoon quick-cooking
  tapioca
1 teaspoon salt
1 cup milk
1 cup grated American cheese

3 egg yolks, well beaten
⅛ teaspoon Worcestershire
  sauce
3 egg whites, stiffly beaten

Combine tapioca, salt, and milk. Cook in top of double boiler 10 minutes, stirring frequently. Add cheese, cook until cheese melts. Add a little hot mixture to egg yolks, then stir in the remaining hot mixture. Add Worcestershire sauce. Cool slightly; fold into egg whites. Bake in an ungreased 1-quart casserole in a slow oven, 300 degrees, for 1 hour and 15 minutes or until cooked all the way through. Serve with canned jellied cranberry sauce. 6 servings.

Bacon 'n' Egg Olive-cheese Pie

1 cup ripe olives
Unbaked pastry for 1 (9-inch)
  shell
4 slices bacon
¼ cup green onion finely
  chopped

1½ cups milk
1 teaspoon salt
½ teaspoon dry mustard
3 eggs
2 cups grated sharp American
  cheese

Cut olives into large pieces. Line 9-inch pie pan with pastry. Fry bacon crisp; drain and crumble coarsely. Pour off all but 1 tablespoon drippings. Add onion; cook slowly until transparent. Add milk, salt, and mustard; heat to scalding. Beat eggs lightly; stir in cheese. Add hot milk mixture slowly. Mix in olives and bacon. Turn into pastry shell.

Bake in 450-degree oven for 10 minutes. Reduce heat to 350 degrees. Bake 25 to 35 minutes longer or until custard is set in center. Cool 5 or 10 minutes before serving. 6 servings.

Bacon 'n' Eggs Supreme

8 slices hickory-smoked bacon
2 cups cubed cooked potatoes

8 eggs
Salt and pepper

Dice the bacon and brown slowly (use iron skillet for best results). Add the potatoes. Beat the eggs. Season. When potatoes are browned lightly, pour beaten eggs over the bacon and potatoes. Stir slowly till the eggs are set. This makes 5 to 6 servings, and what's more, takes only one skillet to cook the whole meal.

Baked Eggs in Cheese Sauce

2 tablespoons minced onion
2 tablespoons butter or
  margarine
2 tablespoons flour
½ teaspoon salt

1 cup milk
½ pound American cheese,
  sliced
6 eggs

Sauté the onion in butter or margarine in the top of a double boiler placed over direct heat. Place over hot water. Add flour and salt and blend well. Add the milk and stir constantly until the sauce is thickened and smooth. Add cheese and stir until melted.

Pour the hot cheese sauce into a 1-quart casserole or baking dish. Carefully break the eggs into the casserole. Bake in a moderately hot oven, 375 degrees, for 15 minutes or until the eggs are firm. 6 servings.

Baked Eggs in Honey Cups

3 tablespoons honey
3 tablespoons butter or
  margarine
8 slices white bread, crusts
  removed

3 slices crisp bacon, crumbled
8 eggs
Salt and pepper to taste

Combine honey and butter in saucepan. Heat until butter is melted and blended with honey. Press out bread with rolling pin and brush with honey-butter mixture. (Grease 8-cup muffin tin very well.) Press a slice of bread into each muffin cup. Sprinkle a few pieces of bacon into bottom of each muffin cup. Break an egg into each. Sprinkle with salt and pepper.

Bake in moderately hot oven, 400 degrees, until eggs have set. 8 servings.

Creamed Eggs New Orleans

Mrs. Phyllis Hairr, Chamblee, Georgia

2 tablespoons butter or
  margarine
2 tablespoons flour
½ teaspoon salt
¼ teaspoon pepper
1 cup milk

1 teaspoon cognac
4 slices hot toast, spread with
  butter and liver pâté
4 hard-cooked eggs, sliced
8 anchovy fillets

Melt butter or margarine in top of double boiler or in copper-clad saucepan. Stir in flour, salt, and pepper, until smooth. Let cook 1 or 2 minutes. Add milk gradually. Stir and cook until slightly thickened. Stir in cognac. Arrange toast on serving plates and cover with sliced egg (1 egg per serving). Spoon hot sauce on top. Crisscross 2 anchovy fillets on each serving. 4 servings.

Curried Eggs in Rice Ring

½ teaspoon Tabasco sauce,
  divided
4 tablespoons butter or
  margarine, divided
6 cups cooked rice
1 medium-size onion, chopped
4 tablespoons flour
1 tablespoon curry powder

2 cups chicken stock or canned
  chicken bouillon
1 cup half and half or light
  cream
1 teaspoon salt
6 hard-cooked eggs, quartered
  lengthwise

Add ¼ teaspoon Tabasco to 2 tablespoons of the butter and stir into cooked rice. Taste and add salt if needed. Pack rice into well-buttered 6-cup ring mold. Set the ring in a pan of hot water 15 minutes before serving time to reheat the rice.

Melt remaining butter in a saucepan and cook onions until they are tender but not brown. Blend in the flour and curry powder, then gradually stir in the stock or bouillon. Bring to the boiling point and cook 5 minutes, stirring constantly.

Add the half and half and season with salt and remaining ¼ teaspoon Tabasco. Stir in the quartered eggs and heat carefully. Unmold the rice ring on serving platter. Place bowl in center and fill with the curry mixture. Serve with buttered peas if desired.

Deviled Eggs

6 hard-cooked eggs
¼ teaspoon dry mustard
½ teaspoon salt
½ teaspoon Worcestershire
   sauce

3 tablespoons sweet pickle
   relish
¼ cup mayonnaise

Carefully cut eggs in half and remove yolks. Add remaining ingredients to yolks and mix well. Pile yolk mixture in halves of egg white. Garnish with thin slices of sweet pickle. 6 servings.

NOTE: Thin wedges of hard-cooked eggs arranged as petals and a sweet pickle relish form a decorative and delicious garnish.

Eggs 'n' Olives Poached in Cream

1 cup milk
1 cup heavy cream
1 cup shredded sharp Cheddar
   cheese
½ cup sliced pimiento-stuffed
   olives
1 tablespoon chopped chives
1 tablespoon butter

⅛ teaspoon salt
Dash Tabasco sauce
1 cup sour cream
8 eggs
Chopped parsley
4 English muffins, halved,
   toasted, and buttered

Combine milk, heavy cream, cheese, olives, chives, butter, salt, and Tabasco in large skillet. Simmer gently, stirring until cheese is melted. Stir in sour cream, blending well. Bring sauce to a gentle simmer; break in eggs, one at a time. Cover and simmer gently 3 to 5 minutes or until egg whites are just set. Garnish with chopped parsley. Serve over muffins with grilled sausage. 4 servings.

Egg and Cottage Cheese Soufflé

4 eggs
1 cup cottage cheese
1 teaspoon salt

¼ teaspoon pepper
1 cup heavy cream or rich milk,
   scalded

Separate eggs. Blend yolks, cottage cheese, and seasonings; then stir in hot cream. Beat whites stiff, but not dry, and fold into cream mixture. Taste, and add more seasonings if desired. Pour into buttered 1-quart casserole, put in pan of hot water. Bake in moderate oven, 350 degrees, until set and slightly browned. Serve from casserole. 4 servings.

Egg and Spinach Casserole

2 pounds fresh spinach or 1
   (10-ounce) package frozen
   spinach
Salt
3 to 5 hard-cooked eggs
Pepper

2 tablespoons prepared mustard
2 tablespoons margarine
2 tablespoons flour
1 cup milk
¼ cup grated cheese

If the spinach is fresh, wash well. Steam until tender in lightly salted water. Remove shells from eggs and cut in half lengthwise. Remove yolks; season with salt, pepper, and mustard. Soften the mixture with milk if necessary. Refill the whites. Melt margarine in a saucepan; add flour. Mix until smooth. Add milk; stir over low heat until creamy and smooth. Season to taste with salt and pepper. Add cheese. Stir. Arrange spinach and stuffed eggs in casserole. Cover with the sauce. Reheat in moderate oven, 350 degrees, for about 10 minutes. Serve at once. 4 servings.

Gourmet Egg Louis

1 cup mayonnaise or salad
   dressing
¼ cup chili sauce or catsup
1 hard-cooked egg, finely
   chopped
2 tablespoons chopped ripe
   olives
1 teaspoon minced chives

1 teaspoon lemon juice
9 hard-cooked eggs, cut in
   pieces
1 large or 2 small ripe
   avocados, peeled and cut in
   slices
2 tomatoes, cut in wedges
½ teaspoon salt

Combine mayonnaise, chili sauce, finely chopped egg, olives, chives, and lemon juice. Chill. Line salad bowl with crisp salad greens. Heap cut eggs on greens and circle with avocado and tomato. Sprinkle with salt. Serve with dressing. 6 servings.

Eggs Benedict

SAUCE

2 egg yolks	*1 tablespoon fresh lemon juice*
¼ teaspoon salt	*6 whole eggs*
¼ teaspoon Tabasco sauce	*6 slices cooked ham*
½ cup melted butter, divided	*3 English muffins, halved*

Measure all ingredients for hollandaise sauce. To prepare sauce, beat egg yolks, salt, and Tabasco with egg beater or electric beater until thick and lemon-colored. Add ¼ cup melted butter, about 1 teaspoon at a time, beating constantly. Combine remaining butter with lemon juice and add slowly, beating constantly. Cover, set aside.

Butter skillet; fill with enough water to cover eggs 1-inch. Bring to boil; lower heat to simmering. Break eggs one at a time into cup; gently let egg slide out of cup into water. Cover skillet.

Cook eggs until whites are solid, about 3 to 5 minutes. While eggs are poaching, heat ham through and toast English muffins. Gently remove poached eggs from skillet with slotted spoon. Place ham on muffins; top with poached eggs; spoon hollandaise over each. Garnish with parsley. 6 servings.

Kentucky Eggs Goldenrod

2 tablespoons butter	*⅔ cup finely grated or finely cut*
2 tablespoons flour	*American cheese*
1 cup milk	*3 hard-cooked eggs*
½ teaspoon salt	*4 slices hot buttered toast*
⅛ teaspoon pepper	

Melt the butter in top of double boiler and blend flour in until smooth. Gradually add milk. Stir sauce constantly until mixture thickens. Add salt and pepper, then cheese, heating and stirring until cheese melts. Keep sauce hot over barely simmering water.

At serving time, shell the eggs and cut in half. Remove yolks. Dice the whites (not too small). Have two plates warm. On each one arrange two slices of hot buttered toast. Top with diced egg whites.

Then pour the cheese sauce evenly over each piece of toast. Force the egg yolks through a fine sieve, directly onto the cheese sauce. That's the goldenrod touch. Serve immediately. 2 servings.

Mexican Picnic Eggs

6 hard-cooked eggs
¼ cup minced onions
2 tablespoons minced green pepper
1 tablespoon chopped stuffed olives

½ teaspoon salt
Dash cayenne pepper
1 tablespoon mayonnaise
Paprika

Cut eggs in half lengthwise. Take out yolks. Mash with other ingredients except paprika. Refill halves, pressing mixture in firmly. Sprinkle with paprika. 6 servings.

Molded Egg Ring

Mrs. Jesse Jackson, Mayfield, Georgia

2 tablespoons unflavored gelatin
½ cup cold water
½ cup boiling water
1½ cups mayonnaise
1 teaspoon salt
1 teaspoon white pepper
6 drops Tabasco

2 tablespoons minced onion
½ cup chopped green pepper
¼ cup chopped parsley
12 hard-cooked eggs
1 teaspoon prepared mustard
Chicken salad

Soften gelatin in cold water, dissolve in boiling water; cool. Add mayonnaise, lemon juice, salt, pepper, Tabasco sauce, onion, green pepper, parsley, and 10 hard-cooked eggs, chopped. Cover bottom of oiled 6-cup mold with 1-inch layer of mixture. Slice the two remaining eggs, arrange around sides of mold, and chill until firm. Add remaining ingredients and chill for at least 2 hours. Unmold, fill center with chicken salad. Garnish with slivered almonds, olives, and tomato wedges. 10 to 12 servings.

Asparagus Omelet

2 to 3 tablespoons olive oil
1 (15-ounce) can white
   asparagus, drained and
   chopped
2 tablespoons chopped onion

4 eggs, beaten
¼ teaspoon salt
1 tablespoon water
Freshly ground black pepper

Place olive oil in a 7- or 8-inch heavy skillet or omelet pan. Add asparagus and onion, cook over moderate heat until onion is soft. Combine eggs, salt, water, and pepper. Add half at a time to the pan, lifting up with spatula as egg firms. When solid throughout, and lightly browned, lift and fold over, slide out onto heated plates. 2 large or 4 moderate servings.

Omelet Creole

1 small onion, minced
¼ cup minced green pepper
4 tablespoons margarine
2½ cups canned or stewed
   tomatoes
¼ cup sliced stuffed olives
Salt and pepper to taste

Dash cayenne pepper
   (optional)
4 eggs
¼ cup milk
½ teaspoon salt
⅛ teaspoon pepper

Cook onion and green pepper in 2 tablespoons margarine, until soft. Add tomatoes and olives. Season with salt and pepper; add a dash of cayenne if desired. Simmer until sauce is rather thick. Keep hot while making omelet as follows:

Beat eggs with milk until mixed. Add ½ teaspoon salt and ⅛ teaspoon pepper. Heat remaining 2 tablespoons margarine in heavy skillet. Add egg mixture and cook slowly over low heat. With a knife lift edge of omelet to let some of the uncooked mixture run under cooked portion. Repeat until cooking is completed. When omelet is set, fold over and remove to a hot platter. Serve with sauce. 2 to 4 servings.

Supper Eggs

¼ cup margarine
¼ cup flour
2 cups milk
1 cup diced American cheese
½ cup chopped pimiento

½ cup chopped ripe olives
½ teaspoon salt
4 to 6 eggs
Toast

Melt margarine in frying pan, add flour, and stir until smooth. Add milk and cook until thick, stirring constantly. Add cheese and stir until melted; add pimiento, ripe olives, and salt, mix thoroughly. Pour into an 8-inch-square baking dish. Break eggs and drop into the hot sauce. Bake uncovered in a hot oven, 400 degrees, until eggs are set, about 15 minutes. Cover to retain heat. Serve on toast. 4 to 6 servings.

6

MEATS

Unless you are one of the fortunates who still live on enough acreage to raise your own livestock, meat is surely the most expensive item in your food budget.

I can remember when meat was no problem. With cured hams and sausage and salt-cured pork in the "smokehouse" you helped yourself. Then at hog-killin' time (two or three during the winter months) we reveled in fresh pork. And occasionally during the year one of the fatted calves was slaughtered for family use. Lamb was not nearly so well known, but I understand that many years ago, around the southeast coastal section, sheep raising was a very big industry.

There is such a vast variety of meats in the markets today that one may pick and choose to fit his pocketbook. One doesn't have to eat filet mignon, porterhouse steak, or standing rib roast to be well fed. The more economical cuts and variety meats are just as nutritious and far less expensive.

All of the recipes here have either been tried at home or served in eating places. You will find something for everyone, from elegant service to "shur nuff" home cooking, and short-order cooking to outdoor grills and picnics.

BEEF

Rib Roast of Beef

1 (5- to 7-pound) rolled or standing rib roast of beef
1 tablespoon monosodium glutamate
Salt and pepper to taste

Wipe meat with damp cloth or paper towel. If standing rib roast, stand on rib bones in shallow open pan; if rolled rib roast, place on rack with fat side up. Sprinkle meat with monosodium glutamate, salt, and pepper. Insert meat thermometer. Make sure pointed end of thermometer does not rest on bone, fat, or gristle.

Roast in a 325-degree oven as follows: For standing rib roast: rare, 22 minutes per pound (internal temperature 140 degrees); medium, 25 minutes per pound (internal temperature 160 degrees); well done, 30 minutes per pound (internal temperature 170 degrees).

For rolled rib roast: rare, 30 minutes per pound (internal temperature 140 degrees); medium, 33 minutes per pound (internal temperature 160 degrees); well done, 40 minutes per pound (internal temperature 170 degrees).

NOTE: Allow ⅓ to ½ pound bone-in roast per serving or ¼ pound boned roast per serving.

Beef Renaissance

Chef John Van Dyke,
Citizens and Southern National Bank, Downtown Atlanta, Georgia

1 rib eye roast, 5 to 6 pounds
1½ pounds fresh mushrooms,
* chopped*
2 tablespoons butter
¼ cup chopped shallots
2 tablespoons dry white wine
¼ cup lemon juice

Salt and pepper
1½ pounds chicken livers,
* cooked puréed*
4 egg yolks, beaten
¼ cup chopped parsley
½ cup dry sherry

Trim rib eye roast of all fat. Place on rack and roast in 325-degree oven until rare; cool to room temperature. Sauté mushrooms in butter with shallots. Add white wine, lemon juice, salt and pepper to taste. Simmer slowly until thickened. Add the puréed chicken livers and the egg yolks. Mix well. Stir in the parsley and sherry. Cool and spread all over the cooled rib eye roast.

Make pastry of:

4 cups self-rising flour	*2 eggs*
½ cup butter (1 stick)	*1½ cups sour cream*
¼ cup sugar	

Combine all ingredients well. Roll out to fit rib eye roast and wrap around roast; seal. Decorate with pastry cutouts if desired and bake 45 minutes at 400 degrees. Slice to serve. 12 to 14 servings.

Barbecued Rib Roast

Mrs. Robert Mouk, Atlanta, Georgia

1 standing rib roast, 8 to 10 pounds	*1 cup beer*
Salt and pepper	*¼ cup Worcestershire sauce*
½ cup (1 stick) butter	*2 tablespoons firmly packed brown sugar*
2 onions, chopped	*Juice of 1 lemon*
2 cups catsup	

Rub roast with salt and pepper. Roast at 325 degrees, allowing 25 minutes per pound for medium beef. Melt butter and sauté onions until golden. Add remaining ingredients and simmer 5 minutes. Brush meat with barbecue sauce several times during the last hour of cooking. Serve with remaining hot barbecue sauce. 12 to 16 servings.

I have had numerous requests for this recipe for it seems not too many cookbooks list it. Beef Wellington makes a handsome entrée for those especially impressive occasions—it is very elegant to eat also.

Beef Wellington

1½ times recipe Puff Paste
5 to 6 pounds fillet of beef,
  trimmed of all fat
½ pound beef suet
2 tablespoons butter or
  margarine
4 chicken livers

½ pound fresh mushrooms,
  finely chopped
¼ pound cooked ham, finely
  ground
1 tablespoon catsup
⅓ cup dry sherry
1 egg, separated

Several days before serving: make Puff Paste, refrigerate wrapped.

On the day before serving, heat oven to 425 degrees. Place fillet on rack in roasting pan; place pieces of suet over it. Insert meat thermometer into center of fillet. Roast to desired degree of doneness. Remove from oven, remove suet, cool and refrigerate.

In hot butter or margarine in skillet, sauté chicken livers until browned; chop fine; return to skillet and add mushrooms, ham, catsup, and sherry. Cook, stirring occasionally, 10 minutes. Cool; stir in beaten egg yolk; remove to bowl, cover and refrigerate.

About 1 hour before serving, on floured board, roll out three-quarters of Puff Paste into a rectangle about 18×18 inches, or large enough to enclose fillet. Place fillet in center of Puff Paste; over top of fillet pat chopped ham mixture. Lift one end of Puff Paste over fillet, overlapping both ends under fillet. Tuck in other ends firmly. Lift fillet and place seam side down on large cookie sheet.

Roll out remaining Puff Paste. With small cookie cutters cut decorative shapes such as leaves, flowers, or triangles, with which to garnish fillet.

Quickly brush pastry surface of fillet with slightly beaten egg white; arrange decorative shapes on it and brush again with egg white.

Bake fillet 30 to 40 minutes or until pastry is golden. With two broad spatulas lift fillet to serving platter; garnish with watercress. In serving, cut into ½-inch-thick slices. 14 servings.

PUFF PASTE

Into large bowl sift 2 cups all-purpose flour. Make well in center. Add ½ cup water and ¾ teaspoon salt. With fork, working quickly and lightly, mix all together, adding ¼ cup more water as the ½ cup water is absorbed into flour.

Refrigerate 15 minutes, then place on a floured board and roll into rectangle, about ¼ inch thick. Shape 1 cup (½ pound) firm, but not hard, butter or margarine into a flat square cake, 1 inch thick. Place butter in center of paste, then fold paste over it, enclosing in an envelope-like shape.

Roll folded paste away from you, into a long, thin rectangle, as thin as possible without letting the butter break through. Fold this rectangle into thirds; bring one end over the center third and the other end over the first. (The rolling and folding, is called a turn.)

Do a second "turn" on dough, then refrigerate 20 minutes. Do two more "turns," then refrigerate dough 30 minutes. Then do two final "turns," wrap the paste in foil and refrigerate. (This makes six "turns" in all.)

HERB PUFF PASTE

Combine 1 tablespoon each of dried dill seed and tarragon with 1 tablespoon snipped parsley; sprinkle over rectangle of Puff Paste before folding steps above.

This is one of the best recipes of the famous resort hotel on one of Georgia's golden isles.

Tenderloin of Beef in Burgundy Aspic
John J. Chalfa, Executive Steward
Herman Yursich, Executive Chef
The Cloister, Sea Island, Georgia

2 pounds rare roast tenderloin of beef

½ cup very fine julienne of green peppers

1 cup very fine julienne of fresh mushrooms

3 envelopes plain gelatin

1 cup warm water

¼ cup very fine julienne of dill pickle

½ cup very fine julienne of pimientos

2 tablespoons lemon juice

1 cup red burgundy wine

½ cup port wine

1 tablespoon monosodium glutamate

Salt and pepper to taste

4 cups strong clear essence of beef

Cut the cooked beef tenderloin into a very fine julienne. Poach the green peppers and mushrooms in a little lemon juice and water. Dissolve gelatin in cup of warm water.

Decorate bottoms of individual molds with slice of black stuffed olive, slice of hard-cooked egg, or as desired. Fill each mold about three-quarters full with this tenderloin mixture. Combine gelatin, lemon juice, wine, monosodium glutamate, salt and pepper, and essence of beef. Pour over other ingredients in mold. Chill in refrigerator overnight. 8 servings.

Barbecued Pot Roast

1 (4-pound) pot roast of beef
2 tablespoons oil
1½ cups sliced onions
1 clove garlic, minced
2 teaspoons salt
½ teaspoon freshly ground
   black pepper
1 (8-ounce) can tomato sauce

¼ cup chili sauce
⅓ cup cider vinegar
2 tablespoons brown sugar
2 teaspoons Worcestershire
   sauce
½ cup water
2 teaspoons chili powder

Trim the fat from the meat. Heat the oil in a Dutch oven or heavy skillet and brown the meat on all sides. Add the onions and garlic; cook until browned. Mix in the salt, pepper, and tomato sauce; cover and cook over low heat 1½ hours. Stir in the chili sauce, vinegar, sugar, Worcestershire sauce, water, and chili powder; cover and cook 1 hour longer or until tender. Skim the fat from the gravy. 8 to 10 servings.

Beef Dill Pot Roast

¼ cup flour
3 teaspoons salt
¼ teaspoon pepper
1 (3- to 4-pound) beef blade
   pot roast

2 tablespoons lard or drippings
1 teaspoon dill seed
¼ cup dill pickle juice
¼ cup water

Mix flour, salt, and pepper. Dredge pot roast in seasoned flour and brown in lard or drippings. Pour off drippings. Sprinkle with dill seed, add dill pickle juice and water. Cover tightly and simmer 2½ to 3 hours or until tender. Thicken cooking liquid for gravy, if desired. 6 to 8 servings.

Italian Pot Roast

Mrs. Robert Rush, Kathleen, Georgia

4 pounds pot roast (chuck, round, or rump)	½ teaspoon marjoram
1 tablespoon olive oil	½ teaspoon thyme
3 large onions, sliced	¼ teaspoon pepper
2 cloves of garlic, speared with wooden picks	½ cup water
	1 (6-ounce) can tomato paste
1½ teaspoons salt	2 tablespoons flour
	1 cup water

Brown meat on all sides over medium heat in hot olive oil in large heavy kettle with close-fitting lid. Add onions, garlic, salt, marjoram, thyme, pepper, water, and ½ can tomato paste. Bring to boiling; reduce heat. Simmer 2 to 2½ hours, or until meat is tender when pierced with two-tine fork. (Add water during cooking, if needed.) Place meat on platter; keep warm. Make gravy. To drippings in pan add flour and water, and remaining tomato paste, stir and cook to thicken slightly. 8 servings.

Sauerbraten

1 (4-pound) beef sirloin butt	1 clove garlic
2 cups vinegar	2 medium-size onions, sliced
1 cup water	1 medium-size orange, sliced
1 teaspoon whole cloves	1 cup dry red wine
1 bay leaf	3 tablespoons cooking oil
1 teaspoon whole black peppercorns	¼ cup tomato purée
1 tablespoon salt	2 tablespoons flour
½ teaspoon ground black pepper	

Cut meat into slices about 1 inch thick or leave in one piece. Combine all ingredients, except tomato purée, to make a marinade and pour over meat. Let stand for 36 hours in refrigerator, turning meat over in marinade two or three times. Remove meat and drain. Brown slices of meat in heated oil. Add strained marinade and tomato purée (enough to cover meat), and simmer until tender, 1 to 3 hours, depending upon whether the meat is in one piece or how tender the cut. Strain sauce, stir in flour, and cook until slightly thickened. 6 servings.

To serve as an appetizer, cut meat into bite-size cubes and serve hot in chafing dish. Serves 36 as appetizer.

Fresh Beef Brisket

1 (4-pound) fresh brisket of beef
2 tablespoons vinegar
2 tablespoons sugar
2 teaspoons salt
3 whole cloves
3 whole black peppercorns
1 small onion, sliced

Cover meat with hot water and add vinegar, sugar, salt, cloves, black peppercorns, and sliced onion. Simmer meat, covered, until tender, 2 to 3 hours. Serve with horseradish sauce. 6 servings.

Corned Beef

Ruth Furman, Columbus, Georgia

1½ cups salt
4 quarts water
1 tablespoon sugar
2 tablespoons pickling spice
½ ounce saltpeter
8 bay leaves
5 pound brisket of beef
8 cloves garlic
2 onions, sliced
2 stalks celery, sliced

Combine salt, water, sugar, pickling spice, saltpeter, and bay leaves in saucepan. Bring to boil and cook 5 minutes. Cool.

Place beef in stone crock or nonmetal bowl. Pour liquid over it and add garlic. If necessary, weight meat down to keep it covered with liquid. Cover with lid or foil. Place in refrigerator and pickle for 12 days. Turn brisket every 3 or 4 days.

To cook, rinse meat, add onions and celery, cover with water. Bring to boil and cook over low heat for 3 hours or until tender. Drain and slice crosswise. 12 to 14 servings.

Corned Beef and Cabbage

*1 (4-pound) corned brisket of
   beef
1 clove garlic, chopped
2 onions, sliced*

*5 whole cloves
2 bay leaves
1 head cabbage, cut in wedges*

In large Dutch oven, heat enough water to cover beef brisket. Add all ingredients except cabbage. Cover and simmer 4 hours or until fork tender. Place meat on a platter; keep warm; add cabbage wedges to liquid, and boil 10 to 15 minutes or until tender. Serve with horseradish sauce. 4 to 6 servings.

Pastrami

Mrs. G. T. Koene, Marietta, Georgia

*5 pounds corned brisket of beef
2 cloves garlic, minced
3 bay leaves
4 small dried hot red peppers
Liquid smoke (optional)*

*1½ teaspoons cracked black
   pepper
¾ teaspoon allspice
¼ teaspoon powdered coriander*

Cover beef with cold water. Add garlic, bay leaves, red peppers; cover and bring to boil quickly. Reduce to simmer and cook 2½ hours or until tender but still firm. Remove from liquid. Cool. Brush with liquid smoke, if desired.

Mix pepper, allspice, and coriander; rub into meat, covering all surfaces. Place in shallow baking pan on low rack or trivet. Bake uncovered at 375 degrees for about 45 minutes. Carve on an angle into paper-thin slices. 8 to 10 servings.

Chicken Fried Steak

*1½ to 2 pounds round steak,
   cut ½ inch thick
2 eggs, beaten
2 tablespoons milk
1 cup fine cracker crumbs
   (cracker meal is what I
   prefer)*

*Salt and pepper to taste
¼ cup vegetable oil*

Cut steak into serving pieces. Pound steak thoroughly. Mix eggs and milk. Dip meat into egg mixture, then into cracker meal.

Salt and pepper. Brown slowly on both sides in hot oil. Cover tightly; cook over very low heat 45 to 60 minutes or until tender. 6 servings.

Pepper Steak

Mrs. M. J. Peruzzi, Forest Park, Georgia

3 green peppers, sliced	Freshly ground black pepper
3 onions, sliced	3 pounds tenderloin steak,
9 large mushrooms, sliced	sliced
3 tomatoes, quartered	½ cup flour
¾ cup butter	6 tablespoons red burgundy
1½ cups Espagnole Sauce	wine (optional)
Salt	

Sauté green pepper, onions, mushrooms, and tomatoes in ½ cup butter for 5 minutes. Add Espagnole Sauce and simmer for 10 minutes. Salt and pepper the sliced steak. Dip in flour and sauté in remaining ¼ cup butter for 2 minutes in large skillet. Add sauce and simmer for 15 minutes, stirring frequently. Add wine and simmer for 3 minutes. 6 servings.

ESPAGNOLE SAUCE

   3 tablespoons butter
   3 tablespoons flour
   1½ cups beef bouillon

Melt butter, add flour, and stir until smooth. Add bouillon gradually and cook, stirring, until thickened. About 1½ cups.

Blade Steak

Mrs. R. W. Jones, Jr., Leslie, Georgia

Have beef shoulder cut in slices ½ inch thick. Sprinkle with meat tenderizer, add garlic salt, and slash edges of fat about every inch to prevent curling. Put little dabs of suet over steak and place under broiler about 1 inch from heat. Cook only a few seconds. When fat is just a little charred, turn. Cut in serving pieces and serve at once. 2 servings per pound of beef shoulder.

This man loves to cook and has won several recipe contests.

Exotic Steak

J. C. Tilly, Rome, Georgia

1 package garlic salad dressing
    mix
1 package exotic herbs salad
    dressing mix
½ teaspoon salt

1 cup cooking oil
2 tablespoons maple syrup
4 T-bone steaks (1½ inches
    thick)

Start charcoal fire in grill bowl 1 hour in advance. Combine salad dressing mixes, salt, oil, and syrup. Brush generously over steaks. Cover grill with foil, turning edges up to catch juices. Place steak on foil on the grill rack, which should be 10 inches above charcoal. Baste often with the mixture and from the juices during the 30 to 45 minutes of cooking to desired degree of doneness.

Browned Swiss Steak

Mrs. Robert Rush, Kathleen, Georgia

1½ pounds round steak, 1½
    inches thick
4 tablespoons flour
2 tablespoons salad oil or
    shortening
½ cup chopped onion
½ cup grated carrot
2 tablespoons chopped parsley

1 teaspoon salt
⅛ teaspoon pepper
¼ teaspoon dried thyme leaves
2 bay leaves
3 whole cloves
½ teaspoon liquid gravy
    seasoning
1 cup water

Wipe steak with damp paper towels. Roll it in flour, coating evenly on both sides; reserve remaining flour. Slowly heat large, heavy skillet. Add oil; heat. In it, brown steak well on both sides, turning with tongs—15 to 20 minutes in all. Add rest of ingredients, except remaining flour, bring to boiling. Reduce heat; simmer, covered, 2 to 2½ hours, or until meat is fork tender. Combine rest of flour with ¼ cup water in small bowl, stirring until smooth. Stir into liquid in skillet; bring to boiling. Reduce heat, simmer 5 minutes. 4 to 6 servings.

SWISS STEAK WITH TOMATOES: Prepare and brown Swiss steak as above. Add 1 (1-pound, 3-ounce) can tomatoes, undrained, along with rest of ingredients, except the remaining flour; omit 1 cup water. Finish cooking as above.

Bean and Steak Stir Fry

1 pound round steak
2 tablespoons salad oil
2 cups diagonally cut green beans
4 green onions, sliced

1 teaspoon salt
½ teaspoon Tabasco sauce
2 medium tomatoes, cut in wedges
2 tablespoons soy sauce

Cut meat across grain into paper-thin slices. Heat oil in heavy skillet; add beans and onions, sprinkle with salt. Stir or shake skillet to sauté beans on all sides. Add meat, stirring to sauté quickly. Sprinkle Tabasco over all. Add tomatoes and soy sauce; stir. Cover and cook 3 minutes. 4 servings.

Beef Kabobs for 8

3 pounds boneless beef sirloin or tenderloin
Marinade for Beef
2 (1 pound each) cans small Irish potatoes
4 zucchini squash, sliced ¾ inch thick
2 green peppers, cleaned and cut into eighths

2 cups precooked carrot chunks
3 medium-size tomatoes, cut into wide wedges (4 to 6 per tomato)
8 small precooked onions
Marinade for Vegetables
Basting Sauce

Cut beef into 1- to 1½-inch cubes; refrigerate in marinade. Drain potatoes, combine with other vegetables. Pour marinade over them and for several hours refrigerate. Thread the beef and vegetables onto skewers. Brush with Basting Sauce. Broil 4 to 5 inches above glowing coals until meat is cooked and vegetables have browned. Turn frequently, brushing with Basting Sauce. 8 servings.

MARINADE FOR BEEF

To each pound of beef cubes, add ⅔ cup cooking oil, 1 teaspoon salt, ¼ teaspoon coarse black pepper, ½ teaspoon thyme, 3 tablespoons lemon juice, ½ cup chopped onion, and about ½ cup red wine vinegar to cover; mix. Cover and refrigerate 2 to 3 hours.

MARINADE FOR VEGETABLES

1 cup cooking oil
¼ cup wine or cider vinegar
½ small clove garlic, crushed
  (optional)
¼ cup minced onion

1 teaspoon salt
½ teaspoon basil
½ teaspoon marjoram
⅛ teaspoon pepper

Combine ingredients; mix, cover, and refrigerate several hours. About 1½ cups.

BASTING SAUCE

¾ cup soft butter or margarine
⅓ cup tarragon or wine vinegar
2 tablespoons minced parsley
2 tablespoons finely chopped
  onion
2 tablespoons catsup

½ teaspoon salt
½ teaspoon paprika
½ teaspoon mustard
¼ teaspoon basil
⅛ teaspoon black pepper

Combine ingredients; mix well. About 1 cup.

Ranch-style Ribs

2 pounds short ribs of beef
2 tablespoons lard or drippings
1 large onion, sliced
1 clove garlic, mashed
¼ cup chopped celery
1 (8-ounce) can tomato sauce

Juice 1 large lemon
1 teaspoon chili powder
1 teaspoon salt
1 tablespoon Worcestershire
  sauce
2 tablespoons flour

Have short ribs cut in 2-inch lengths. Heat lard in Dutch oven; brown meat slowly on all sides. Add remaining ingredients with the exception of flour. Cover closely and simmer for 1½ hours. Transfer meat to a hot platter. Skim off excess fat, mix flour with a little cold water, and add to juices in the pan. Cook until thickened, stirring constantly. 4 servings.

Short Ribs

3 pounds short ribs of beef
2 tablespoons lard or drippings
3 cups water
1 (1½-ounce) package
    dehydrated onion soup
½ cup diced celery
¼ teaspoon thyme
Corn Meal Dumplings

Brown short ribs on all sides in lard or drippings. Pour off drippings. Add water, dehydrated onion soup, celery, and thyme. Cover tightly and cook slowly 2 hours, or until tender. Drop Corn Meal Dumplings by spoonfuls on short ribs. Cover tightly, steam for 15 minutes. Thicken liquid for gravy, if desired. 4 to 6 servings.

Corn Meal Dumplings

¾ cup sifted enriched flour
¼ cup corn meal
1½ teaspoons baking powder
½ teaspoon salt
1 tablespoon minced parsley
1 egg
⅓ cup milk
2 tablespoons melted lard

Sift together flour, corn meal, baking powder, and salt. Add parsley. Combine egg and milk. Add to dry ingredients and stir in melted lard. 10 to 12 dumplings.

Beef Short Ribs—Raisin Sauce

4 pounds short ribs of beef
2 teaspoons salt
⅛ teaspoon pepper
1 onion, quartered
½ cup brown sugar
1 teaspoon dry mustard
1 tablespoon flour
2 tablespoons vinegar
2 tablespoons lemon juice
¼ teaspoon grated lemon rind
1 bay leaf
1½ cups water
½ cup raisins

Brown short ribs in own fat, cover tightly, and cook slowly 1½ hours. Pour off drippings. Season ribs with salt and pepper. Add quartered onion.

Combine remaining ingredients and bring to a boil. Pour over short ribs. Cover tightly and cook slowly about 2 hours or until meat is tender. Thicken sauce, if desired. 6 servings.

Skillet Round-up

Mrs. Willett Robinson, Sylvania, Georgia

*2 pounds flank steak or beef
   cubes
2 tomatoes
2 sweet green peppers
2 tablespoons salad oil
1 garlic clove
1 teaspoon salt
Dash of pepper*

*¼ teaspoon ground ginger
¼ cup soy sauce
½ teaspoon sugar
1 (1-pound) can bean sprouts,
   optional
1 tablespoon cornstarch
¼ cup water*

Cut flank steak in thin strips, across the grain of the meat; cut tomatoes in quarters; trim away seeds and ribs from peppers and cut peppers into big chunks. Heat oil in large skillet. Add strips of beef, crushed garlic, salt, pepper, and ginger. Sauté over high heat until light brown on all sides. Season with soy sauce and sugar. Cover tightly and cook slowly 5 minutes. At this point toss in tomatoes, peppers, drained bean sprouts. Bring to a boil, cover and cook briskly for 5 minutes. Make smooth paste of cornstarch and water. Add to beef mixture and cook until sauce thickens slightly. Stir occasionally. 6 servings.

The Rush family raise cattle.

Beef Stroganoff

Mrs. Robert Rush, Kathleen, Georgia

*2 pounds round steak, cut ¾
   inch thick
2 tablespoons fat
2 tablespoons dry mustard
1 teaspoon salt*

*⅛ teaspoon pepper
2 cups water
Flour
1 cup sour cream*

Cut meat in long, narrow strips; brown on all sides over medium heat in hot fat in large heavy frying pan with tight-fitting cover, or Dutch oven. Blend in mustard, salt, and pepper, stir in 1 cup water; cover tightly. Bring to boiling, reduce heat. Simmer, stirring occasionally, 1 hour, or until meat is tender when pierced with two-tined fork. Remove meat from pan, stir in 1 to 2 tablespoons flour and 1 cup water, stir and cook to thicken slightly. Return meat to gravy; stir in sour cream. Simmer, stirring constantly, just until hot. (Do not boil mixture or cream will curdle.) Serve in ring of hot mashed potatoes, if desired.

Julienne Beef in Sour Cream

Marion Hunt Hays, University of Florida

1 small onion, sliced	*Dash of pepper*
1 tablespoon butter	*1 teaspoon salt*
1 pound round steak, ½ inch	*1 cup sour cream*
thick, cut in Julienne strips	*2 tablespoons flour*
⅛ teaspoon ginger	

Sauté onion slices in butter, add meat and seasonings. Cook, stirring constantly, until meat is browned on all sides and thoroughly cooked—10 to 15 minutes. Combine sour cream and flour; add to meat. Cook, stirring constantly, until sour cream is heated. Serve with Chinese noodles, rice, toast points, or green peas. 4 servings.

Sukiyaki

2 beef round steaks, cut ½ inch thick, about 1½ pounds	*10 to 12 green onions, cut in 2-inch pieces*
¼ cup lard or drippings	*1½ cups sliced celery*
1 beef bouillon cube	*1 cup (8 ounces) bamboo shoots*
¼ cup hot water	*3 cups cooked rice*
3 tablespoons sugar	
½ cup soy sauce	

Pound round steaks and cut into strips about 2 inches long and ½ inch wide. Brown meat in lard or drippings. Pour off drippings. Dissolve bouillon cube in hot water. Combine bouillon, sugar, and soy sauce. Mix well. Pour mixture over meat. Cover tightly and cook slowly 1 hour.

Push meat to one side. Add vegetables, keeping each separate. Cover and cook slowly 15 minutes. Serve immediately with rice as an accompaniment. 4 to 6 servings.

The Joneses own a cattle ranch.

Beef Casserole
Mrs. R. W. Jones, Jr., Leslie, Georgia

3 large onions, sliced or
  chopped
2 tablespoons bacon fat
3½ pounds beef, cut in 1-inch
  cubes
1 quart tomatoes
2 cups cut-up fresh or frozen
  okra
2 sweet green peppers, cut in
  pieces
3 teaspoons salt
⅛ teaspoon pepper
½ teaspoon garlic powder
½ bay leaf

Sauté onion in bacon fat. Remove onion, add meat and
brown. Remove meat and heat tomatoes, okra, onion, pepper and
seasonings. Arrange together in 3-quart casserole and bake for 5
hours at 325 degrees, or 3½ hours at 400 degrees, or all day at 250
degrees. 8 servings.

NOTE: This recipe is one that can wait for guests as long as you
like.

Beef Stew with Herb Dumplings

2 tablespoons melted fat
¼ cup finely chopped onion
1 pound ground beef
1½ teaspoons salt
⅛ teaspoon black pepper
¼ teaspoon basil
¼ teaspoon thyme
2 teaspoons finely chopped
  green pepper
1 cup sliced carrots
¾ cup peas
2¼ cups water
Herb Dumplings
2 tablespoons flour

Heat fat in saucepan. Add onion and beef and cook until well
browned. Add salt, pepper, basil, thyme, green pepper, carrots, peas,
and 2 cups of water. Simmer 20 minutes or until vegetables are
tender. Meanwhile prepare herb dumplings. Combine flour and remaining ¼ cup water to make a smooth paste. Add gradually to
stew, stirring constantly. Cook until slightly thickened. Drop Herb
Dumplings by spoonfuls into simmering stew, being careful to drop
each dumpling onto a piece of meat or vegetable so that it will not

be immersed in the liquid. Cover tightly and cook without removing cover for 12 minutes. Serve immediately. 6 servings.

HERB DUMPLINGS

1½ cups sifted flour	*½ teaspoon marjoram*
2 teaspoons baking powder	*¾ cup water*
1 teaspoon salt	

Sift together flour, baking powder, and salt. Add marjoram and water and mix only enough to dampen all flour. 12 small dumplings.

Sweet 'n' Sour Beef

Mrs. Kenneth Krause, Atlanta, Georgia

⅓ cup vinegar	*1 medium onion, sliced thin*
¼ cup water	*Salt and pepper*
2 tablespoons sugar	
Leftover roast beef, sliced	
(about 1 pound)	

Combine vinegar, water, and sugar in cup. Cover bottom of dish with a third of the sliced beef. Place a third of the onion slices on top of meat; salt and pepper to taste. Pour some of vinegar mixture over this. Add another layer of meat, then onion, seasoning and sauce as before. Continue until all are used. Cover dish tightly and refrigerate. 4 servings.

Beef Ragout

Mrs. F. Stuart Gould, III, Atlanta, Georgia

5 pounds boneless chuck, cut in	*4 bay leaves*
1-inch cubes	*6 whole cloves*
4 medium onions, sliced	*6 peppercorns*
5 bell peppers, sliced	*1 tablespoon sugar*
3 (1 pound each) cans whole	*1 tablespoon salt*
tomatoes	

Brown beef, turning often, about 20 minutes. Add onions, bell peppers, and tomatoes. Add remaining ingredients. Cover and simmer for 2 hours. Serve over rice. 10 servings.

Country-style Beef Stew

4 slices bacon
2 pounds boneless beef for
   stew, cut in 1½-inch cubes
2 teaspoons salt
¼ teaspoon pepper
½ teaspoon marjoram
1 clove garlic, minced

2 cups water
4 medium potatoes
6 medium carrots
1 small turnip
6 small onions
3 tablespoons flour

Cut bacon into 1-inch pieces. Cook until lightly browned. Remove bacon pieces and brown beef in bacon drippings. Add bacon, salt, pepper, marjoram, garlic, and water. Cover tightly and cook slowly 2 hours. Cut potatoes and carrots in half and turnip in quarters.

Add vegetables and cook an additional 45 minutes or until meat is tender and vegetables are done. Remove meat and vegetables to serving platter. Add water to cooking liquid to make 2 cups. Thicken liquid with flour for gravy. 6 servings.

Summer Beef Stew

3 tablespoons flour
2 teaspoons salt
1 teaspoon paprika
2 pounds boneless beef for
   stew, cut in 1-inch pieces
3 tablespoons lard or drippings
2 cups hot water
½ teaspoon basil

6 to 8 new red potatoes
6 to 8 carrots, each cut
   diagonally in 3 pieces
8 green onions, cut in 2-inch
   pieces
3 tablespoons flour
¼ cup water

Combine flour, salt, and paprika. Dredge meat in seasoned flour. Brown in lard or drippings. Pour off drippings. Add hot water and basil. Cover tightly and cook slowly 1 hour. Add potatoes and carrots. Cover and continue cooking 1 hour or until meat is tender and vegetables are done. Add green onions, cover and cook an additional 10 minutes. Remove meat and vegetables to serving platter. Mix flour and water and thicken cooking liquid with flour mixture for gravy. Serve half of the gravy over the meat and vegetables. Serve remaining gravy separately. 6 to 8 servings.

Beef Goulash

2 pounds boneless beef for
   stew, cut in pieces
2 medium onions, sliced
3 tablespoons lard or drippings
1 bouillon cube
1 cup hot water
1½ teaspoons salt
⅛ teaspoon pepper

2 teaspoons paprika
2 bay leaves
1 tablespoon vinegar
3 medium carrots, cut in strips
1 (10-ounce) package frozen
   Italian green beans
½ cup chopped dill pickle
Flour for gravy (optional)

Brown beef and onion rings in lard or drippings. Pour off drippings.

Dissolve bouillon cube in hot water. Add bouillon, salt, pepper, paprika, bay leaves, and vinegar to meat.

Cover tightly and cook slowly 2 hours. Add carrots and continue cooking 30 minutes. Add green beans and continue cooking 15 to 20 minutes or until meat is tender and vegetables are done.

Add dill pickle and cook just until heated through. Thicken with flour for gravy, if desired. 6 to 8 servings.

Round Steak Casserole

1½ pounds top round steak, cut
   in 2-inch strips, or cooked
   roast beef, cut in 2-inch
   chunks
Meat tenderizer
4 ears sweet corn, cut in thirds
1 (1-pound) can stewed
   tomatoes

½ teaspoon sweet basil
½ teaspoon oregano
Pinch sugar
Pinch nutmeg
Salt and pepper to taste
2 cups cooked rice

First, treat round steak with meat tenderizer, as directed on container. Sauté round steak in cooking oil. If cooked roast beef is used, place in casserole. Cook corn in boiling water 6 minutes. Drain. In oiled casserole, combine meat, corn, tomatoes, and seasonings. Bake in 350-degree oven for 25 minutes, or until corn is tender. Serve with rice. 4 servings.

Old South Meat Dinner

*2 pounds top round steak, cut
    in 1-inch cubes*
⅓ cup chopped onion
1 teaspoon brown sugar
½ cup catsup
⅓ cup chili sauce
*1 teaspoon Worcestershire
    sauce*

1 teaspoon salt
Dash garlic salt
Pinch dry mustard
1 teaspoon vinegar
1 cup water
Cooked noodles

Sauté beef and onions in small amount of cooking oil, remove
from pan. Add to drippings, brown sugar, catsup, chili sauce, Worcestershire, salt, garlic salt, mustard, vinegar, and water. Stir and cook a
few minutes. Return meat to pan; let simmer in sauce 1 hour; add
more water if necessary. Serve over cooked noodles. 4 to 6 servings.

Marinated Hamburgers

1 tablespoon salad oil
*3 tablespoons finely chopped
    onion*
1 cup catsup
¼ cup dark corn syrup
*¼ cup burgundy, claret, or
    other red dinner wine*
*1 tablespoon Worcestershire
    sauce*

*2 tablespoons horseradish
    mustard*
1 tablespoon sweet pickle relish
*¼ tablespoon mixed Italian
    herbs*
2 pounds lean ground beef

Heat oil and add onion; cook several minutes. Add all ingredients,
except beef. Simmer about 15 minutes. Cool. Shape beef into 6 to 8
patties. Pour marinade over patties; cover and refrigerate several
hours. Broil to desired doneness, basting occasionally with remaining
marinade. Serve on buns. 6 to 8 servings.

Poor Man's Filet Mignon

1½ pounds ground beef
1 teaspoon salt
1 teaspoon sugar

⅛ teaspoon pepper
4 strips bacon
Poor Man's Sauce

Combine beef, salt, sugar, and pepper and form into four flat, round cakes an inch thick. Wrap a strip of bacon around edge of each patty and fasten with toothpick. Place the patties in Poor Man's Sauce in a flat pan and let stand in refrigerator 30 minutes. Turn the cakes and let stand for another 30 minutes marinating on the other side. Remove from marinade and grill slowly. Serve with hot mushroom sauce or hot catsup. 4 servings.

POOR MAN'S SAUCE

4 tablespoons salad oil
2 tablespoons vinegar
⅛ teaspoon salt
⅛ teaspoon sugar

⅛ teaspoon pepper
*½ teaspoon Worcestershire
    sauce*

Combine all ingredients well and pour into a flat pan.

Sloppy Joes on Corn Bread

1 pound ground beef
¾ cup chopped onion
½ cup chopped green pepper
½ cup chopped celery
1 carrot, grated

1 (No. 2) can tomatoes
*1 (6-ounce) can tomato purée
    or ½ cup catsup, if you prefer*
¾ teaspoon salt
¼ teaspoon pepper

Brown ground beef in big skillet, stir in onion, green pepper, and celery and brown. Add carrot, tomatoes, and purée. Stir mixture well; season with salt and pepper. Simmer for 1 hour and serve hot over corn bread. 4 servings.

Barbecued Hamburgers

1 pound ground beef
¼ cup finely chopped onion
1 teaspoon salt
¼ teaspoon pepper
1 tablespoon shortening

1 cup catsup
1 sliced onion
¼ cup vinegar
1 tablespoon sugar
½ teaspoon dry mustard

Mix together ground beef, finely chopped onion, salt, and pepper. Shape into four large or six smaller patties. Pan fry in hot shortening to brown both sides. Combine catsup, sliced onion, vinegar, sugar, and dry mustard. Pour over hamburgers. Cover and simmer 20 minutes. Serve over toasted buns or fluffy rice. 4 to 6 servings.

Sweet and Sour Meatballs

Mrs. Robert Rush, Kathleen, Georgia

2 pounds ground beef	½ cup milk
1 cup fine bread crumbs	2 tablespoons grated onion
1 egg, slightly beaten	Salad oil
½ teaspoon salt	Sweet and Sour Sauce
½ teaspoon pepper	

Combine meat, bread crumbs, egg, salt, pepper, milk, and onion. Brown on all sides in small amount of salad oil. Drain off oil, add Sweet and Sour Sauce, and simmer over low heat for 30 minutes. Or place meatballs in baking dish, cover with sauce, and bake at 350 degrees for 30 minutes. Serve with wooden picks. 4 to 6 servings. May also be served as appetizer.

SWEET AND SOUR SAUCE

1 (*No. 2*) can pineapple juice
1 cup barbecue sauce
2 tablespoons flour

Combine ingredients well.

Meatballs and Tomato Rice

1 pound ground beef	¼ cup shortening
¼ cup corn meal	¼ cup chopped green pepper
1 medium onion, chopped	1 teaspoon chili powder
2 teaspoons salt	(optional)
Dash pepper	2 (No. 2) cans (4½ cups)
⅔ cup evaporated milk	tomato juice
2 tablespoons flour	1 cup uncooked rice

Mix together thoroughly the meat, corn meal, half of the onion, 1 teaspoon salt, pepper, and evaporated milk. Shape mixture into twelve balls. Roll each ball in the flour to coat.

Melt shortening in a large frying pan over medium heat; add meatballs, and brown on both sides. Push balls to sides of pan. Add the remaining onion and green pepper, and cook until tender. Add the remaining teaspoon salt and chili powder.

Pour tomato juice over balls, and bring to a boil over high heat. Add rice, and stir to moisten. Cover pan, reduce heat as low as possible, and cook 40 minutes, or until rice is tender. 6 servings.

A most interesting and tasty dish.

Gingered Beef 'n' Tato Balls
James C. Tilly, Rome, Georgia

1 (10¾-ounce) can cream of
 mushroom soup
½ cup water
1 pound ground beef
1 cup finely crushed potato
 chips

3 teaspoons curry powder
2 teaspoons minced onion
1 egg, lightly beaten
2 tablespoons shortening
2 teaspoons chopped candied
 ginger

Blend soup with water. Mix ¼ cup of the mixture with beef, potato chips, curry powder, onion, and egg; blend thoroughly. Shape into 16 balls. Brown in shortening in a skillet. Pour off fat, add remaining soup mixture; cover and simmer for 10 minutes. Add ginger and simmer 5 minutes longer, gently stirring often. 4 servings.

Family Liver Loaf

4 slices bacon
1½ pounds sliced beef liver
1 stalk celery
½ cup chopped onion
1½ cups whole wheat bread
 crumbs

1 teaspoon salt
⅛ teaspoon pepper
2 eggs, well beaten
1 (10½-ounce) can condensed
 tomato soup

Brown bacon lightly. Drain. Pour off drippings, reserving 2 tablespoons. Brown liver lightly in the 2 tablespoons drippings. Grind together liver, bacon, and celery.

Combine liver mixture, onion, bread crumbs, salt, pepper, eggs, and soup. Pack mixture into a greased 9×5-inch loaf pan. Bake in a moderate 350-degree oven for 1½ hours.

Meat Loaf

E. W. Robinson, Florence, Alabama

1½ pounds ground beef
1 egg, beaten
1 cup bread crumbs
1 medium-size onion, chopped
1¼ teaspoons salt

¼ teaspoon pepper
¼ teaspoon herb blend
½ (8-ounce) can tomato sauce
2 tablespoons chopped green
    pepper, optional

Mix ingredients and form a loaf. Place in a shallow pan in moderate 350-degree oven. While the loaf is baking, about 20 minutes, combine the following to make gravy:

½ (8-ounce) can tomato sauce
2 tablespoons vinegar
2 tablespoons prepared mustard

1 cup water
2 tablespoons brown sugar or
    molasses

Pour over meat loaf in oven and continue baking 1½ hours longer, basting occasionally. 6 to 8 servings.

Party Meat Loaf

2 eggs, slightly beaten
⅓ cup evaporated milk
⅓ cup well drained pickle relish
1 tablespoon instant minced
    onion or 1 onion, chopped
1½ pounds ground beef
½ pound sausage meat
1 cup fine dry bread crumbs
2 tablespoons Worcestershire
    sauce

2 tablespoons catsup
1 (2-ounce) can pimiento,
    drained and chopped
Salt and pepper to taste
6 olives (any kind), chopped
    (optional)
½ to ¾ cup ¼- to ½-inch
    cubes American cheese
Barbecue Sauce

Mix well all the ingredients except cheese. Shape with wet hands into a loaf about 9×5×3 inches. With knife blade make holes in loaf, tuck cheese into holes, and cover with meat. Place in greased loaf pan; cover with half of Barbecue Sauce. Bake near center of oven at 350 degrees for 70 to 75 minutes. Remove from oven and serve with remaining sauce. 8 servings.

BARBECUE SAUCE

½ cup catsup
2 tablespoons brown sugar
1 tablespoon Worcestershire
  sauce
2 to 3 tablespoons well-drained
  pickle relish

1 (8-ounce) can tomato sauce
2 tablespoons finely chopped
  onion
2 tablespoons water
2 tablespoons vinegar
Pepper

Combine all ingredients in 1-quart saucepan. Heat until steaming. About 2 cups.

Meat Loaf

Mrs. R. J. Dufano, Mableton, Georgia

2 eggs
2 cups fresh bread crumbs
¾ cup minced onion
¼ cup minced green pepper
½ pound ground pork shoulder
1½ pounds ground chuck

2 tablespoons horseradish
2½ teaspoons salt
1 teaspoon dry mustard
¼ cup milk
¾ cup catsup, divided
1 slice bacon (optional)

Beat eggs slightly; mix in crumbs, onion, pepper, and meats. Add horseradish, salt, mustard, milk, and ¼ cup catsup; combine lightly but well.

Shape meat into oval loaf; place in shallow baking dish or broil-and-serve platter. Top with remaining catsup and slice of bacon, if desired. Bake 50 minutes to 1 hour at 400 degrees. 6 to 8 servings.

Banana Meat Loaf

1 pound ground beef
1 tablespoon chopped onion
1 teaspoon salt
¼ teaspoon pepper

1 cup soft bread crumbs
¾ cup (about 2) mashed
  bananas
2 teaspoons prepared mustard

Mix meat, onion, salt, pepper, and crumbs. Combine bananas and mustard, add to meat mixture and mix well. Form into loaf and place in baking dish or fill small loaf pan. Bake at 350 degrees for about 1 hour, or until meat is thoroughly cooked. 4 to 6 servings.

Apple Upside-down Meat Loaf

1 pound ground beef chuck
2 pounds ground lean ham
1 cup fine bread crumbs
2 eggs
½ cup milk
1 teaspoon mild dry mustard
3 to 4 green onions, chopped
  (tops included)

½ cup chopped celery
½ to 1 cup brown sugar
½ teaspoon ground cloves
¼ teaspoon cinnamon
2 apples

Combine beef and ham with bread crumbs. Slightly beat eggs into milk, add to meat mixture. Add mustard, onions, and celery; mix well. Combine brown sugar and spices, spread on bottom of a 3-quart mold. Core, but do not peel apples and slice into rings; cut rings in half crosswise and place in bottom of mold. Pack meat mixture firmly into mold on top of apples. Bake at 350 degrees for 1 to 1½ hours.

(There will be some juices, so when done let set for about 5 minutes, then tip mold to pour off excess juices before turning upside down on serving platter.) For serving a buffet, place loaf in center of platter, surround with poached apple halves filled with horseradish sauce. 10 to 12 servings.

Pimiento Meat Loaflets

1½ pounds ground beef
½ pound pork sausage meat
1 egg
½ cup evaporated milk
¼ cup chili sauce
1½ teaspoons salt
¼ teaspoon seasoned pepper
¼ teaspoon chili powder
1 small onion, chopped
2 tablespoons chopped green
  pepper

3 tablespoons fine dry bread
  crumbs
2 (4 ounces each) cans or jars
  whole pimientos
¼ cup ice water
6 unbaked individual pie shells
3 slices process cheese
Salad oil

Thoroughly combine meats, egg, milk, chili sauce, seasonings, onion, green pepper, and crumbs. Mince two pimientos (or equivalent in pieces), and add to meat mixture. Cut remaining pimientos into wedges or triangles and reserve for topping. Use heavy fork to beat ice water into meat mixture. This helps to give filling lighter and more porous texture. Add additional and/or hotter seasonings, if desired.

Fill unbaked pie shells with meat mixture and bake at 350 degrees for about 35 minutes or until filling is firm and crust browned. Cover tops of pies with alternating triangles of pimiento and cheese and brush with a little oil. Return to oven and continue baking 10 to 15 minutes more. Serve piping hot. 6 servings.

Pedernales River Chili

Lady Bird Johnson's recipe,
submitted by Mrs. Hamilton, Forest Park, Georgia

*4 pounds boneless chuck, cut
    into 1½-inch cubes*
1 large onion, chopped
2 cloves garlic, chopped
1 teaspoon ground oregano
1 teaspoon cumin seed

*6 teaspoons chili powder (more
    if needed)*
2 (No. 303) cans tomatoes
Salt to taste
2 cups hot water

Put meat, onion, and garlic in large heavy saucepan or skillet. Sear meat until light-colored. Add oregano, cumin seed, chili powder, tomatoes, salt, and water.

Bring to a boil, lower heat, and simmer about 1 hour. As fat cooks out, skim off. 10 to 12 servings.

Yam-burger Pie

Mrs. R. E. Thacker, Waleska, Georgia

1 pound ground beef
1 egg, beaten
1 medium onion, chopped
½ cup chopped green pepper
⅓ cup fine dry bread crumbs
1 teaspoon salt
⅛ teaspoon pepper

*2½ cups mashed cooked sweet
    potatoes*
¼ teaspoon seasoned salt
⅛ teaspoon allspice
*2 tablespoons grated medium
    sharp cheese*

Combine beef, egg, onion, green pepper, crumbs, salt, and pepper
and mix well. Press meat mixture on bottom and sides of 9-inch pie
plate.

Combine mashed sweet potatoes with seasoned salt, allspice, and 1
tablespoon of cheese.

Mix well and arrange potato mixture over meat mixture. Top with
remaining 1 tablespoon of cheese.

Bake in moderate 350-degree oven for 50 minutes. 4 servings.

Cowboy's Country Pie

Mrs. J. A. Garrison, Montezuma, Georgia

CRUST

½ cup tomato sauce	½ teaspoon salt
½ cup bread crumbs	⅛ teaspoon oregano
1 pound ground beef	⅛ teaspoon black pepper
¼ cup chopped onion	
¼ cup chopped sweet green pepper	

Combine all ingredients. Mix well. Pat meat mixture into 9-inch
pie plate.

FILLING

1 cup steamed rice	1 cup grated Cheddar cheese
1½ cups tomato sauce	½ teaspoon salt

Combine above ingredients using one quarter of cheese; pour into
meat shell. Cover with aluminum foil and bake 25 minutes at 350
degrees. Remove foil, sprinkle with remainder of cheese. Return to
oven 10 to 15 minutes longer. 4 to 6 servings.

Hamburger Cabbage Skillet

3 tablespoons fat	¼ cup flour
¾ pound ground beef	1½ teaspoons salt
½ cup diced onion	¼ teaspoon paprika
4 cups coarsely chopped cabbage	½ teaspoon celery seed
	1 cup milk

Heat fat in skillet; add meat and onions. Stir until meat is gray and begins to brown. Add cabbage and fry lightly. Sprinkle flour, salt, paprika, and celery seed over mixture; stir into mixture. Pour in milk, cover and simmer 15 to 20 minutes, or until cabbage is done. 4 servings.

Gregg's Dish

Mrs. I. C. Smith, Athens, Georgia

8 ounces shell macaroni
2 pounds ground beef chuck
¼ pound (1 stick) margarine
3 medium-sized onions, chopped
1 sweet green pepper, minced
3 cloves garlic, minced
1 can whole kernel corn, undrained
1 (3-ounce) can mushrooms, undrained
1 cup grated Cheddar cheese
1 tablespoon brown sugar
1 tablespoon Worcestershire sauce
1 tablespoon chili powder
2 teaspoons salt
¼ teaspoon pepper

The day before, cook macaroni according to package directions and drain. Brown meat in margarine, with onions, pepper, and garlic. Stir in other ingredients. Add macaroni and toss together lightly. Refrigerate to mellow.

Following day, bake in 350-degree oven for 1½ to 2 hours or until bubbling. 6 servings.

Polynesian Beef

Mrs. Joseph Alperin

1 pound ground beef
2 tablespoons shortening
1 (10-ounce) package frozen green peas
½ cup sliced water chestnuts
1 (3-ounce) can sliced mushrooms with liquid
½ cup golden raisins
½ cup beef bouillon or water
1 teaspoon curry powder
1 teaspoon soy sauce
1 unpeeled orange, cut crosswise in 6 slices
½ cup salted cashews
Fried Rice

Brown beef in hot fat in skillet. Separate the peas. Add peas, water chestnuts, mushrooms, raisins, bouillon, curry powder, and soy sauce to beef in skillet. Toss mixture with fork to blend. Top with orange slices; cover tightly and cook over low heat about 15 minutes. Lightly mix with cashews and serve with Fried Rice.

Fried Rice

½ cup chopped onion
2 tablespoons margarine
1 egg, beaten
2 cups cooked rice

½ cup diced chicken, or other
*   meat (optional)*
2 tablespoons soy sauce

Sauté onion in margarine until golden. Add egg and scramble mixture. Stir in rice, meat, and soy sauce; cook over low heat 5 minutes. 4 servings.

Creamed Chipped Beef

¼ cup butter
1 small onion, chopped
1 (3½-ounce) package smoked
*   sliced beef*
¼ cup green pepper strips
2 tablespoons coarsely chopped
*   pimiento*

3 tablespoons flour
1 (13-ounce) can (1⅔ cups)
*   evaporated milk*
⅓ cup water

Melt butter in skillet over low heat. Add onion and cook until tender but not brown. Tear beef slices into pieces and add to onion along with green pepper and pimiento. Cook 2 to 3 minutes, stirring occasionally. Remove from heat. Sprinkle in flour a little at a time, blending smoothly. Gradually stir in evaporated milk, then water. Cook over low heat, stirring occasionally, until thickened, about 10 minutes. Serve hot over baked potatoes. 4 servings.

The late Mrs. Morris knew how to stretch a dollar to feed her family of nine. Eldest daughter Mrs. Gertie Hallman learned the lesson well and when she fed this to her own sons, Garner and Morris, there was never a crumb left. It became Grandma's hash.

Grandma's Hash

Mrs. N. M. Morris, Marietta, Georgia

¾ pound round steak
Salt and pepper
Flour for dredging plus 4
  tablespoons flour

3 to 4 tablespoons fat
1 small onion (may be omitted)
1 pint milk

Season steak with salt and pepper and roll in flour. Drop into hot fat and fry until medium brown on both sides. While still hot run through a food chopper on medium blade along with onion (if desired). To the fat in the skillet, add 4 tablespoons flour and milk, stirring until smooth. To this add the steak and onion and cook slowly 15 to 20 minutes. Serve hot with hot biscuits. 4 servings.

NOTE: This flavorsome dish cannot be made with leftover roast, nor can it be started with ground raw steak if you wish to get the same delicious result as the original.

Beef Hash

Mrs. Hugh Cates, Snellville, Georgia

3 cups chopped leftover roast
  beef
4 medium potatoes, diced
1 onion, chopped

1 teaspoon salt
Pepper to taste
2 tablespoons flour
½ cup water

Place beef, potatoes, and onion in pan. Add salt and pepper and enough water to cover ingredients (broth may be used if you have it). Simmer until potatoes are tender. Dissolve flour in ½ cup water and add to hash. Boil until slightly thickened. Delicious served on crisp toast! 6 servings.

Corned Beef Hash

Mrs. James Crumley, Cornelia, Georgia

1 pound cooked corned beef
3 to 4 medium potatoes, cooked
1 small onion

½ large green pepper
1 small stalk celery
1 or 2 sprigs parsley

Preheat oven to 425 degrees. Grind all ingredients in food grinder. Mix well. Turn into a shallow greased 9-inch pan. Bake until brown crust is formed 20 to 25 minutes. Fold as you would an omelet. Serve with poached eggs, catsup, or thickened tomato sauce. 4 servings.

PORK

Marinated Fresh Pork Roast

Mrs. W. A. McGuffey, Columbus, Georgia

1 teaspoon salt
½ teaspoon ground sage
½ teaspoon thyme
½ teaspoon black pepper
1 teaspoon whole cloves
1½ teaspoons allspice
1 bay leaf, crumbled
1 tablespoon slivered lemon rind

2 beef bouillon cubes
2 cups hot water
5- or 6-pound pork roast or ham
1 tablespoon fat
½ cup sliced carrots
2 tablespoons instant minced onion
3 tablespoons flour

Combine first ten ingredients and heat to boiling. Place pork in pan and pour marinade over it. Place in refrigerator for 24 hours, turning several times. When roast is removed from marinade, set liquid aside. Brown roast on all sides in hot fat. Add liquid. Add carrots and minced onion. Cover and simmer until meat is tender, about 3 to 3½ hours. Remove meat from pan. Strain juices and thicken with flour for spicy gravy. 10 to 12 servings.

Smoked Fresh Ham

Mrs. L. E. Harris, Milledgeville, Georgia

Salt a fresh ham well and set aside until it reaches room temperature. Make fire in broiler-smoker with charcoal. Add green hickory leaves and wood to make fire smoke. Smoke cooking is cooking by hot smoke only. It is a slow process, but a deliciously different experience. A 10- to 12-pound ham requires 12 to 24 hours' cooking time, depending on the temperature. The slower, 150 to 200 degrees, gives best results. *Allow plenty of time.*

Chicken halves require 5 hours, ribs 4 hours, and turkeys, hams, and larger chickens 8 to 12 hours.

Island-style Pork Roast

1 tablespoon shortening
1 (4-pound) piece center-cut
  pork loin
½ teaspoon salt
¼ teaspoon seasoned pepper
⅛ teaspoon ground ginger
Dash Tabasco sauce
½ cup water
¼ cup pineapple juice

1 onion, thinly sliced
6 firm yams, pared
½ cup dry sherry
6 slices pineapple
1 lime, thinly sliced
Grated coconut (optional)
2 teaspoons cornstarch
  (optional)

Heat pressure cooker and add shortening. Brown pork well on all sides, remove, and add rack to cooker; replace pork roast on rack. Sprinkle with seasonings, add liquids and onion. Arrange yams around pork on rack. Close cover securely. Place pressure regulator on vent pipe and cook 50 minutes. Let pressure drop of its own accord. Remove roast and yams to a serving platter and keep hot.

Add sherry, pineapple, and a few slices of lime to liquid in cooker; bring to a boil. Cook 2 to 3 minutes (thicken with 2 teaspoons cornstarch if desired). Add hot pineapple to platter and discard cooked lime. Pour sauce over and garnish with remaining fresh lime slices. Sprinkle with grated coconut. 6 servings.

Country-cured Ham

Mrs. Richard T. Russell

Soak 10-to-12-pound ham overnight in water. This is not a must but helps to soften it. A lard can is ideal for cooking it in. You may have to cut off the shank end to get the top to fasten on the can. Cover the ham in can with water. Bring to boil and boil 2 minutes per pound.

Take can off heat and cover and wrap well with newspaper, maga-
zines, blankets, and the like. Let stand for 24 hours. When you
unwrap the ham the water will still be quite hot.

Trim fat from ham and glaze as you wish. A brown sugar and
pineapple glaze is excellent.

Baked Ham

Senator and Mrs. Herman Talmadge, Lovejoy, Georgia

Wash a country-cured ham thoroughly and put into a covered
roaster, fat side up. Pour 2 inches of water into the pan. Wine, ginger
ale, apple, orange, pineapple, or grapefruit juice, cola, or champagne
may be substituted for water. Roast at 350 degrees approximately 20
minutes per pound or until done. Baste often. When nearly done,
remove rind from ham and trim off some fat. Score the surface of fat
and use one of the following glazes.

1. Cover fat with paste made of 1 generous teaspoon dry mustard
and 1 tablespoon prepared mustard. Pour 1 cup orange, pineapple,
or grapefruit juice over ham and return to 450-degree oven to finish
baking. Baste frequently until lightly browned.

2. Stud the diamond scores with cloves and cover with brown
sugar and honey. Add apple juice or cider. Glaze in 450-degree
oven, basting gently and often.

3. Pour 8 ounces of sweet wine over ham and spread with dark
molasses. Glaze in 450-degree oven for 8 to 10 minutes. Baste.

A favorite old southern sauce to serve with the ham combines 1
quart apple cider, 1 pound brown sugar, 6 cloves, and the juice of 2
oranges. Bring to a boil. Remove from heat and add 2 ounces
brandy.

Baked Ham Steak, Country Style

1 ham steak, cut 1-inch thick   *¼ cup minced onions*
Pepper   *1 bay leaf*
Pinch thyme   *4 sprigs fresh parsley*
1½ cups canned tomatoes
¼ pound grated American
*   cheese*

Place ham in greased casserole or baking dish with a closely fitting cover. Sprinkle with pepper and thyme, then cover with the remaining ingredients all blended together. Cover closely and bake in moderate oven, 350 degrees, about 45 minutes, turning once during the cooking process. Serve with plain boiled potatoes and cabbage or a green salad. 4 servings.

Ham Slice with Fruit Stuffing

3 cups soft bread crumbs
1 cup diced apple
½ cup seedless raisins
⅔ cup orange juice
¼ cup melted ham or bacon
   drippings

¼ cup granulated sugar
2 ham slices, each cut ½ inch
   thick
Brown sugar
Whole cloves

Combine bread crumbs, apple, raisins, orange juice, drippings, and granulated sugar. Mix lightly.

Spread one ham slice with fruit stuffing. Place the second ham slice on top. Stick wooden picks through one slice into the other to hold slices in place. Spread surface of top ham slice with brown sugar and stick with cloves. Place on rack in open roasting pan. Roast in a slow oven, 325 degrees, for 1¼ hours. Remove picks. 6 servings.

Mrs. John Glenn's Ham Loaf

Miss Irene Burkhalter, Warrenton, Georgia

1 pound ground cured ham
1 pound ground fresh pork
2 eggs
⅔ cup cracker crumbs or rolled
   oats

1¼ cups milk
⅓ cup minute tapioca

DRESSING

¼ cup vinegar
½ cup water

½ cup brown sugar
1 tablespoon prepared mustard

Mix ingredients and form into a loaf. Boil dressing a few minutes. Pour over loaf and bake in 350-degree oven about 2 hours, basting occasionally. Dressing should become thick and syrupy. 6 servings.

Excellent way to use leftover baked ham remaining on bone after slicing.

Creamed Ham

3 cups diced cooked ham
6 tablespoons butter
3 to 4½ tablespoons flour

2¼ cups milk
2 tablespoons chopped parsley
Salt and pepper to taste

Sauté ham in butter 5 minutes. Add flour and stir until smooth. Add milk gradually, stirring constantly. Cook and stir until thickened.

Add parsley; season with salt and pepper. 6 servings.

Ham Roll-ups

2 cups mashed cooked sweet
   potatoes
3 tablespoons melted margarine
½ cup crushed pineapple
¼ cup chopped pecans

½ cup cracker crumbs
3 tablespoons brown sugar
6 slices ham, ⅛ inch thick
¾ cup pineapple juice

Combine potatoes, margarine, pineapple, pecans, cracker crumbs, and brown sugar. Mix well. Spread filling on each slice of ham, rolling as for jelly roll. Fasten with toothpicks or tie with string. Place in baking dish. Add pineapple juice. For smoked ham, bake at 350 degrees for 1 hour; 20 minutes for boiled ham. Baste frequently. 6 servings.

Ham Banana Rolls

4 thin slices boiled ham
Prepared mustard
4 firm bananas

2 to 4 teaspoons melted butter
   or margarine
Cheese Sauce

Spread each ham slice with mustard. Peel bananas and wrap each one in a slice of ham. Brush banana ends and ham with melted butter. Place in greased shallow baking dish; cover with Cheese Sauce. Bake 30 minutes at 350 degrees or until bananas are easily pierced with a fork. Serve hot. 4 servings.

CHEESE SAUCE

1 tablespoon butter or margarine
1 tablespoon flour
¾ cup milk
1½ cups grated sharp Cheddar cheese

Melt butter in saucepan. Blend in flour, making a smooth paste. Slowly add milk, stirring constantly until thickened. Remove from heat. Add cheese and stir until cheese is melted. About 1 cup.

Baked Ham Timbales

2 cups ground cooked ham
1½ cups milk
½ teaspoon paprika
½ teaspoon celery salt
1 tablespoon minced onion
½ teaspoon dry mustard

½ teaspoon Worcestershire sauce
4 eggs, slightly beaten
6 pineapple rings
Parsley

Butter six 6½-ounce baking cups. In mixing bowl, combine ham, milk, paprika, celery salt, onion, mustard, Worcestershire sauce, and mix well. Stir in eggs and pour into baking cups. Set cups in pan of warm water. Bake 1 hour at 325 degrees or until metal knife inserted in center of mixture comes out clean. Unmold on pineapple rings; garnish with parsley. 6 servings.

Ham Hash

1 slice stale bread
1 ounce diced Parmesan cheese
2 cups diced cooked ham
½ small onion
½ medium green pepper

½ cup milk
1 egg
¼ teaspoon dry mustard
2 tablespoons butter

Break bread into container of electric blender. Cover and blend on high speed for 6 seconds. Empty crumbs onto piece of waxed paper. Put cheese in container, cover and blend for 6 seconds. Empty grated cheese on top of bread crumbs.

Shred ham by blending not more than ½ cup at a time and emptying into a shallow casserole. Then put onion, pepper, milk, egg, and mustard into container. Cover and blend at high speed for 6 seconds. Pour blended mixture over ham in casserole. Sprinkle with bread crumbs mixed with the cheese; dot with butter and bake at 350 degrees for 20 minutes. 4 servings.

Pork Chops with Corn Bread Dressing

Chef Will Harris, General Forrest Hotel, Rome, Georgia

6 pork chops, 1 to 1½ inches
   thick
Salt and pepper to taste
Corn bread, about 3 cups
1 egg
¼ cup chopped celery
¾ teaspoon sage
2 tablespoons finely chopped
   onion

¼ to ⅓ cup chicken broth
2 tablespoons melted butter
Flour
Paprika
½ cup milk
½ cup water

Have pocket cut in each chop by slitting from fat side and cutting almost to bone edge. Season with salt and pepper. Crumble corn bread and combine with egg, celery, sage, onion, and chicken broth, using enough broth to moisten well. Fill pockets of pork chops lightly. Fasten with wooden picks or skewers. Butter a baking pan, place chops in pan, and brush tops with butter; sprinkle with a little flour and paprika. Add milk and water. Bake at 350 degrees for 1 hour. 6 servings.

Corn-stuffed Pork Chops

Mrs. J. Andy Rape, McDonough, Georgia

4 double-thick rib pork chops
Salt and pepper
¾ cup drained whole kernel
   corn
1 tablespoon chopped celery

1 tablespoon chopped green
   pepper
2 tablespoons chopped onion
¼ cup dry bread crumbs
½ cup hot water

Have pocket cut in each chop by slitting from fat side and cutting almost to bone edge. Season with salt and pepper. Mix remaining ingredients except water and stuff into chop pockets. Close openings with toothpicks along fat edge. Insert picks at angle so they do not keep chops from resting in skillet. Add hot water; cover tightly and simmer until tender, about 1½ hours. Add more water if necessary. Remove picks before serving. 4 servings.

Easy main dish. So good served with fluffy white rice.

Oven-barbecued Pork Chops

8 loin pork chops, cut 1-inch
   thick
Salt and pepper to taste
8 slices lemon, ¼ inch thick

8 slices onion, ¼ inch thick
½ cup brown sugar
1 (8-ounce) can tomato sauce

Brown chops in skillet; arrange in casserole and season with salt and pepper. Top with lemon and onion slices. Mix brown sugar and tomato sauce together. Pour over meat. Cover and bake at 325 degrees for 1 hour.

Baste occasionally. Remove cover and bake 15 minutes longer. 8 servings.

Yam Chops

8 pork chops, cut ¾ inch thick
2 tablespoons cornstarch
½ cup firmly packed brown
   sugar
½ teaspoon salt

1 cup orange juice
1 cup lemon juice
2 tablespoons grated orange
   rind
8 medium yams, cooked

Brown chops on both sides in skillet; transfer to baking dish. Cover, bake in 350-degree oven for 1 hour. Mix cornstarch, sugar, and salt. Add to drippings in skillet.

Gradually add fruit juices and rind. Stir over medium heat until sauce boils and thickens. Place 1 yam on each chop. Pour sauce over the chops. Continue baking uncovered 30 minutes, basting frequently. 8 servings.

Pork Chops with Apple Raisin Sauce

1 cup flour	*4 teaspoons brown sugar*
½ teaspoon salt	*1½ teaspoons cornstarch*
½ teaspoon thyme	*⅛ teaspoon salt*
4 pork chops	*Dash cinnamon*
½ cup evaporated milk	*⅓ cup apple cider*
2 tablespoons butter	*2 teaspoons fresh lemon juice*
½ cup water	*2 tablespoons raisins*

Combine flour, salt, and thyme in a paper bag. Set aside. Dip chops in ¼ cup evaporated milk; then shake in flour mixture to coat thoroughly. Melt butter in skillet; sauté chops in butter until lightly browned. Add water; cover. Reduce heat and cook 1 hour and 15 minutes or until tender.

Remove chops from skillet. Stir brown sugar, cornstarch, salt, and cinnamon into meat drippings. Add cider, lemon juice, remaining ¼ cup evaporated milk, and raisins. Cook, stirring constantly, until thick. Serve sauce over chops.

Gourmet Pork Chops

6 rib pork chops, cut ¾ to 1 inch thick	*3 tablespoons butter or margarine*
2 tablespoons lard or drippings	*2 beef bouillon cubes*
1¼ teaspoons salt	*2 cups cooked wild rice (about ¾ cup uncooked)*
⅛ teaspoon pepper	*⅓ cup light cream*
⅓ cup chopped onion	
¾ cup chopped celery	
1 (6-ounce) package fresh mushrooms, quartered	

Grease a 12×8-inch baking dish. Brown chops in lard or drippings. Pour off drippings. Season chops with 1 teaspoon salt and pepper.

Cook onion, celery, and mushrooms in butter or margarine until onions and celery are tender and mushrooms are lightly browned. Add bouillon cubes to hot mushroom mixture. Crush cubes and stir until dissolved.

Add remaining ¼ teaspoon salt, rice, and cream. Put rice mixture in baking dish and place chops on top. Cover tightly and bake in a moderate oven, 350 degrees, for 30 minutes. Uncover and continue baking 15 minutes or until chops are done. 6 servings.

Pork Chops with Dressing Balls

6 rib pork chops, cut 1 inch
  thick
2 tablespoons lard or drippings

1½ teaspoons salt
⅛ teaspoon pepper
Dressing Balls

Brown chops in lard or drippings. Season and place in baking dish. Arrange Dressing Balls around chops. Cover tightly and bake in a moderate oven, 350 degrees, for 30 minutes. Remove cover and continue baking 15 minutes. 6 servings.

DRESSING BALLS

1 cup chopped celery
1 tablespoon minced onion
1 tablespoon minced parsley
1 tablespoon butter or
  margarine
2½ cups bread crumbs

⅛ teaspoon marjoram
⅛ teaspoon celery seed
1 teaspoon salt
⅛ teaspoon pepper
Water or stock

Cook celery, onion, and parsley in butter or margarine until lightly browned. Add bread crumbs, marjoram, celery seed, salt, pepper, and enough water or stock to moisten. Shape into 1½-inch balls. 12 balls.

Cheese-stuffed Pork Chops

3 tablespoons butter
1 teaspoon minced onion
¼ cup finely sliced mushrooms
½ cup (about 3 ounces)
  crumbled blue cheese

¾ cup fine dry bread crumbs
Dash salt
6 double-thick pork loin chops,
  with pockets

Melt butter in skillet. Add onion and mushrooms. Cook 5 minutes. Remove from heat and stir in blue cheese, bread crumbs, and salt.

Stuff pockets of each chop with dressing. Secure with picks. Bake at 325 degrees for 1 hour or until meat is nicely browned and cooked through. 6 servings.

Southern Pork Chops

4 pork loin chops, ½ inch thick
Fat for browning
1 medium onion, cut in 4 slices
¼ cup peanut butter smooth or crunchy
½ (10½-ounce) can cream of mushroom soup
½ cup milk
1 teaspoon Worcestershire sauce
1 teaspoon salt
⅛ teaspoon pepper

Brown pork chops quickly on both sides in small amount of fat. Pour off excess fat and return pork chops to skillet. Top each pork chop with onion slice.

Mix peanut butter with remaining ingredients. Pour over pork chops. Cover and cook over very low heat for about 45 minutes or until tender. 4 servings.

Savory Barbecue Pork Loin with Bacon Dressing

1 (4- to 5-pound) pork loin roast
½ cup chopped onion
3 tablespoons fat
¾ cup water
¾ cup catsup
½ cup cider vinegar
3 tablespoons brown sugar
4 teaspoons Worcestershire sauce
¾ teaspoon oregano
¾ teaspoon paprika
¾ teaspoon garlic salt
½ teaspoon salt
¼ teaspoon dry mustard
⅛ teaspoon black pepper
⅛ teaspoon ground cloves

Place pork loin on a rack in a shallow roasting pan. Roast in slow oven at 325 degrees about 3 to 3⅓ hours, until thoroughly done or until meat thermometer reads 185 degrees.

Meanwhile, sauté onion in hot fat until tender. Add remaining ingredients; mix. Simmer to blend flavors about 15 minutes. Baste meat with sauce several times during last 30 minutes' roasting time. Serve remaining sauce and Bacon Dressing with meat. 8 servings.

BACON DRESSING

6 slices bacon
1½ cups sliced celery
½ cup chopped onion
6 cups ½-inch bread cubes
2 tablespoons chopped parsley

¼ teaspoon salt
2 tablespoons hot water
2 tablespoons barbecue sauce
   (recipe above)

Fry bacon until crisp. Drain and crumble into bits. Save ⅓ cup bacon drippings. Add celery and onion to drippings; sauté until onion is tender. Add to remaining ingredients and toss lightly. Place in 2-quart baking dish and cover tightly. Bake with meat during last 30 minutes' roasting time. 8 servings.

Party Spareribs

5 to 6 pounds spareribs, cut
   into serving pieces
Salt
1 lemon, thinly sliced
¼ cup molasses
¼ cup prepared mustard
2 tablespoons vinegar

2 tablespoons lemon juice
1 teaspoon chili powder
1 tablespoon celery seed
2 tablespoons Worcestershire
   sauce
½ cup catsup

Place spareribs, meat side up, in shallow baking pan. Sprinkle with salt. Top with lemon slices. Bake in a 350-degree oven 30 minutes. Combine remaining ingredients. Brush spareribs with mixture. Turn and continue baking 1 hour longer, basting frequently. 4 to 6 servings.

Sweet and Sour Spareribs

3 pounds spareribs, cut into
   serving pieces
1 cup water
1 (10½-ounce) can consommé,
   undiluted
1 cup pineapple juice
¼ cup vinegar

¼ cup water
2 tablespoons brown sugar
2 tablespoons cornstarch
1 tablespoon soy sauce
¼ teaspoon ginger
⅛ teaspoon garlic powder

Place spareribs and water in kettle and steam for 45 minutes or until tender. Combine remaining ingredients and cook until thick and transparent. Pour cooked sauce over steamed spareribs in baking pan and bake in 350-degree oven for 1 hour. 3 to 4 servings.

When I serve these there is always a rush for second helpings and requests for the recipe.

Barbecued Spareribs

3 pounds fresh pork spareribs
½ cup chili sauce or catsup
½ cup firmly packed brown
 sugar
1 tablespoon vinegar

2 tablespoons Worcestershire
 sauce
⅛ teaspoon cayenne pepper or
 hot pepper sauce

Cook spareribs in boiling salted water (just barely to cover) about 1½ hours or until tender. Drain and place in a shallow baking dish. Mix together chili sauce, brown sugar, vinegar, Worcestershire sauce, and cayenne. Spread over top of spareribs. Place under preheated broiler and brown slowly under low heat about 15 minutes—or bake in 350-degree oven and about 20 minutes or until spareribs are browned. Serve with sauce from the dish poured over the spareribs. 6 servings.

Mr. and Mrs. Bowdoin are noted for the excellence of their barbecue and Brunswick stew.

Barbecue Meat

Mr. Frank D. Bowdoin, Cabiness Community, Georgia

Split cleaned and dressed pig carcass down middle and place over coals in open pit, flesh side down. The oak and hickory coals should be about 12 inches below meat. Cook until all fat is broken down. It will take at least 8 hours for even a small pig. At the last part of cooking time, throw lots of coals under meat, turn and brown skin.

When cool enough to handle, cut meat from bone, season with salt, and add sauce to taste. Put in oven to heat through. Package and thoroughly chill before freezing.

BARBECUE SAUCE

1 gallon pure apple vinegar　　　*5 tablespoons red pepper*
2 pounds butter　　　　　　　　*Salt to season*
1 tablespoon black pepper

Combine all ingredients; bring to boil and simmer 1 hour at very low heat. About 1 gallon sauce.

Brunswick Stew

Mrs. Frank D. Bowdoin, Cabiness Community, Georgia

1 (5-pound) hen　　　　　　　*4 (No. 303) cans (1 pound*
1 hog's head　　　　　　　　　　*each) cream-style corn*
5 pounds potatoes　　　　　　*1 quart barbecue sauce*
4 pounds ground beef
5 (No. 303) cans (1 pound
each) tomatoes

Cook hen and hog's head in small amount water and take meat from bones; grind meat. Grind peeled potatoes, add beef and other ingredients, and cook 2 to 2½ hours at low heat. Stir often to keep from sticking. About 10 quarts.

Pork Tenderloin with Sour Cream Gravy

6 to 8 (about 1 pound) pork　　*2 teaspoons flour*
tenderloin patties　　　　　　*⅓ cup milk*
¼ cup flour　　　　　　　　　*1 cup sour cream*
3 tablespoons lard or drippings　*1 teaspoon Worcestershire*
1 teaspoon salt　　　　　　　　*sauce*
⅛ teaspoon pepper　　　　　　*1 tablespoon chopped parsley*
2 tablespoons chopped onion　　*½ teaspoon sage*
2 tablespoons water

Dredge patties in flour. Brown in lard or drippings. Pour off drippings. Season patties with salt and pepper. Add onion and water. Cover tightly and cook slowly 45 minutes. Remove patties from frying pan. Stir flour into drippings. Add milk and cook, stirring constantly, until thickened.

Stir in sour cream, Worcestershire sauce, parsley, and sage. Cook just until heated through. Serve with patties. 4 servings.

A handsome and tasty platter. Great for special occasions.

Pork Tenderloin with Orange Sauce

2 (2 pounds each) pork
　tenderloins
2 tablespoons butter or
　margarine
¾ cup chopped onion
2 teaspoons salt
¼ teaspoon pepper

½ cup white wine
3 oranges
3 tablespoons sugar
1 bay leaf
1 tablespoon chopped parsley
1½ teaspoons cornstarch
4 cups hot cooked rice

Sauté tenderloins in butter until golden. Remove from pan and set aside. Cook onion, salt, and pepper in butter until onion is tender. Return meat to pan. Pour wine and juice from two oranges over meat. Add sugar, bay leaf, and parsley. Cover and simmer for about 45 minutes, or until meat is tender. Peel remaining orange and section. Cut peel into very thin strips; boil in small amount of water and add to broth. Add cornstarch, stirring until thickened and smooth. Cut tenderloin in thick slices; place on platter of cooked rice. Pour sauce over meat. Garnish with orange slices and cooked peel. 6 servings.

Sweet and Sour Pork

Joseph R. Webb, Atlanta, Georgia

5 tablespoons sugar
¼ teaspoon salt
½ cup plus 2 tablespoons water
3 tablespoons vinegar
½ teaspoon lemon juice
5 tablespoons tomato juice
1 or 2 pineapple slices, cut in
　chunks
1 large carrot, cut in sticks
12 green snap beans, snapped

1½ tablespoons cornstarch
½ pound fresh pork, boneless
　and lean, cut in ½-inch
　squares
Egg whites
Flour
Pepper
Garlic salt
Oil for frying

Mix sugar, salt, water, vinegar, lemon juice, tomato juice, pineapple, carrot sticks, and beans in a boiler. Bring to boil and thicken slightly with cornstarch. Do not cook further. All quantities may be increased according to taste.

Dip pork in egg white, then roll in flour with a little black pepper and garlic salt. Cook 3 minutes in hot oil or until done. Pour off oil. Add sauce mixture, cover and cook 1 minute. 2 servings.

Sausage and Squash Bake

4 acorn squash
1 pound bulk pork sausage
1 cup chopped celery
¼ cup chopped onion

¼ cup chopped green pepper
⅝ cup grated Parmesan cheese
3 tablespoons sour cream

Halve and seed squash; place cut-side down in pan and bake in 375-degree oven about 45 minutes or until fairly tender. Meanwhile, in skillet, brown sausage well; pour off drippings. Stir in celery, onion, green pepper, ⅓ cup Parmesan cheese, and sour cream. Turn squash, fill with sausage mixture, and sprinkle with remaining cheese. Bake 15 more minutes. 8 servings.

Sausage Cornbake

Mrs. Fred McCord, Atlanta, Georgia

1 egg, beaten
1¼ cups milk
¼ cup sausage fat or other
  shortening
2 cups self-rising corn meal

1 teaspoon sugar
½ pound sausage, lightly
  browned in skillet

Heat oven to 450 degrees. Grease and heat muffin pans, corn-stick molds, or skillet. To egg, add milk and shortening. Stir in meal, sugar, and sausage and blend thoroughly. Pour batter into hot greased pans and bake 25 to 30 minutes. This should be baked thin and brown. 4 servings.

NOTE: If using plain meal, add 3 teaspoons baking powder and 1 teaspoon salt.

Sausage Scrapple

Mrs. Fritz Orr, Jr., Palmetto, Georgia

½ pound pork sausage	*¼ teaspoon pepper*
2½ cups meat broth or water	*1 teaspoon poultry seasoning*
1 cup corn meal	*Fat for frying*
1 teaspoon salt	

Cook sausage in large frying pan about 5 minutes, stirring and tossing it about in pan with a fork. Drain off excess fat. Add liquid; bring to boiling point, then sift in corn meal slowly, stirring constantly. Cook until mixture thickens. Season, cover and cook slowly 15 minutes. Turn into small, wet loaf pan. Cool, chill, slice, and brown in a little hot fat. 4 servings.

Deep South—hearty, filling, and *satisfying* breakfast.

Salt Pork with Sawmill Gravy

1 pound salt pork, thinly sliced	*⅛ teaspoon pepper*
2 tablespoons flour	*1½ cups milk*

Over medium heat slowly pan fry salt pork slices until crisp. Remove from pan and keep warm. Pour off all but 2 tablespoons fat. Add flour and pepper and blend. Add milk and stir until thickened. Serve on hot biscuits or grits with fried pork slices. 4 servings.

Liver Pudding

Mrs. MacDonald Johnson (Sara), Decatur, Georgia
one of my numerous first cousins

Cook 1 hog liver and 1 hog heart together until well done. Throw away the water. Cook 2 hog faces until done. Skim off surplus fat and save water. Pick meat from bones, then run meat through coarse food chopper. Grind up liver and heart in same way.

Mix all three meats together and put back into water saved. Heat to boiling and add meal to thicken. Then add onions, sage, salt, black and red pepper to taste and cook for 20 minutes. Pour into pans to cool and set. For serving, cut slices, dip in flour, and fry in bacon fat or lard until brown on both sides. Serve hot.

Souse

Mrs. MacDonald Johnson, Decatur, Georgia

Cook hog face, after cleaning well, in water until well done. Skim off fat and leave water. Pick meat off bones and run through coarse food chopper. Season with vinegar, sage, black and red pepper. Mix meat and seasonings and put back into cooking water. Pour into pans or molds and let cool and set. Slice for serving and put vinegar in serving dish.

VEAL

Veal Cutlets Piquant with Mushroom Sauce

2 pounds veal cutlets, ¼ inch thick	*1 tablespoon lemon juice*
2 teaspoons bottled brown sauce	*¼ cup butter or cooking oil*
¼ teaspoon ginger	*1 lemon*
⅛ teaspoon pepper	*2 sweet pickles or 6 small gherkins*
1 teaspoon salt	*Mushroom Sauce*

Divide cutlets into 6 portions. Combine bottled sauce, ginger, pepper, salt, and lemon juice. Brush cutlets with combined seasonings. Melt fat in skillet with tight-fitting cover, then cook cutlets, uncovered, over moderate heat until well browned. Cover and cook until tender, about 25 minutes. Remove to hot platter and top each piece with thin slice of lemon topped with thin slice of pickle or a gherkin. Serve with Mushroom Sauce. 6 servings.

MUSHROOM SAUCE

3 tablespoons flour
½ teaspoon salt
1 cup milk
1 (6-ounce) can sliced broiled mushrooms

Add flour and salt to drippings in skillet. Stir until smoothly blended. Add milk, stirring constantly. Add mushrooms, including broth, and cook over low heat until thickened. 1 pint.

Veal Rolls Parmigiana

8 (about 1½ pounds) veal
    cutlets, cut ¼ inch thick
2 tablespoons finely chopped
    parsley
1 teaspoon salt
½ teaspoon seasoned pepper
½ cup grated Parmesan cheese
Flour
2 tablespoons oil
1 tablespoon butter

1 small clove garlic, minced
1 small onion, finely chopped
6 large mushrooms, sliced
2 teaspoons cornstarch
1 (1-pound) can stewed
    tomatoes
½ teaspoon crumbled dried
    oregano or rosemary
¼ pound mozzarella cheese

Season one side of each piece of veal with parsley, salt, ¼
teaspoon pepper, and 3 tablespoons Parmesan cheese. Roll up
enclosing seasonings. Skewer each roll with a small wooden pick to
hold them together. Dust lightly with flour.

Brown in heated oil and butter. Lift rolls to large rectangle of
heavy-duty foil, cupping edges slightly. Add garlic and onion to drippings remaining in pan. Cook and stir until vegetables begin to soften. Add mushrooms, cornstarch, tomatoes, oregano or rosemary,
and remaining salt and pepper.

Heat to simmering. Spoon sauce over veal. Dot meat with pieces
of mozzarella cheese. Sprinkle with remaining Parmesan cheese.
Close foil over meat, using double fold at edges; leave room for
steam which forms during cooking. Place on shallow baking pan.
Bake in moderate oven, 350 degrees, for 35 minutes. 4 servings.

LAMB

Rolled Shoulder of Lamb with Vegetables

1 (5-pound) boned shoulder of
    lamb, rolled and tied
Salt
Pepper
¼ cup butter or margarine
1 beef bouillon cube

1 (1-pound) can whole onions,
    drained
½ pound mushrooms
2 cups diced cooked turnips
2 (10 ounces each) packages
    French-cut green beans,
    thawed

Sprinkle lamb with salt and pepper. Place on rack in roasting pan. Bake in slow oven, 300 degrees, for 2 to 2½ hours. About 1 hour before lamb will be ready, melt butter or margarine. Add bouillon cube and cook over low heat, stirring constantly, until bouillon cube dissolves.

Arrange onions, mushrooms, turnips, and green beans around lamb. Brush vegetables with butter mixture. Bake 30 minutes to 1 hour, or until meat thermometer registers 175 to 180 degrees, depending upon desired degree of doneness. 6 to 8 servings.

Leg of Lamb with Minted Stuffing

1 (7- to 8-pound) leg of lamb, boned
Salt
Pepper
2 tablespoons chopped onion
½ cup chopped celery
2 tablespoons butter or margarine

1 teaspoon salt
1 tablespoon dried mint or 2 tablespoons chopped fresh mint
2 cups bread cubes
¼ cup water

Sprinkle lamb inside and outside with salt and pepper. Cook onion and celery in butter or margarine until lightly browned. Add 1 teaspoon salt and mint. Toss with bread cubes and water. Spoon stuffing into both openings of leg; sew with thread or secure with skewer. Roast at 325 degrees about 3 hours or to desired doneness. 8 servings.

Grilled Lamb Chops

4 loin lamb chops, cut 1 inch thick
¼ cup lemon juice
¼ cup chopped fresh mint leaves or 1¾ tablespoons dried mint leaves

1 teaspoon grated lemon rind
¼ teaspoon sugar
½ teaspoon salt
⅓ cup olive oil

Trim fat from lamb chops and make several slits around edges. Pour lemon juice into blender container. Add mint leaves, lemon rind, sugar, and salt. Blend at high speed for 5 seconds. Pour into bowl and mix well with olive oil. Place chops on china or glass platter and pour mint mixture over them, turning to coat thoroughly. Let stand for at least an hour at room temperature to season, turning occasionally.

Remove chops from mint sauce and grill over medium hot coals for 7 to 8 minutes on each side, basting with sauce. 4 servings.

Succulent Lamb Chops

6 loin lamb chops, cut 1½
　inches thick
Salt, pepper, and monosodium
　glutamate
⅔ cup bottled Italian salad
　dressing

1 tablespoon lemon juice
1 tablespoon soy sauce
½ teaspoon oregano leaves
⅛ teaspoon ginger

Sprinkle lamb with salt, pepper, and monosodium glutamate. Combine remaining ingredients; mix well. Broil chops 5 to 6 inches from source of heat, 10 to 12 minutes per side or until desired degree of doneness. Brush frequently with sauce. Garnish with lemon slices, if desired. 6 servings.

Shashlik

1 cup olive oil
1 cup dry red wine
3 tablespoons red wine vinegar
¼ cup chopped fresh dill
¼ cup chopped fresh parsley

1 tablespoon oregano
Salt and pepper to taste
3 medium-size onions, sliced
1 (4-pound) leg of lamb, boned
　and cut into 1½-inch cubes

Mix oil, wine, and vinegar. Add dill, parsley, oregano, salt, and pepper. Add the sliced onions and lamb cubes and coat thoroughly with the mixture. Allow to marinate overnight, stirring at least 4 or 5 times.

About 4 or 5 hours before grilling, the accompanying vegetables can be added to the marinade to absorb additional flavor. Tiny tomatoes, mushrooms, eggplant cubes, green peppers, and small white onions are all appropriate for this dish. The vegetables should be skewered and cooked a shorter time than the meat.

Place lamb cubes on skewers, allowing a ½-inch space between pieces. Broil over hot charcoal, turning frequently and brushing with marinade, about 8 to 10 minutes. Do not overcook. 8 servings.

NOTE: This marinade also makes a delicious dressing for a tossed green salad.

Lamb Spareribs en Brochette

½ cup sweet and pungent
  barbecue sauce
½ cup salad oil
½ cup water
1 tablespoon lemon juice
½ teaspoon ginger
4½ pounds lamb spareribs, cut
  up

12 (about ½ pound)
  mushrooms
1 large cucumber, cut in 6
  pieces
6 pieces fresh fruit in season

Mix together barbecue sauce, oil, water, lemon juice, and ginger. Pour over lamb. Marinate several hours or overnight, turning occasionally. Place lamb on skewers. Grill 15 to 20 minutes or until tender, brushing frequently with marinade. Place mushrooms and cucumbers on skewers and fruit on separate skewers. Grill vegetables about 10 minutes and fruit about 5 minutes or until desired doneness, brushing both frequently with marinade. 6 servings.

Baked Lamb Shanks

4 lamb shanks
4 tablespoons flour
1 tablespoon salad oil
1 cup water
2 teaspoons prepared
  horseradish

2 teaspoons bottled steak sauce
2 teaspoons vinegar
½ teaspoon salt
Dash pepper

Dredge shanks in 3 tablespoons flour; brown in salad oil in skillet. Place in baking dish. Blend remaining flour into salad oil, add water. Cook, stirring constantly, until thick. Add horseradish, bottled steak sauce, vinegar, salt, and pepper. Pour gravy over shanks; cover. Bake at 300 degrees for 2 hours. 4 servings.

Irish Stew

2 pounds boneless lamb for
   stew
½ cup diced carrots
½ cup diced turnips

1 onion, sliced
4 cups sliced or diced potatoes
Salt and pepper to taste
¼ cup flour

Cut lamb in cubes and simmer 1 hour in water to cover. Add vegetables, salt, and pepper and simmer for 30 minutes longer. Thicken gravy with flour. Serve hot. 6 servings.

Lamb Curry with Coconut Rice

⅓ cup flour
1 tablespoon salt
½ teaspoon pepper
¼ cup butter
3 pounds boneless lamb for
   stew, cut in 1-inch pieces
2 cups chopped onion
3 cloves garlic, crushed
2 tomatoes, peeled and chopped

2 tablespoons curry powder
1 tablespoon paprika
2 teaspoons salt
1 teaspoon coriander
5 whole cloves
Dash cinnamon
4 cups hot water
Coconut Rice

Combine flour, 1 tablespoon salt, and ½ teaspoon pepper. Melt butter in large skillet. Roll lamb in flour mixture. Then brown quickly in butter over high heat. Push meat to one side of skillet. Add onions and crushed garlic; brown lightly. Stir in tomatoes, seasonings, and hot water. Cover and cook over low heat until lamb is tender, about 1½ hours. Serve with Coconut Rice. Garnish with watermelon rind pickle slices if desired. 6 servings.

COCONUT RICE

Combine 2⅔ cups flaked coconut and 2⅔ cups milk in saucepan. Simmer over low heat, stirring occasionally until mixture foams, about 2 minutes. Add 1⅓ cups packaged precooked rice, 2 tablespoons butter, and ½ teaspoon salt. Cover loosely. Boil gently, stirring occasionally, until milk is absorbed, about 15 minutes. Press into well-buttered 1-quart mold and let stand a few minutes. Loosen sides and unmold on serving plate. Surround with lamb mixture. 6 servings.

Lamb Stew

2 pounds boneless lamb for
   stew
3 tablespoons flour
1 tablespoon meat drippings
1½ cups boiling water
1 clove garlic, minced
½ cup cut-up celery
4 tablespoons tomato paste
2 teaspoons salt

1 bay leaf
⅛ teaspoon pepper
⅛ teaspoon rosemary
6 carrots
6 small onions
6 potatoes, quartered
2 cups frozen peas
2 tablespoons chopped parsley

Cut meat in cubes; roll in flour and brown in fat in skillet. Add boiling water, garlic, celery, tomato paste, and seasonings. Simmer for 30 minutes. Add carrots, onions, and potatoes; simmer for about 40 minutes longer, or until all vegetables are tender. Peas should be added in last 10 minutes of cooking period. Sprinkle with parsley and serve. 6 servings.

Lamb Curry with Bananas

1 medium onion, thinly sliced
½ green pepper, chopped
1 small clove garlic, finely
   chopped
3 tablespoons olive oil, butter,
   or margarine
2 tablespoons flour
2 cups meat stock or bouillon
½ cup tomato sauce
2 tablespoons minced parsley
1 tablespoon curry powder

1 teaspoon salt
⅛ teaspoon pepper
1 large bay leaf
1 pinch thyme
2 whole cloves
Dash ground mace
2½ to 3 cups cubed cooked
   lamb
3 bananas, sliced about ½ inch
   thick
Saffron Rice

Sauté onion, green pepper, and garlic in 2 tablespoons oil until golden brown. Sprinkle flour on top. Stir until well blended, then add the meat stock or bouillon. Simmer until thick and smooth. Add tomato sauce, parsley, and seasonings; simmer about 15 minutes. Stir in the cubed lamb and let stand in the sauce—preferably overnight but at least an hour.

Shortly before serving, sauté the banana slices in remaining 1 tablespoon oil or butter. Heat lamb mixture just long enough to get it really hot. Serve over Saffron Rice and garnish with sautéed banana slices. 6 servings.

SAFFRON RICE

1 cup uncooked rice	*1 teaspoon salt*
2 cups water	*¼ teaspoon saffron*

Combine rice, water, salt, and saffron in a saucepan. Bring to a boil. Stir. Cover and cook over low heat until rice is tender, about 15 minutes. 6 servings.

GAME AND VARIETY MEATS

This recipe comes from Stone Mountain Inn, Stone Mountain, Georgia

Barbecued 'Coon

1 dressed raccoon	*1 apple*
2 tablespoons salt	*1 teaspoon black pepper*
1 whole onion	*Dash Tabasco*
1 carrot	

Soak dressed raccoon in water with 1 tablespoon salt overnight. Parboil in water to cover with 1 tablespoon salt and remaining ingredients. Cook until meat falls off bones.

Pull meat from bones, separating lean from fat; discard fat. Add lean meat to sauce made of the following:

3 onions, sliced	*¼ cup cane syrup*
½ cup chopped celery leaves	*1½ teaspoons salt*
3 tablespoons bacon drippings	*¼ cup cider vinegar*
2 teaspoons dry mustard	*¼ cup dry white wine*
1 teaspoon chili powder	*1½ cups tomato juice*

Sauté onions and celery leaves in heated bacon drippings. Add remaining ingredients, cook for 20 minutes. Add 'coon meat and heat thoroughly. 6 to 8 servings.

Missouri Venison Stew

Mrs. Henry Schuman, Hagan, Georgia

3 to 4 pounds venison	1 large onion, sliced
Flour	1½ teaspoons salt
3 tablespoons bacon fat	½ teaspoon coarse pepper
1½ cups hot water	3 carrots, scraped and
1 cup dry red wine	quartered
1 teaspoon mixed dried thyme,	3 potatoes, peeled and
marjoram, and basil	quartered
1 teaspoon dried parsley	

Remove sinews and bones from venison, cut meat into bite-size pieces, and roll in flour. Brown in bacon fat in deep kettle. Add hot water, wine, herbs, onions, salt, and pepper. Cover pot and bring to a boil. Lower heat and simmer 2 hours. Add carrots and potatoes. Cover and simmer 1 hour, adding more hot water if needed. When meat is tender and vegetables done, serve hot. 6 servings.

Roast Leg of Venison

Mrs. J. L. Bright, Brunswick, Georgia

1 (4-pound) leg venison	⅛ teaspoon thyme
6 thin slices salt pork	Salt
2 cups dry white wine	2 carrots, scraped and sliced
6 peppercorns	2 onions, peeled and sliced
2 bay leaves	¼ cup light cream

Trim excess fat from venison. Cut gashes in meat and lard with slivers of salt pork. Place in deep dish; add wine, seasonings, and vegetables. Let stand in cold spot or refrigerator 1 to 2 days, turning meat several times. Preheat oven to 300 degrees. Remove meat from marinade drain and dry. Place meat in open roasting pan. Strain marinade and reserve.

Pat vegetables dry. Place around roast. Roast meat uncovered 1 hour; raise temperature to 450 degrees. Bake 15 minutes longer. Remove meat to heated platter; keep hot. Strain pan juices into marinade; skim any fat; simmer until about three quarters of liquid remains. Add cream, season to taste; reheat. Do not boil. Serve sauce hot with meat. 4 to 6 servings.

Mrs. Schuman's husband "likes to hunt better than nearly any-thing." He kept bringing home so much venison, which she didn't re-ally like, that she felt compelled to find some tasty ways of prepara-tion. She found the following recipes in an old Remington gun cookbook. We sampled them and can say "delicious."

Hawaiian Venison

Mrs. Henry Schuman, Hagan, Georgia

1 pound venison steaks	1 teaspoon salt
¼ cup flour	2 or 3 green peppers
¼ cup butter	½ cup pineapple chunks
½ cup boiling water	Hawaiian Sauce

Cut steak into 1-inch cubes, dredge with flour, and brown in hot butter. Add water and salt and simmer until tender. Clean peppers, cut into 1-inch squares, and boil in water to cover 10 minutes; drain. Add pineapple chunks and pepper squares to browned meat. Pour Hawaiian Sauce over meat mixture and simmer 5 minutes. Serve over Chinese noodles or cooked rice. 4 to 6 servings.

HAWAIIAN SAUCE

2½ teaspoons cornstarch	½ cup sugar
½ cup pineapple juice	2½ teaspoons soy sauce
¼ cup vinegar	

Combine ingredients and cook until sauce thickens. 1 cup.

Broiled Pheasant

2 young pheasants
Salt and pepper to taste
Butter, melted

Split the birds, season with salt and pepper. If they are large, split into two pieces; if small, split and lay flat on a preheated broiler rack, skin side down. Brush with melted butter. Broil for 10 to 15 minutes, 2 inches from broiler unit. Then turn birds skin side up and broil slowly 6 to 7 inches from broiler unit. Broil 10 to 20 minutes on second side, depending on size of bird. Baste with melted butter and turn so the pheasant is browned on all sides. 4 servings.

This recipe comes from the marshes around Savannah and Brunswick.

Mud or Marsh Hens

1 mud or marsh hen   *Salt and pepper to taste*
¼ cup salt   *Paprika*
½ cup vinegar   *2 slices bacon*
4 cups water   *2 tablespoons fat*
1 apple   *1 cup stock from giblets*
1 onion   *2 tablespoons sour cream*

Remove skin and plumage by slitting breast skin and pulling from hen. Dress and wash thoroughly. Soak hen in salt, vinegar, and water for 3 hours. Wash thoroughly again. Place apple and onion inside hen. Tie hen together and cover with water and boil 10 to 15 minutes. Drain, add seasonings, tie bacon across breast, and place in deep skillet with fat. Simmer for 2 hours. Add stock to meat. The last 5 to 10 minutes of cooking time add sour cream. 1 to 2 servings.

Garlic Rabbit in Sour Cream

1 (1¾- to 2½-pounds) cut-up   *¼ teaspoon oregano*
*   fryer rabbit*   *1 bay leaf*
1 teaspoon salt   *2 tablespoons vegetable oil*
¼ teaspoon pepper   *1 cup commercial sour cream*
2 cups dry sauterne or chablis *3 tablespoons butter or*
*   wine*   *   margarine*
1 medium onion   *3 tablespoons flour*
1 clove garlic, grated

Place cut-up rabbit in large bowl (not metal). Add salt, pepper, and wine. Slice onion over the meat; add garlic, oregano, and bay leaf and marinate at room temperature for several hours, turning frequently. Remove onions and place in skillet with oil. Cook slowly until onions are golden brown.

Remove rabbit from marinade; add sour cream and coat each piece with mixture. Brown in skillet, turning frequently. Low heat must be used or the gravy will be scorched. When rabbit is browned, remove to hot platter. Pour sour cream marinade mix into gravy base; stir smooth and cook briefly. Remove bay leaf. Melt butter in small skillet; add flour and cook, stirring constantly, until brown. Turn into the simmering gravy base and stir until smooth. Pour gravy over rabbit and serve. 2 to 4 servings.

Rabbit Potpourri

1 (1- to 3-pound) dressed rabbit	2 cups sliced carrots
	½ cup diced celery
¼ pound salt pork	½ cup chopped onion
2 cups cold water	2 teaspoons salt
4 cups cubed potatoes	½ teaspoon pepper
1 cup tomatoes, canned or fresh	3 tablespoons flour

Cut rabbit into pieces for serving. Put into covered pan with salt pork and 1½ cups water. Boil slowly 1½ hours or until tender. Drain and save broth. Remove meat from bones and cut into 2-inch pieces. Combine meat, broth, potatoes, tomatoes, carrots, celery, and onion in large covered pan.

Bring to a boil and cook slowly for about 15 to 20 minutes or until vegetables are tender. Add seasoning and flour moistened with remaining ¼ cup cold water. Stir until broth is slightly thickened. 4 servings.

This recipe comes from a very good and well-known Atlanta photographer (now deceased) especially famous for his portraits.

Potchki V Madeiry
(Russian Veal Kidney in Madeira)

Leonid Skivrsky, Atlanta, Georgia

4 to 5 veal kidneys	½ tablespoon flour
Salt and pepper to taste	1 to 1½ cups stock
3 tablespoons butter or margarine	½ cup madeira wine

Soak and pare veal kidneys; salt and pepper to taste. Brown 2 tablespoons butter and sauté kidneys 10 minutes. Make sauce from remaining 1 tablespoon butter, flour, and stock; when smooth stir in wine. Pour over kidneys and simmer for 20 minutes. 4 servings.

Frankfurter Apple Yam Bake

6 medium yams, cooked,   *8 to 10 frankfurters, scored*
* peeled, and sliced*   *¼ teaspoon salt*
2½ cups canned applesauce   *¼ cup butter or margarine*
¼ teaspoon nutmeg

In lightly buttered shallow casserole, arrange layer of yam slices; cover with applesauce and sprinkle with nutmeg. Arrange frankfurters on top of applesauce with remainder of yam slices. Sprinkle with salt and dot with butter. Bake in a moderate oven, 350 degrees, for 25 to 30 minutes. 6 servings.

Liver Mush

Mrs. G. E. Griggs, Atlanta, Georgia

1 pound pork liver   *8 cups water*
1 pound sausage   *Corn meal*
Salt and pepper to taste

Cook liver and sausage with salt and pepper in water until liver can be mashed with a fork or potato masher. There should be about 2 quarts of liquid left.

Return mashed meat to liquid and cook slowly while stirring in enough corn meal to make it of thick consistency. Stir constantly. When mush begins to pull away from sides of the pan, it is done. It may be eaten hot or chilled, or sliced and fried golden brown. 6 servings.

French-fried Sweetbreads

1 pound sweetbreads   *1 egg, beaten*
1 teaspoon salt   *½ cup dry bread or cracker*
1 tablespoon vinegar   * crumbs*
1 quart water   *Lard for deep-fat frying*

Wash sweetbreads. Add salt and vinegar to water. Simmer 20 minutes. Drain and plunge in cold water. Remove membrane.

Break into 2-inch pieces. Roll sweetbreads in egg, then in bread or cracker crumbs. Fry in deep hot fat, 360 degrees, until well browned. Drain on absorbent paper. 6 servings.

7

POULTRY AND STUFFINGS

Some of the best eating on earth begins with poultry. If the point needs proving that poultry is the base of the most creative cookery being done today, the recipes in this section are ample evidence. Poultry is truly the most accommodating meat on the market, as its delicious flavor is so congenial to other ingredients. It combines successfully with many foods, herbs, and spices to make unique, delightful dishes.

When I was a child, poultry was considered a special occasion or Sunday dish. We awaited with much enthusiasm the time when the spring chicks became "frying size." What a feast that was—even if each of us only got one piece of chicken! It was adequately supplemented with cream gravy and hot biscuits.

Chicken traditionally has produced very elegant dishes, "fit for a king," and was often served to kings in the past. Only in the last few decades since the poultry industry has mushroomed has it been considered an "everyday dish."

CHICKEN

Roast Chicken for Two
Mrs. Claud Cofield, Monroe, Georgia

2½-pound frying chicken
2 tablespoons shortening
¼ cup chopped onion
¼ cup chopped celery
1 quart soft bread crumbs

1 teaspoon salt
Dash pepper
1 teaspoon poultry seasoning
⅓ cup water or chicken bouillon

Have chicken split down the back only. Rinse and pat dry. Melt shortening in a skillet; add onion and celery. Sauté in hot fat for 5 minutes. Pour mixture over soft bread cubes, salt, pepper, and poultry seasoning. Add water or chicken bouillon. Mix well. Spread chicken apart, fill cavity with bread stuffing. Close chicken with skewers or toothpicks. Pull neck skin over back and secure with skewers. Lace twine around skewers from neck, down center back, to tail, and fasten. Tie drumsticks together tightly. Brush skin with fat. Place chicken on rack in baking pan. Roast uncovered in moderate oven, 350 degrees, for 1½ hours. 2 servings.

Mr. Walters barbecues for many community outings.

Barbecuing Chicken
J. C. Walters, Tifton, Georgia

Use small fryers (2 pounds 2 ounces to 2 pounds 6 ounces ideal size). Split in half, salt, and place in pans for 1 to 4 hours (about 2 teaspoons salt per chicken or 1 pound salt for 25 chickens).

Place chicken halves on rack 15 to 18 inches above coals. As soon as chicken begins to cook (15 to 20 minutes) baste with sauce and turn. Continue basting and turning until chicken is done, 2½ hours to 4 hours. Slow cooking retains moisture, thus improving flavor. Chicken is done when the hip joint gives when twisted.

During the last 30 minutes of cooking, use oak twigs on coals to add smoked flavor. A commercial preparation may be used instead of twigs.

If the skins of the chickens blister or if sauce turns dark during cooking, reduce heat by raising rack. Slow cooking is essential. Use sauce sparingly so that it does not drip on coals and burn, creating an unpleasant smoke.

Barbecue Sauce for Chicken

1 pound margarine
4 cups finely chopped celery
2⅔ tablespoons salt
2 teaspoons black pepper
Tabasco sauce to taste (2 tablespoons or more)

2 (2¼ ounces each) bottles chili powder
1 cup peanut butter
1½ quarts vinegar
1½ quarts lemon juice

Melt margarine over low heat. Add celery, salt, pepper, Tabasco, chili powder, and peanut butter, stirring constantly. Add vinegar slowly and bring to simmer. Remove from heat and cool. Then add lemon juice. This will keep in refrigerator indefinitely. About 1 gallon sauce.

Chicken Barbecue

David Sorrell, Monroe, Georgia

⅓ cup vinegar
⅓ cup cooking oil
¼ teaspoon black pepper
½ teaspoon poultry seasoning

2 tablespoons salt
3 broiler-fryer chickens, split in half

Combine sauce ingredients well. Baste chicken halves with the sauce; place on heated grill. Baste with sauce every 15 minutes, turn. Grill about 1 hour. 6 servings.

Oven-baked Chicken

Mrs. Yates Green, New Perry Hotel, Perry, Georgia

2½-pound broiler-fryer
Salt and pepper
⅓ cup flour
Water

2 tablespoons butter
4 slices ham
Slivered almonds

Cut fryer into four sections. Season with salt and pepper and coat lightly with flour. Place in baking dish 4 inches deep. Add water to ¼-inch depth. Spread butter over top of chicken.

Cover with foil and bake at 325 degrees about 2 hours. Remove foil about 30 minutes before end of baking period so chicken will brown. Remove to hot platter and use drippings to make gravy. Serve chicken over pieces of fried country ham and sprinkle toasted slivered almonds on top. 4 servings.

NOTE: Ham slivers may be added to chicken 30 minutes before end of baking period for a very tasty dish.

Buttermilk Fried Chicken

Mrs. D. L. Jenkins, Atlanta, Georgia

1 broiler-fryer, cut up	*1 cup self-rising flour*
Salt and pepper	*½ teaspoon thyme*
Buttermilk	*Cooking oil or shortening*

Wash and drain chicken; add salt and pepper to taste. Place chicken in bowl and cover with buttermilk. Let stand for about 30 minutes. Season flour with thyme and roll chicken pieces in it until well coated. Cook in deep hot fat in large frying pan until golden brown. Turn once and cover with lid. Continue cooking until chicken is tender (about 30 minutes). 4 servings.

Oven-fried Pecan Chicken

Mrs. Delmas Rushing, Jr., Register, Georgia

1 broiler-fryer (2½ to 4 pounds)	*½ teaspoon poultry seasoning*
1 cup biscuit mix	*½ cup finely chopped pecans*
1½ teaspoons salt	*½ cup evaporated milk*
1 teaspoon paprika	*½ cup melted butter or margarine*

Wash chicken pieces, drain and pat dry. Combine biscuit mix, seasoning, and chopped pecans. Dip chicken into milk; coat well with dry mixture. Place in 13×9×2-inch baking dish. Pour melted butter or margarine over chicken. Bake uncovered at 375 degrees for 1 hour or in a slow oven at 200 degrees for 2 hours. 4 to 6 servings.

Fried Chicken with Gravy

1 (3-pound) broiler-fryer, cut
   in pieces
Salt
Pepper
Flour for dredging
Shortening

4 tablespoons flour
6 tablespoons nonfat dry milk
1 teaspoon salt
⅛ teaspoon pepper
½ teaspoon paprika (optional)
2 cups water

Sprinkle pieces of chicken with salt and pepper; dredge with flour. Fry chicken in 2 inches of hot fat in skillet. Brown well on both sides. Lower heat and cover tightly with lid. Cook slowly, turning each piece once until chicken is tender. Remove chicken to hot platter and keep warm while making gravy.

To make gravy, remove all but 5 tablespoons of drippings from pan. Combine flour, milk, salt, pepper, and paprika. Add to drippings in pan and stir until well blended. Gradually stir in water. Cook over low heat, stirring constantly until thickened and smooth. Serve with chicken. 4 servings.

Chicken Breasts with Almonds

Mrs. Steve Alexander, Atlanta, Georgia

4 boneless chicken breasts
Salt and pepper
⅓ cup butter or margarine,
   divided
½ cup chopped onion

¼ cup slivered almonds
1 tablespoon tomato paste
1 tablespoon flour
1 cup chicken broth
Pinch of dried tarragon

Sprinkle chicken breasts with salt and pepper. Melt 4 tablespoons of the butter in skillet; add chicken breasts and brown, turning occasionally, about 25 minutes; remove chicken. To juices in pan add remaining butter, onion, and almonds. Blend in tomato paste and flour. Gradually add chicken broth and cook, stirring constantly, until mixture thickens and comes to a boil. Add cooked chicken breasts and tarragon; cover and simmer 20 minutes. Serve hot over fluffy white rice. 4 servings.

A green vegetable such as buttered broccoli, crisp vegetable salad, and beverage completes the meal. A light dessert may be added, if desired.

Chicken Breast Fillets on Bed of Green Peas
Mrs. Steve Alexander, Atlanta, Georgia

8 boneless chicken breasts
3 tablespoons butter
4 cups puréed fresh peas or 2
  (*10 ounces each*) *packages*
  frozen peas, cooked and put
  through sieve

1 small onion, chopped fine
3 eggs, separated
1 tablespoon wine vinegar
Salt and pepper

Either sauté chicken breasts in the butter until brown on both sides, cover and cook over low heat until tender, or roast in the oven at 350 degrees with the butter, basting from time to time until chicken is tender.

Mix puréed peas with onion, egg yolks, vinegar, salt, and pepper. Fold in gently the stiffly beaten egg whites and spread in a large, shallow baking dish. Arrange chicken breasts on top of it. They will sink slightly to bottom and be half covered with soufflé-like mixture. Bake in medium oven, 350 degrees, 45 to 50 minutes or until purée is puffy and brown. 4 generous servings.

Glazed Stuffed Chicken Breasts

2 teaspoons salt
¼ teaspoon pepper
2 tablespoons flour
3 whole chicken breasts
1 cup diced unpared York
  apples
3 cups toasted bread cubes

¼ cup melted margarine
2 tablespoons honey
1 teaspoon grated lemon peel
¼ teaspoon paprika
¼ teaspoon cinnamon
¼ cup apple juice
Honey Spice Glaze

Combine salt, pepper, and flour. Rub chicken breasts with mixture. Combine remaining ingredients except for honey spice glaze and fill chicken breast cavities. Skewer together and place top side up in baking pan. Roast in 325-degree oven about 1 hour. Baste often with Honey Spice Glaze throughout baking period.

HONEY SPICE GLAZE

In saucepan combine ½ cup honey, 2 tablespoons water, 1 tablespoon butter or margarine, ¼ teaspoon nutmeg, and ¼ teaspoon ginger. Bring to boil. Use for basting.

Baked Stuffed Chicken Breasts

Mrs. A. L. Reynolds, Mayfield, Georgia

6 whole chicken breasts,
  backbones removed
1 (4-ounce) can mushrooms
  with liquid
⅓ cup chopped onion
1 cup chopped celery
6 tablespoons butter
1½ cups corn bread crumbs
1 cup white bread crumbs
2 tablespoons catsup
1 teaspoon Worcestershire
  sauce
¼ teaspoon poultry seasoning

½ teaspoon monosodium
  glutamate
1 teaspoon salt
½ teaspoon black pepper
½ cup chopped pecans
2 cups hot water or chicken
  broth
¾ cup dry sherry
3 chicken bouillon cubes
2 tablespoons cornstarch
¼ cup cold water
Sliced mushrooms (optional)

Carefully remove rib bones and shoulder blade bones from breasts, leaving pulley bone and long breast bone intact—do not remove any skin. Drain on paper towels.

To make stuffing, drain and chop the mushrooms, reserving liquid for basting sauce. Sauté mushrooms, onions, and celery in 2 tablespoons butter until golden; do not brown. Add mushroom mixture to bread crumbs, catsup, Worcestershire, poultry seasoning, monosodium glutamate, salt, pepper, and pecans. Mix thoroughly but lightly. Use about ½ cup stuffing for each breast.

Use boned rib sections and skin to hold stuffing. Secure with round wooden toothpicks, broken in half. Put 1 teaspoon stuffing in neck cavity, pulling skin over and securing it at the back with toothpicks. Melt remaining butter in frying pan and lightly brown stuffed breasts. Place in baking pan.

To make basting sauce combine liquid from mushrooms, hot water or broth, sherry, and bouillon cubes.

Pour sauce into pan where breasts were browned, then pour over breasts in baking pan. Cover and bake at 300 degrees for 1½ hours, basting occasionally. When done, remove toothpicks and place chicken on heated platter. Mix 2 tablespoons cornstarch with ¼ cup cold water and add gravy to thicken. Check seasonings. Sliced button mushrooms may be added to sauce. Pour over breasts or serve in sauceboat. If served separately, pour 1 tablespoon gravy over each breast. Garnish with parsley. These may be served whole to hearty eaters or carved in half lengthwise for ample servings. 6 to 12 servings.

So very good—and satisfying.

Breast of Chicken with Browned Rice

Mrs. R. N. Beasley, Millen, Georgia

> 4 chicken breasts, split in half
> ¼ cup butter
> 2 cups sliced mushrooms
> 2 (10¾ ounces each) cans
>   cream of chicken soup
> 1 large clove garlic, minced
> Dash crushed thyme
> ⅛ teaspoon crushed rosemary
> ⅔ cup light cream
> Browned Rice

Brown chicken in butter. Remove chicken. Brown mushrooms, stir in soup, garlic, and seasonings. Add chicken. Cover and cook over low heat 45 minutes. Blend in cream; heat slowly. Serve with Browned Rice and garnish with toasted, slivered almonds.

BROWNED RICE

> 1 cup uncooked rice
> 3 tablespoons chopped onion
> 1 stick butter
> 2 (10¾ ounces each) cans beef
>   consommé
> 1 consommé can water
> Salt and pepper to taste
> ½ cup slivered almonds

Brown rice and onion in butter. Put in 1½-quart casserole with all of the other ingredients; cover. Bake 1 hour at 350 degrees.

Chicken in Cucumber Sauce

Mrs. Steve Alexander, Atlanta, Georgia

> 1 cup sour cream
> 1 cucumber, peeled and sliced
> 6 boneless chicken breasts
> ⅓ cup bacon drippings
> 1 medium-size onion, chopped
>   fine
> Salt and pepper

Combine sour cream and cucumber; let stand 1 hour. Brown chicken breasts on all sides in bacon fat in a heavy skillet. Add onion, salt, and pepper and cook until onion is tender; add sour cream and cucumber mix. Cover pan tightly and cook over very low heat until tender, about 30 to 40 minutes.

Serve in the sauce with brown rice and tomato aspic to accompany it. The sour cream will separate slightly in the cooking, which is as it should be. 4 servings.

Pat and I grew up together at Meansville, Georgia. She, too, is a home economist and an excellent cook.

Brunswick Stew

Pat Collier Morse (Mrs. Harley), Eustice, Florida

1 small hen
2 pounds boneless stew meat
1 quart water
1 pound onions
3 pounds potatoes
2 (16 ounces each) cans
  cream-style corn
1 (1-pound) can green peas
1 (1-pound) can lima beans

1½ (14 ounces each) bottles
  catsup
1 (6-ounce) bottle
  Worcestershire sauce
½ cup vinegar
¾ cup lemon juice
4 teaspoons Tabasco sauce
2 tablespoons salt
Black pepper

Cook the hen and stew meat in water until well done or meat leaves the bone. Discard bones. Grind, and set meat aside. Put onions and potatoes through food grinder, and add to broth in which meat was cooked. Cook until well done.

Add meat and other ingredients. Cook on low heat until well done and thick (about 2 hours). Serve hot. May be frozen if desired. 5 to 6 quarts. 20 servings.

Quick Brunswick Stew with Corn Meal Dumplings

3 pounds cut-up chicken
2 (1 pound each) cans
  tomatoes
2 cups water
1 tablespoon salt

½ teaspoon oregano
½ teaspoon pepper
1 (10-ounce) package frozen
  baby lima beans
Corn Meal Dumplings

In Dutch oven or large saucepan combine chicken, tomatoes, water, salt, oregano, and pepper. Bring mixture to boil. Reduce heat, cover, and simmer 30 minutes or until chicken is tender. If necessary, remove excess fat. Stir in lima beans and bring to boil. Reduce heat and simmer while preparing corn meal dumplings. Drop dumplings by rounded tablespoons onto boiling mixture. Cover and steam gently 10 minutes. Remove cover and cook 10 minutes longer. Serve hot. 6 servings.

CORN MEAL DUMPLINGS

¾ cup self-rising corn meal　　　*½ cup chopped onion*
¾ cup sifted, self-rising flour　*1 egg, beaten*
2 tablespoons butter or　　　　*3 to 6 tablespoons milk*
*　margarine*

In mixing bowl stir together corn meal and flour. Cut in butter or margarine until mixture resembles coarse crumbs. Stir in onion. Blend together egg and 3 tablespoons milk. Add liquid all at once to corn meal mixture, stirring to blend. If necessary, add more milk to make a thick drop batter. Drop onto hot chicken mixture. 12 to 15 dumplings.

Hartley Reunion Brunswick Stew

4 pounds boneless chicken　　*2 (1 pound each) cans lima*
2 pounds boneless beef　　　　*　beans*
2 pounds boneless pork　　　　*1 (14-ounce) bottle catsup*
4 (1 pound each) cans　　　　　*1 cup vinegar*
*　tomatoes*　　　　　　　　　　*6 medium onions, chopped*
2 to 3 (1 pound each) cans　　*½ cup Worchestershire sauce*
*　cream-style corn*　　　　　　*Salt to taste*

Cook the meats. Chill overnight and skim off all the fat. Chop the meats (some people use a food chopper; I like mine cut in small pieces). Add remaining ingredients and simmer until well done, 1 to 1½ hours at least. If stew is too thin, a few finely crushed cracker crumbs or toasted bread crumbs make a good thickener. 24 servings.

NOTE: I like to use fresh corn, tomatoes, and limas, if available. They should be precooked before adding to the stew.

Easy Chicken Cacciatore
Mrs. J. A. Herndon, Moultrie, Georgia

1 (3-pound) chicken, cut up	*Salt and pepper*
2 tablespoons olive oil	*1 to 1½ cups sliced mushrooms*
1 medium clove of garlic	*1 (No. 303) can stewed*
1 teaspoon oregano, crumbled	*tomatoes*

Brown chicken in olive oil with garlic. Before turning the chicken, sprinkle with oregano, salt, and pepper, then add mushrooms. Brown lightly; add stewed tomatoes. Cover and simmer 30 minutes. Uncover and continue cooking until sauce is reduced to desired consistency and chicken is tender. Good with rice or spaghetti. 6 servings.

Chicken Divan
Chef Leroy Pollen, Nancy Hanks Dining Car,
Central of Georgia train, Atlanta to Savannah

2 chicken breasts, halved	*2 tablespoons flour*
6 tablespoons butter or	*½ teaspoon salt*
margarine	*¼ teaspoon pepper*
½ cup water	*1 cup light cream*
16 spears fresh or frozen	*¼ cup dry white wine*
asparagus	*¼ cup grated Parmesan cheese*
3 green onions, thinly sliced	

Skin and bone chicken breasts. Brown in 3 tablespoons butter or margarine in skillet. Add ½ cup water; cover. Lower heat, cook slowly until tender. While chicken cooks, cook asparagus (if fresh) until barely tender in boiling, salted water. Drain. Heat oven to 350 degrees. Melt remaining 3 tablespoons butter or margarine in small saucepan; add green onions; sauté about 2 minutes. Blend in flour, salt, and pepper. Stir in cream gradually, whipping constantly with wire whisk or fork to keep mixture smooth. Add wine, bring to boiling. Remove from heat. Add 2 tablespoons Parmesan cheese; stir until cheese melts. Arrange asparagus in four portions in a shallow, greased baking dish. Place a half chicken breast on each portion. Pour sauce over. Sprinkle with remaining cheese. Bake 15 minutes or until bubbly and slightly browned. 4 servings.

Casuela Quién Sabe

Rosemary DeCamp, Redondo Beach, California,
Actress and TV Personality

1 dozen corn tortillas, diced
2 (10 ounces each) cans
chicken gravy
½ cup water or chicken stock
1 large (4 to 5 pounds) stewing
hen, cooked, deboned, and
chopped

1 (2-ounce) can salsa (very
hot, red and green pepper
sauce)
½ cup chopped red or green
onion
1 can mushroom soup
(optional)

Soak diced tortillas in gravy and water for 24 hours. Add chicken, salsa, and onions. Place in earthenware or iron casserole and bake at 300 degrees for 3 hours.

Ham, cut fine, is a good substitute for chicken and if the salsa makes the sauce too hot, add the can of mushroom soup. 8 servings.

NOTE: Without the tortillas, meat, and onions, the sauce of gravy, water, salsa, and mushroom soup is wonderful alone for vegetables or fish, or jellied in a shrimp or crab ring.

Corn-stuffed Chicken

Mrs. W. E. Harris, Milledgeville, Georgia

2 (1½ pounds each) chickens,
cut up or halved
Salt and pepper to taste
¾ cup melted butter, divided
1 teaspoon paprika
2 (10-ounces each) packages
whole kernel frozen corn

2 cups bread crumbs
1 large onion, chopped
1 cup finely chopped celery
¼ cup chopped green pepper
1½ teaspoons salt
¼ teaspoon pepper

Season chicken with salt and pepper. Brush with ½ cup butter and paprika. Place foil in 2-quart baking dish or grease well. In separate bowl thaw corn enough to separate and combine with ¼ cup butter and remaining ingredients. Make four mounds of mixture in baking dish or spread evenly if cut-up chicken is used. Place cut side of chicken over each mound. Bake at 350 degrees for 1½ hours or until tender. 6 to 8 servings.

Country Captain Chicken

Mrs. Eldon Fancher, Fayetteville, Georgia

¼ cup flour	1 (8-ounce) can tomato sauce
1½ teaspoons salt	2 cups water
1 fryer, disjointed	¼ teaspoon Tabasco
¼ cup vegetable oil	1 teaspoon curry powder
1 onion, chopped	½ cup currants or raisins
1 green pepper, sliced	Cooked rice
1 clove garlic, minced	Toasted slivered almonds

Flour and salt chicken. Brown in vegetable oil; remove. Add onion, green pepper, and garlic. Cool 3 minutes. Blend in tomato sauce, water, seasonings, and currants.

Cover, simmer 30 minutes, until done. Delicious with rice and garnish of almonds. 4 to 6 servings.

Creole Chicken

Mrs. Perry L. Bridges, Blakely, Georgia

¼ pound margarine	1 (3-ounce) can mushrooms
1 broiler-fryer, cut in serving pieces	1 tablespoon Worcestershire sauce
1 large onion, chopped	1 tablespoon sugar
1 green pepper, chopped	Dash Tabasco sauce
1 cup chopped celery	1 tablespoon parsley flakes
2 (1 pound each) cans tomatoes	1 teaspoon oregano
	Salt and pepper to taste

Melt margarine in large skillet. Sauté chicken pieces. Remove chicken and sauté onion, pepper, and celery. To this add tomatoes, mushrooms, and seasonings. Replace chicken in the sauce, cover tightly, and simmer 30 minutes or until done. 4 servings.

Chicken 'n' Dumplings

1 (3- to 4-pound) chicken, disjointed	2 teaspoons baking powder
2½ teaspoons salt	⅓ cup shortening
2 cups sifted flour	½ cup milk

Place chicken in large saucepan. Barely cover with water, add 1½ teaspoons salt; simmer until meat is tender, 1 to 2 hours, depending on age and size of chicken.

Sift together flour, baking powder, and remaining salt; cut in shortening. Add milk to make stiff dough. Roll out thin and cut into squares, strips, or diamonds. Sprinkle lightly with flour and drop a few at a time into boiling liquid over chicken.

Close tightly after each addition and continue adding (keeping at full boil) until all dumplings are added. Cover tightly and continue cooking about 12 to 15 minutes. Serve at once. 6 servings.

Hawaiian Chicken

Mrs. Harriett Kendrick, Macon, Georgia

1 (4-pound) hen	*3 tablespoons margarine*
1 tablespoon dried parsley	*¾ tablespoon curry powder (or*
Celery leaves	*to taste)*
2½ teaspoons salt	*½ (10¾-ounce) can cream of*
¾ teaspoon pepper	*mushroom soup*
½ teaspoon crushed thyme	*1 chicken bouillon cube*
1 small whole onion	*1 (7-ounce) package precooked*
2 small fresh pineapples	*rice*
1 small onion, chopped	*Paprika*
2 stalks celery, chopped	*½ cup blanched toasted*
½ cup thin strips green pepper	*almonds*

Disjoint hen and simmer with dried parsley, celery leaves, 2 teaspoons salt, ½ teaspoon pepper, thyme, and onion in enough water to cover. Cook until tender. Cool in broth. Save ½ cup of broth.

Halve pineapples lengthwise, cutting through and leaving on green tops. Scoop out fruit, leaving shells about ½ inch thick. Cut pineapple into small pieces. Sauté onion, celery, pepper, and pineapple in margarine. Stir in curry powder, ½ teaspoon salt, and ¼ teaspoon pepper. Add mushroom soup and bouillon cube dissolved in hot chicken broth. Add chicken. Cook one small package minute rice according to directions. Add chicken curry to rice. Serve in pineapple halves which have been warmed in the oven. Sprinkle generously with paprika and slivered almonds before serving. 10 servings.

Chicken Livers with Apple Rings

3 tablespoons butter or
　margarine
2 cloves garlic, slashed
½ cup chopped onion
1 cup chopped apple
2 pounds chicken livers
½ teaspoon salt
Few grains pepper
1 teaspoon oregano

Dash Tabasco sauce
1 (3-ounce) can sliced broiled
　mushrooms
1 (10¼-ounce) can mushroom
　gravy
2 tablespoons vegetable oil
2 large red apples
Flour
Cinnamon-sugar

Melt butter or margarine in skillet. Add garlic cloves, onion, and chopped apple. Cook gently over low heat until soft and golden brown. Remove garlic cloves. Add chicken livers, salt, pepper, oregano, and Tabasco. Cook over low heat, turning frequently until chicken livers are cooked to desired degree of doneness. Add mushrooms with their broth and gravy. Simmer gently about 15 minutes.

Meanwhile heat oil in another skillet. Core unpeeled apples; slice crosswise; dust lightly with flour and brown on both sides in oil. Drain; sprinkle with cinnamon-sugar. Serve with chicken livers on fluffy rice. 8 servings.

Orange Chicken

Mrs. J. C. Walters, Tifton, Georgia

4 chicken breasts or chicken
　legs with thighs
1 teaspoon salt
¼ teaspoon pepper
¼ cup orange juice

1 tablespoon honey
¼ teaspoon Worcestershire
　sauce
¼ teaspoon dry mustard

Place chicken, skin side up, in a single layer in a shallow baking pan; sprinkle with salt and pepper. Bake in moderate oven, 375 degrees, for 30 minutes. Blend orange juice, honey, Worcestershire sauce, and mustard in a cup. Brush some over chicken. Continue baking, brushing again with remaining orange mixture after 20 minutes. Repeat until chicken is tender and richly glazed. 4 servings.

Chicken Pan-American

Mrs. Leland H. Bagwell, Canton, Georgia

⅓ cup cooking oil	*¼ teaspoon pepper*
6 or 8 pieces chicken	*1 tablespoon sugar*
1 cup raw yellow rice	*2 cups chicken broth or hot*
1 medium onion, chopped	*water (if bouillon cubes are*
1 clove garlic, chopped	*used, reduce salt ½ teaspoon)*
1 cup sliced mushrooms	*1 bay leaf*
2 cups canned tomatoes	*1 cup canned or fresh shrimp*
2 teaspoons salt	*1 (6-ounce) can crab meat*

Heat oil in Dutch oven, skillet, or casserole. Brown chicken and remove. In same pan, sauté rice (do not wash) until golden brown. Add onions, garlic, and mushrooms; sauté lightly. Add tomatoes, salt, pepper, sugar, chicken broth, and bay leaf. Arrange pieces of chicken on top of rice mixture. Add shrimp and crab meat. Cover and bake at 350 degrees for 1 hour. Garnish with pimiento strips and parsley. 6 to 8 servings.

Party Perfect Chicken

Mrs. Carl Sanders, Atlanta, Former First Lady of Georgia

6 tablespoons flour	*1 stick butter or margarine*
1½ teaspoons salt	*Curry Glaze*
1 teaspoon ground ginger	
2 broiler-fryers (about 3	
pounds each), quartered	

Combine flour, salt, and ginger in paper bag. Add chicken and shake to coat well. Melt butter or margarine in large shallow pan. Roll chicken in melted butter to coat well, then arrange skin side up in single layer in pan. Bake uncovered in hot oven, 400 degrees, 20 minutes or until it begins to turn golden brown.

Prepare Curry Glaze. Spoon about half of glaze on top of chicken to make thick coating; bake 20 minutes. Spoon on remaining glaze and bake 20 minutes longer, or until chicken is tender and richly browned. Arrange chicken around a mound of buttered hot rice on serving platter. 8 servings.

CURRY GLAZE

1 medium-size onion, chopped	2 tablespoons flaked coconut
2 tablespoons flour	2 tablespoons applesauce
6 slices bacon, finely diced	2 tablespoons catsup
1 tablespoon curry powder	2 tablespoons lemon juice
1 tablespoon sugar	
1 (10¾-ounce) can condensed beef broth	

Combine all ingredients in medium-size saucepan. Heat to boiling, stirring constantly; then simmer uncovered, stirring often, about 15 minutes or until thickened. About 1½ cups.

Very different and unusual—and so very good.

Bertha's Chicken Pie

Mrs. B. W. Harrison, Monroe, Georgia

1 (2½-pound) broiler-fryer	1 cup shortening
Salt and pepper to taste	½ pound butter or margarine
5 cups self-rising flour	2 quarts (about) boiling water
2 cups buttermilk	

Cut chicken into serving pieces. Salt and pepper and let set 30 minutes. Make pastry as for biscuits, using flour, buttermilk, and shortening. Knead harder than for biscuits. Roll out half of dough thin, cut into strips, and line sides of buttered 6-quart roasting pan or any large pan. Place about half the chicken in bottom of pan; using about half of the butter, between pieces of chicken and sprinkle with pepper to taste. Place half the remaining strips of pastry on chicken until it is completely covered. Then place remaining chicken on this pastry and repeat the butter and pepper. Save 2 tablespoons butter to butter two crusts. With half the remaining dough roll a crust large enough to cover the chicken and seal it to the side crust by pressing with finger tips. Dampen crust well with water. Make a small hole in the center of crust and pour enough boiling water barely to float the crust. Put in 450-degree oven and cook until brown, about 25 minutes. Remove from oven and brush crust well with butter. Use remaining dough and roll out another crust and place on top of the first crust; return to oven and brown (about 10 minutes), then brush top crust with butter. Reduce oven heat to very low (250 degrees) and cook until chicken is tender when tested with a fork. (Test right through the crust.) The pie may be removed from oven and the cooking completed on top of range on low heat. More water may be added if the pie gets too dry. Cooking time is about 1½ hours. 4 servings.

NOTE: Dumplings may be used in place of pastry strips.

Mrs. Mansell discovered this recipe by accident. She forgot the biscuit dough and left it in the refrigerator. Not to be outdone, she decided to use it in chicken pie. It was an instant success, so it became a family favorite. This pie is a must at family reunions and church dinners. (The Mansell boys were in the egg-producing business.) Mrs. Mansell in now 93 years old and going strong.

Mrs. Mansell's Sour Dough Chicken Pie

Mrs. Robert (Maude) Mansell, Roswell, Georgia

2 recipes (2 cups flour each) plain biscuit dough	*Black pepper*
	10 hard-cooked eggs, sliced
2 chickens (about 3 pounds each), cooked and boned	*2½ to 3 cups chicken stock*
	2 tablespoons flour
½ pound butter	*2 cups milk*

Cover biscuit dough and leave in the refrigerator for 2 days, to become sour.

Line sides of a very large baking pan with one third of the sour dough rolled thin. Place about one third of the chicken in pan and dot with butter. Roll sour dough very thin, cut into dumplings, and place over the chicken. Sprinkle generously with black pepper. To this add a layer of sliced eggs and dot with butter. Repeat layers of chicken, butter, and dumplings. Add remainder of eggs and chicken. Dot with butter and cover with chicken stock seasoned to taste. Sprinkle 2 tablespoons flour over top and add 2 cups milk.

Roll out remainder of sour dough and cut into four equal pieces. Place on top of pie, trim off excess and press edges together to seal. Dot with butter. Bake at 300 degrees for 1½ to 2 hours. 15 servings. But it is so good eight people can devour it.

Sweet and Sour Chicken Wings

2½ pounds chicken wings
⅓ cup solid all-vegetable
  shortening
⅓ cup vinegar
½ cup firmly packed dark
  brown sugar

1 (10-ounce) can unsweetened
  pineapple juice
¾ cup catsup
1 tablespoon soy sauce
1 tablespoon prepared mustard
⅛ teaspoon salt

Brown a third of the chicken wings at a time in hot shortening in a skillet, adding more shortening if necessary. Remove chicken wings as they brown. Discard drippings from skillet and add vinegar, sugar, juice, catsup, soy sauce, mustard, and salt to skillet. Bring to boil, stirring occasionally, then boil gently 5 minutes. Add browned chicken wings. Simmer, covered, 15 minutes. Turn wings and cook uncovered 15 minutes longer. Remove chicken to serving dish. Skim fat from sauce, if necessary. Pour sauce over chicken. Serve with rice, if desired. 4 servings.

Chicken Tetrazzini

Mrs. H. O. Eason, Thomaston, Georgia

½ pound spaghetti
1 cup sliced mushrooms
6 tablespoons butter
3 tablespoons flour
2 cups chicken broth
1 cup heavy cream

Salt and pepper
3 cups cubed cooked chicken
½ cup grated American,
  Parmesan, or Swiss cheese
⅓ cup toasted slivered almonds

Cook spaghetti in extra chicken broth until tender; then drain and keep warm. Sauté the mushrooms in 3 tablespoons butter. Make sauce by melting remaining 3 tablespoons butter, adding flour, and stirring in broth slowly. Heat cream and add to sauce along with salt and pepper. To one half of the sauce add chicken and to the remaining half add the well-drained spaghetti and mushrooms. Place half the spaghetti in shallow baking dish, add layer of chicken, and sprinkle with half of the cheese. Repeat. Top with almonds. Bake in 350-degree oven until lightly browned, about 12 to 15 minutes. 8 servings.

Chicken Sauterne

Mrs. Michael A. Wilson, Gainesville, Georgia

3 tablespoons butter	*4 cloves*
8 pieces chicken	*¼ tablespoon powdered thyme*
2 tablespoons flour	*3 or 4 sprigs parsley*
1 cup dry white wine	*Salt and pepper*
(sauterne)	*8 small potatoes, peeled*
1 cup chicken broth	*12 small white onions*
Dash nutmeg	

Melt butter in heavy saucepan. Brown chicken, and remove from pan. Stir flour into drippings, add wine, chicken broth, and seasonings. Return chicken to sauce, add potatoes and onions. Simmer for 1 hour. 4 servings.

Yellow Rice and Chicken

Harold G. Blocker, Atlanta, Georgia

1 4-pound hen, cut up	*2 tablespoons chopped pimiento*
Salt	*1 or 2 cloves garlic, chopped*
Paprika	*1 teaspoon chili powder*
⅓ cup fat	*¼ teaspoon saffron*
¼ pound ground beef	*1 teaspoon Worcestershire*
2½ cups water	*sauce*
1 green pepper, chopped	*1 teaspoon salt*
⅓ cup chopped celery	*¾ cup uncooked rice*
2 small onions, chopped	

Cut chicken into serving pieces, sprinkle fleshy pieces with salt and paprika, saving wings, neck, liver, etc., for use with other meals. In frying pan quickly brown chicken in hot fat. Remove chicken and pour off all but about 1 tablespoon fat and "scramble" ground beef until slightly brown. Pour entire contents of frying pan and chicken into large pot containing water and add all remaining ingredients, except rice, to pot.

Cook slowly 45 minutes or until chicken is tender, then turn up heat and add rice to vigorously boiling mixture. When mixture is again boiling reduce heat and simmer with lid on for 30 minutes more. Serve with crisp salad, coffee, and Cuban or French bread. 6 generous servings.

Baked Chicken Loaf

1 cup chicken broth
2 eggs
¾ cup soft bread crumbs
⅛ teaspoon salt
¼ teaspoon paprika
½ teaspoon Worcestershire
sauce

2 cups finely diced, cooked
chicken
¼ cup minced celery
2 tablespoons chopped green
pepper
½ teaspoon grated onion
¾ tablespoon lemon juice

Pour hot chicken broth over slightly beaten eggs while stirring. Add bread crumbs, salt, paprika, Worcestershire sauce, chicken, celery, pepper, onion, and lemon juice. Mix well. Pour into greased loaf pan or individual molds. Set in a pan of hot water and bake at 350 degrees until inserted knife comes out clean, about 1 hour. 4 to 6 servings.

Chicken Rice Casserole

Mrs. J. Forrester Zipperer, Savannah, Georgia

6 tablespoons butter or chicken
fat
6 tablespoons flour
3 cups milk or half chicken
broth
½ pound Cheddar cheese,
grated
Salt to taste
1½ cups cooked rice
2 cups bite-size pieces chicken
or turkey

½ cup chopped pecans
1 (3-ounce) can mushroom
pieces
1 medium onion, chopped fine
1 (4-ounce) can pimiento,
chopped
1 cup toasted bread crumbs
Paprika
Celery salt

Melt butter, add flour, and stir until smooth. Add milk and stir until thick. Blend in grated cheese and add remaining ingredients except bread crumbs, paprika, and celery salt. Butter casserole and place half of bread crumbs on bottom. Pour in chicken mixture and sprinkle remaining crumbs on top. Sprinkle with paprika and lots of celery salt. Bake at 350 degrees until bubbly. 8 servings.

Chicken Patties

Mrs. R. E. Thacker, Waleska, Georgia

1½ cups cooked chicken,
   ground
3 tablespoons chopped green
   pepper
¾ cup ground coconut
1 teaspoon chopped celery
   leaves

½ cup milk
1 teaspoon chopped parsley
¾ teaspoon dry mustard
½ teaspoon paprika
1 egg, slightly beaten
6 slices bacon
6 slices pineapple

Mix chicken, green pepper, coconut, celery leaves, milk, parsley, seasonings, and egg together. Shape into patties. Wrap a slice of bacon around each and secure with toothpicks. Arrange on pineapple slices in a shallow greased baking pan. Bake for 30 to 40 minutes in 350-degree oven. 6 servings.

Chicken Scallop

Mrs. James A. Whitehurst, Macon, Georgia, (Mrs. Georgia 1963)

⅓ cup uncooked rice
2 cups chicken broth
2½ cups diced cooked chicken
¾ teaspoon salt
⅓ cup chopped celery

¼ cup chopped pimiento
2 eggs, beaten
⅛ teaspoon poultry seasoning
Mushroom Sauce

Cook rice in chicken broth 10 minutes until partially tender. Combine with remaining ingredients. Pour into a greased 10×6×1½-inch baking dish. Bake in slow oven, 325 degrees, 45 to 50 minutes or until set. Serve hot with Mushroom Sauce. 6 to 8 servings.

MUSHROOM SAUCE

Mince ½ onion and cook in 3 tablespoons butter or margarine until tender. Blend in 3 tablespoons flour. Stir in 1 cup chicken broth and ½ cup heavy cream. Cook, stirring constantly, until thick. Add two 3-ounce cans sliced mushrooms, drained, ¼ teaspoon salt, dash of pepper. About 2½ cups.

Golden Chicken Roll

Mrs. Don McConnell, Atlanta, Georgia

¼ cup margarine
¼ cup minced onion
¼ cup flour
1½ teaspoons salt
Dash cayenne pepper
1 cup chicken stock or bouillon
3 cups chopped cooked chicken

2 cups cooked rice
¼ cup diced pimiento
2 tablespoons grated Parmesan
 cheese
1 cup cornflake crumbs
3 tablespoons melted butter or
 margarine

Melt margarine in saucepan; sauté onion until soft. Blend in flour, salt, and pepper; slowly add chicken stock. Cook, stirring constantly, until bubbly and thickened; cool. Chill several hours. Combine chicken, rice, pimiento, cheese, and cooled sauce. Chill several hours. Combine cornflake crumbs and melted butter; spread evenly on waxed paper to cover a 12×15-inch area. Shape chilled chicken mixture in a firm roll about 10 inches long; place in center of crumbs. Roll gently back and forth until well coated. Bake at 350 degrees 40 minutes. 8 to 10 servings.

TURKEY

Roast Turkey with Corn Bread Stuffing and Giblet Gravy

Mrs. James E. Thaxton, Watkinsville, Georgia

CHART FOR ROASTING TURKEY

8 to 10 pounds	325 degrees	3 to 3½ hours
10 to 14 pounds	325 degrees	3½ to 4 hours
14 to 18 pounds	300 degrees	4 to 4½ hours
18 to 20 pounds	300 degrees	4½ to 6 hours

Brush entire turkey well with butter and salt. Fill lightly with stuffing if desired. Wrap in heavy foil with breast up Avoid having it touch top or sides. When turkey has cooked to within 15 or 20 minutes of total cooking time, fold back the foil so the bird may become golden brown.

CORN BREAD STUFFING

1 (8-ounce) package dry corn
  bread
⅓ cup butter or margarine
1 cup chopped onion
1 (4-ounce) can sliced
  mushrooms and liquid

2 tablespoons diced pimiento
2 tablespoons dried parsley
  flakes
1½ teaspoons savory
1½ teaspoons thyme
¾ cup turkey broth

Put corn bread into large bowl. In skillet melt butter and sauté onions until softened and golden. Add onions and pan juices to corn bread. Add remaining ingredients, stirring in broth last. Stuff turkey lightly or place stuffing in greased 1½-quart casserole. Bake covered 15 minutes; uncover and bake 10 minutes longer. 6 servings.

This is a golden, crumbly, richly flavored stuffing. For a more moist stuffing add a beaten egg.

GIBLET GRAVY

2 (10½ ounces each) cans
  chicken gravy
½ cup turkey drippings

1 teaspoon dry instant coffee
Chopped giblets

Combine all ingredients and heat to bubbling. 6 servings.

Oven-smoked Turkey or Hen

1 small (about 6 pounds)
  turkey, ready to cook, cut up
¼ cup water
1 cup vinegar
½ cup salad oil

¼ cup brown sugar
2 tablespoons liquid smoke
  seasoning
1 tablespoon salt

Place turkey parts skin side down in shallow casserole. Blend sauce ingredients and pour one half over turkey. Bake covered in a slow oven, 325 degrees, for 1 hour. Turn skin side up. Baste and continue cooking uncovered about 1½ to 2 hours or until thickest parts are fork tender. Turn turkey parts as necessary to brown evenly. Baste occasionally until all the sauce is used. Serve with drippings as sauce. 6 to 8 servings.

Hickory-smoked Turkey

Mrs. W. D. Harrington, Eastman, Georgia

Choose a 10- to 15-pound turkey, thaw completely if frozen. Brush entire bird with cooking oil and sprinkle with garlic salt. Place 3 or 4 stalks of celery and 1 tablespoon parsley flakes in cavity. Secure wings and legs of the bird. Place on grill at low heat, breast side up; lower hood and cook for 4 to 5 hours until golden brown all over.

Add hickory chips to the charcoal as desired for flavor. Soak chips 30 minutes before using.

It takes 48 to 50 briquets per turkey, adding as needed, allowing them to become gray before placing bird on the grill.

Thomas Kellam's Barbecued Turkey

Thomas Kellam, Dublin, Georgia

1 (12-pound) turkey	*Juice of ½ lemon*
2 cups sauterne wine	*1 clove garlic, minced*
1 cup soy sauce	*1 cup salad oil*

Allow turkey, if frozen, to thaw in refrigerator. Clip end of bag, open, and remove neck from body cavity. Insert tightly closed jar to fill space in body cavity, to keep marinade from getting inside.

Return turkey to bag and stand it open end up in large bowl. Pour marinade made with remaining ingredients into bag with turkey. Allow to marinate 3 to 4 hours. Pour off marinade and reserve. Remove turkey from bag, remove giblets from neck cavity, and take out jar. Prepare turkey for spit barbecue.

After starting grill fire, insert spit rod above tail of bird, run through diagonally, coming out at breast bone. Tighten spit fork, roll rod in palms to check balance. Tie securely. Insert thermometer through thickest part of thigh. Place drip pan of heavy aluminum foil above coals; adjust spit.

Baste occasionally with reserved marinade, adding drippings from foil pan to basting mixture. Add charcoal as needed to maintain cooking heat. Turkey is done when thermometer reaches 185 degrees or when thickest part of drumstick feels soft, 5 to 6 hours.

The marinade ingredients are enough for any average-sized turkey. The soy sauce makes it quite dark but this is an unusually juicy and delicious turkey.

Turkey Corn Bread Bake

TURKEY FILLING

2 cups chopped cooked turkey
1 cup chopped celery
1 teaspoon lemon juice
½ teaspoon salt
½ teaspoon poultry seasoning
2 tablespoons minced pimiento
¼ cup mayonnaise

CORN BREAD

2 cups enriched self-rising corn meal
½ cup sifted enriched self-rising flour
2 tablespoons sugar
1 egg, beaten
¼ cup melted shortening or salad oil
1¾ cup milk
1 (10½-ounce) can condensed cream of mushroom soup

Combine all ingredients for turkey filling. Mix thoroughly. Let stand while preparing corn bread.

Combine corn meal, flour, and sugar. Combine egg, melted shortening or salad oil, and 1 cup milk. Add to dry ingredients and mix well. Turn half of batter into well-greased 9-inch square pan. Spoon turkey filling over batter. Top filling with remaining batter. Bake in hot oven, 425 degrees, for 25 minutes or until golden brown. Serve with sauce made with mushroom soup and remaining ¾ cup milk. 6 servings.

Turkey Apple Pie

¼ cup chopped onion
2 tablespoons butter or margarine
2 (10½ ounces each) cans condensed cream of mushroom soup, undiluted
2 cups cubed cooked turkey or chicken
2 cups cubed, cored, unpared apples
⅓ cup raisins
¼ teaspoon ground nutmeg

FLAKY PASTRY

2 cups flour	*⅔ cup shortening*
1 teaspoon salt	*4 tablespoons cold water*

Sauté onion in butter until tender. Combine onion, soup, turkey, apples, raisins, and nutmeg. Spoon into 6 individual casseroles or one large casserole. Prepare pastry. Roll to ⅛-inch thickness. Cut pastry to fit over casseroles. Make decorative slits for steam to escape. Lay pastry over turkey mixture; tuck pastry under to fit casserole. Seal with tines of fork. Bake 30 minutes at 425 degrees or until golden brown. 6 servings.

BIGARADE

Hart's—one of Atlanta's first really fine restaurants—was housed in an old gray-stone mansion which had been the home of one of the owners of *The Atlanta Journal*. This property has now been razed for other commercial industry.

Roast Duckling à la Bigarade

Hart's Restaurant, Atlanta, Georgia

Wipe a 5- to 6-pound duckling with a damp cloth; truss. Rub with salt and pepper and roast in a 450-degree oven for 15 minutes. Reduce heat to 350 degrees and continue to roast, allowing 20 minutes to the pound.

Baste several times during cooking period with 1 cup dry white wine.

In a small pan, melt 1 tablespoon sugar and blend in 1 tablespoon vinegar until thoroughly combined. Remove roasted duck from oven and set aside on platter to keep warm. Remove all but 3 tablespoons fat from pan and, to that, add slowly 1 cup milk with 3 tablespoons flour, scraping bottom of pan well.

Add juice of four oranges and one small lemon and 2 tablespoons brandy. Blend well and add the sugar caramel. Cook sauce slowly for 10 minutes.

Carve duckling and arrange on large platter. Pour sauce over it and sprinkle grated rind of 2 bitter oranges over duck. Garnish with orange slices, blanched almonds, and watercress. 4 servings.

Glazed Duckling

1 (4- to 5-pound) duckling, quartered
1 (1-pound) can apricot halves
¼ cup honey
2 tablespoons soy sauce
½ teaspoon ginger

Place duckling on rack in shallow roasting pan, skin side down. Roast at 450 degrees for 15 to 20 minutes. Drain apricots, reserve syrup. Combine syrup and remaining ingredients, except apricots. Drain fat from pan. Reduce temperature to 325 degrees, roast 1 hour. Brush duckling with glaze every 15 minutes during roasting. Turn skin side up and roast 1 hour longer. Combine apricots with remaining glaze. Pour over duckling last 15 minutes of roasting. 4 servings.

GOOSE

Roast Goose

1 (8- to 10-pound) fresh or frozen goose
Salt
1 to 2 teaspoons caraway seed
2 small oranges
3 or 4 small onions
1 stalk celery

Thaw goose if frozen. Clean and remove any fat from body cavity. Rinse and dry. Sprinkle cavity with salt and caraway seed. Quarter oranges; cut onions into halves and celery into 2-inch pieces. Stuff body cavity loosely with them. Close cavity with skewers and lace with cord. Fasten neck skin to back with skewer. Fold wing tips across back; skewer wings securely to body. Loop cord around legs and tighten slightly. Roast, breast side up, on rack in baking pan in 325-degree oven for 3½ to 4 hours, removing fat from pan several times. To serve, remove skewers and cord. Transfer goose to serving platter. Discard stuffing or serve with goose if you wish. 8 servings.

QUAIL

Quail with Grapes

Make a paste of the following ingredients: quail livers, chopped bacon, some bread crumbs soaked in cognac. Fill each bird with 2 tablespoons of this mixture, wrap each in a vine leaf soaked beforehand in cognac, and add a covering of bacon. Cook in butter (1 tablespoon per bird) in hot oven, 400 degrees, for about 10 minutes. Then add a dozen grapes for each bird to the baking dish. Add 2 ounces of brandy and cover the pan, leaving it in 375-degree oven for another 5 or 6 minutes. Take the quails out and remove the bacon wrappings. Put quails in a serving dish with the grapes and brandy with which they were cooked and serve hot. 1 quail per serving.

Quail Baked in Wine

½ cup fat	2 cups white wine
2 small onions, cut fine	½ teaspoon salt
2 whole cloves	⅛ teaspoon pepper
1 teaspoon peppercorns	Few grains cayenne pepper
2 cloves garlic, cut fine	1 teaspoon minced chives
½ bay leaf	2 cups light cream
6 quail, trussed	

Melt fat, add onions, cloves, peppercorns, garlic, and bay leaf and cook for several minutes. Add quail and brown on all sides. Add wine, salt, pepper, cayenne, and chives and simmer until tender, about 30 minutes. Remove quail to hot serving dish. Strain sauce, add cream, and heat to boiling point. Pour over quail. 1 quail per serving.

Crunchy Quail Breast

Mrs. W. P. Hendricks, Metter, Georgia

Remove back and legs from quail and reserve for Quail Steam Cook. Pour buttermilk over breasts and let stand for several hours. Pour off milk; season quail with salt and pepper, sprinkle a little flour over all (this adds extra crunch). Then roll each piece of quail in flour to coat. Fry in hot fat until golden brown; lower heat and cook until very tender, about 30 to 40 minutes.

Quail Steam Cook

Mrs. W. P. Hendricks, Metter, Georgia

18 quail back and leg parts	⅔ cup cold water
1 quart water	1½ cups milk
1½ teaspoons salt	½ cup cream
3 tablespoons salad oil	2 tablespoons butter
⅓ cup flour	Pepper to taste

In large saucepan combine quail parts, 1 quart water, salt, and salad oil. Cook over medium heat until meat is very tender. Make a thin paste of flour and cold water (shake in a jar with lid to mix). Add to the cooked quail parts to thicken broth. Stir in milk, cream, and butter. Cook for only a short time. Season with pepper. Serve over grits or homemade biscuits. 6 servings.

Grilled Quail

2 (*or more*) small quail, ready for cooking	2 small pieces celery and leaves
	2 slices onion
Salt and pepper to taste	2 slices salt pork or bacon

Rub quail inside and out with salt and pepper mixture. Place a piece of celery and slice of onion inside each bird. Wrap with a slice of salt pork or bacon and secure with a small skewer.

Grill in oven at high heat, turning once, just until well browned. Then reduce heat and broil slowly 10 minutes or until done. Do not pierce birds or juice will run out. 1 quail per serving.

Casserole of Quail with Cherries

6 quail	5 tablespoons veal stock
Butter	2 tablespoons currant jelly
1 teaspoon brandy	5 dozen sour cherries
3 tablespoons port	Lemon juice (*optional*)
1 tablespoon grated orange rind	

Prepare the quail as for roasting. Pan roast in casserole in plenty of butter for about 25 minutes. Lift out the birds and keep hot. To the butter in the casserole, add brandy and port and stir until mixture boils up; then add orange rind, stock, jelly, and sour cherries. Return the quail to this sauce, cover and heat to boiling point. If too sweet, add a few drops of lemon juice. 3 servings.

Roast Rock Cornish Game Hen

⅓ cup uncooked wild rice mix
Giblets and liver from hen
1 small onion, diced
1 small green pepper, diced
1 (1- to 1¼-pounds) Cornish hen

Pinch garlic powder
Salt and pepper to taste
Paprika

Cook rice according to package directions and combine with diced giblets and livers, onion, and pepper. Sauté rice and vegetables in cooking oil for 8 minutes. Stuff hen and close opening. Brush hen with oil seasoned with garlic powder, salt, pepper, and paprika. Roast hen on rack in open roaster at 350 degrees for about 45 minutes or until done. 2 servings.

STUFFINGS

Chestnut Stuffing

1½ cups finely chopped onion
1½ cups finely chopped celery
5 tablespoons butter
8 cups dry bread cubes
1 cup chopped cooked chestnuts

1½ teaspoons salt
⅛ teaspoon pepper
½ teaspoon poultry seasoning
½ teaspoon sage
¼ cup water
1 egg, well beaten

Cook onion and celery in butter in a skillet until tender. Add mixture to bread cubes, which have been placed in a large pan. Add chestnuts and sprinkle with seasonings. Combine. Add water and egg. Toss together with forks. Stuff bird immediately and roast. Enough for a 12-pound bird.

Chicken Dressing

Mrs. Lamar G. Russell, McDonough, Georgia
1965 Mrs. Georgia Homemaker

3 tablespoons shortening	*1 egg*
2 cups flour	*2½ cups (about) chicken broth*
1 cup corn meal	*2 eggs, slightly beaten*
1 tablespoon baking powder	*1 teaspoon black pepper*
½ teaspoon soda	*½ cup finely chopped celery*
1 teaspoon salt	*¼ cup finely chopped onion*
1⅔ cups buttermilk	*2 tablespoons (about) butter*

Melt shortening in 9-inch square baking pan. Sift together flour, meal, baking powder, soda, and salt. Stir in buttermilk and egg. Pour into baking pan and bake in 400-degree oven for 30 minutes. Let cool and crumble.

Add chicken broth to corn bread. Add rest of ingredients except butter. Pour into greased baking pan and dot with butter. Bake at 450 degrees for about 45 minutes. Enough for a 12-pound bird.

Corn Bread and Grits Dressing

Mrs. Vivian Webb, for Georgia School Food Service Training Course

1 cup chopped onion	*1½ cups cooked grits*
1 cup chopped celery	*3 cups or more broth*
¼ cup fat	*¼ cup melted fat or margarine*
1 cup day-old or stale bread	*3 eggs*
crumbs	*Salt, pepper, and poultry*
5 cups crumbled egg corn bread	*seasoning to taste*
1 cup coarse cracker crumbs	

Sauté onion and celery in ¼ cup fat. Combine all ingredients, using enough broth to make heavy custard consistency. Bake in greased 9×12-inch pan at 425 degrees until brown and firm. This is a moist and very delicious dressing. 8 to 10 servings.

Corn Stuffing

2 cups diced celery
⅔ cup chopped onion
⅓ cup butter
2 (16 ounces each) cans whole
   kernel corn, drained, liquid
   reserved

1 teaspoon dried sage
6 cups soft bread crumbs
2½ teaspoons salt
¾ teaspoon pepper
1½ cups boiling liquid (use
   corn liquid plus water)

Sauté celery and onion in butter. Add remaining ingredients and mix well. Enough for an 8- to 10-pound bird.

Cranberry Stuffing

2 cups fresh cranberries
½ cup butter
½ cup sugar
8 cups bread crumbs or cubes
2 teaspoons salt

1 tablespoon sage
2 tablespoons thyme
½ cup chopped celery
3 tablespoons minced parsley
1 cup water

Chop cranberries and cook slowly in butter for 5 minutes. Stir in sugar. Mix together crumbs, seasonings, celery, and parsley. Add water and combine with cranberry mixture.

Cook about 5 minutes or until blended. Stir constantly. 6 cups stuffing—enough for a 12-pound turkey or 8-pound pork crown roast.

Mincemeat Turkey Stuffing

1 cup chopped onion
¾ cup butter
1 (28 ounce) jar (2⅔ cups)
   mincemeat

2 (7-ounces each) packages
   croutons
¾ cup water

Sauté onions in butter until golden brown. In large bowl mix sautéed onions, mincemeat, and croutons. Add water. Toss lightly. Stuff turkey. Place extra stuffing in a casserole. Bake in oven during last 30 minutes of baking turkey. Enough for a 10-pound turkey.

Mushroom Stuffing

2 tablespoons instant minced
  onion
2 tablespoons water
½ cup butter or margarine
2 cups sliced fresh mushrooms
2 cups sliced celery
1 teaspoon salt

½ teaspoon powdered thyme
¼ teaspoon powdered
  marjoram
¼ teaspoon pepper
6 cups day-old whole wheat
  bread cubes

Combine instant mixed onion and water and let stand a few minutes. Melt butter. Add mushrooms, celery, and onion and cook slowly about 5 minutes. Add salt, thyme, marjoram, and pepper. Pour mixture over bread cubes, tossing to blend evenly. Stuff lightly into chicken or turkey for roasting or turn into greased casserole, cover and bake about 1 hour in a moderate 350-degree oven. About 6 cups stuffing—enough for a 12-pound bird.

Oyster and Celery Stuffing

¾ cup fat
2 tablespoons chopped onion
3 tablespoons chopped parsley
1½ cups chopped celery

6 cups soft bread crumbs
1 pint oysters, chopped
Salt and pepper to taste

Melt fat. Add onion, parsley, and celery and cook until tender. Add bread crumbs and heat well. Add chopped oysters and seasonings and mix lightly but thoroughly. About 5 cups stuffing—enough for a 10-pound bird.

Sausage Dressing

½ pound pork sausage meat
1 cup water
7 cups bread cubes
2 tablespoons diced onion

1 teaspoon salt
4 tablespoons chopped parsley
1 cup diced celery

Pan fry sausage until browned. Combine all ingredients, mixing well. Stuff prepared turkey. About 6 cups stuffing—enough for a 12- to 14-pound turkey.

Turkey Dressing

1 cup diced celery	1 tablespoon poultry seasoning
2 medium onions, diced	1 teaspoon sage
½ cup butter or margarine	Cooked giblets, finely chopped
2 pounds (21 cups) cubed	(optional)
bread, measured after cubing	1 cup liquid from cooking
1 tablespoon salt	giblets
½ teaspoon pepper	3 eggs, beaten

Slowly simmer celery and onions in butter or margarine until soft but not brown. To bread cubes, add salt, pepper, poultry seasoning, and sage. Add celery, onions, and giblets.

Then add giblet liquid and eggs. Gently fold into dressing. Stuff into turkey. About 10 cups stuffing—enough for a 15- to 18-pound turkey.

8

FISH, SHELLFISH,
AND STUFFINGS

I can remember when we folks who lived inland had little access to other than fresh-water fish caught in our creeks, rivers, and lakes. But how we loved those fish! Some of my fondest memories center around community fish fries. Our mamas would cook up all kinds of goodies like salads and desserts. These were packed up and off we went to the river or creek bank. While the men and boys took off with their fishing poles and seines, the campsite was readied, fires started, fat heating in huge frying pans for fish and hush puppies. Oh, yes, they always caught enough fish! After this wonderful out-door feast, there was singing and storytelling. By the time we rode back home, several miles in a surrey, we were a tired, very full, but happy bunch.

The recipes in this chapter are extra special, we think. They come from numerous famous eating places in the South as well as from friends throughout the area. I have personally been served most of these dishes.

Many of the recipes had never been given until published in *The Atlanta Journal* food sections. Some of the restaurants no longer exist and some of the donors have passed away. The recipes continue to be ever popular and have been requested over and over.

FISH

A good cook can cook anything, according to Mrs. Fendig, one of the finest cooks to be found. She serves her special cracklin' bread with this.

Bass Marguery

Mrs. Edwin Fendig, Sr., St. Simons Island, Georgia

12 fillets of bass
Salt and pepper
1 cup dry white wine
Juice of 1 or 2 lemons
½ pint oysters
1 pound shrimp, cooked and
cleaned

2 or 3 rock lobster tails, cooked
Grated Parmesan cheese
Paprika
4 cups (1 quart) white sauce

Cut fillets into serving-size pieces, sprinkle with salt and pepper, and lay in shallow baking pan. Over them pour the wine and lemon juice. Place in 350-degree oven and gently poach about 15 minutes.

Gently lift out fillets, draining as well as possible, and lay in bottom of a casserole that can go to the table for serving.

Simmer oysters in own liquid 3 minutes. Combine with the shrimp and cut-up lobster meat. Place carefully over fillets.

Make 4 cups of your best white sauce using liquid from fish pan as part of liquid. Spoon sauce over casserole; sprinkle generously with Parmesan cheese and paprika. Place in 350-degree oven for 20 to 30 minutes until brown. 12 servings.

Catfish Stew

Mrs. W. D. Warren, Woodbine, Georgia

½ pound white bacon
5 pounds catfish, cut in serving
pieces

Salt and black pepper
2 bunches green onions (use
some tops), chopped

Cut bacon in small pieces and fry until crisp. Season fish with salt and pepper and add with onions to bacon and drippings with enough water to cover. Bring to boil; simmer 30 to 45 minutes. Do not over-cook and if necessary to stir try to avoid breaking the fish. 6 serv-ings.

Catfish Stew—South-Georgia Style

Mrs. O. B. Clifton, Statesboro, Georgia

3 medium-size (10- to 12-inch)
  catfish
1 pint milk
1 (13-ounce) can evaporated
  milk

1 or 2 tablespoons butter, as
  needed
Salt
Pepper

Place fish in a 3-quart saucepan and add just enough water to cover the fish. Cook until tender, but do not overcook. Remove the meat from the bones and return to the broth. Add both kinds of milk, season with butter, salt, and pepper to taste, and heat to boil-ing. Serve with oyster crackers or thin pieces of corn bread. 3 serv-ings.

Flounder Baked in Foil

Mark Sedlack, Golden Palms Restaurant, Atlanta, Georgia

½ pound sliced mushrooms
1 teaspoon chopped shallot or
  onion
4 tablespoons butter
1 cup cooked tomatoes
Salt and ground black pepper
¼ teaspoon sugar
3 (2 pounds each) dressed,
  striped flounder

2 tablespoons oil
¼ cup dry white wine
1 tablespoon lemon juice
18 black pitted olives
¾ pound ready-to-cook shellfish
  (shrimp, crab, or lobster)

Cook mushrooms and shallots or onions in 2 tablespoons of the butter until all the liquid has evaporated. Add tomatoes, salt and pepper to taste, and sugar. Cook 2 to 3 minutes, stirring constantly. Sprinkle fish with salt and pepper. Heat remaining 2 tablespoons butter and the oil in a long baking pan; add fish and cook in a preheated, 350-degree oven for 20 minutes or until fish is golden.

Spread the mushroom mixture over a long piece of foil the length and width of the fish. Place fish on mixture. Cook the remaining ingredients together over low heat 5 minutes and spoon the mixture over the fish. Bring both ends of foil up over the fish and make a lengthwise drugstore fold over it. Turn up the ends, folding them three times. Place fish on a baking sheet and cook in a 400-degree oven 10 to 12 minutes or until the steam has inflated the foil. Transfer the foil-wrapped fish to a platter and serve it in the foil, turning foil back. 6 servings.

Stuffed Baked Mackerel

2 cups cooked crab meat or shrimp	*2 teaspoons chopped chives*
	1 tablespoon flour
2 eggs	*1 (3- to 4-pound) mackerel, cleaned and boned*
1 cup light cream	
2 tablespoons butter	*Salt and paprika*
½ cup chopped mushrooms	*4 tablespoons sherry*

Combine crab meat, eggs, and ½ cup cream. Melt butter, add mushrooms and chives. Sauté until soft. Add flour, stir and cook until bubbly. Stir in crab meat mixture and cook until thick. Place mackerel in buttered baking dish and spread the crab meat mixture between the two sides of fish. Pour remaining cream over mackerel; sprinkle with salt and paprika. Add sherry and bake at 350 degrees for 45 minutes. 4 servings.

Pompano en Papillotes

Ambassador Restaurant, Atlanta, Georgia

1 tablespoon butter	*¼ teaspoon salt*
1 tablespoon flour	*Dash Tabasco sauce*
1 onion, minced	*1 egg yolk*
½ cup boiled shrimp, chopped	*6 pompano fillets*
⅔ cup crab meat, chopped	

Melt butter, stir in flour, and add onion, browning mixture lightly. Add shrimp and crab meat. Cook for 3 minutes and add salt and Tabasco. Remove from heat; stir in egg yolk. Parboil pompano fillets 5 minutes. Place each fillet, opened flat, on individual sheet of parchment paper. Divide sauce among fillets, by placing spoonfuls on fold. Fold fillets and then fold parchment papers so that each fillet is encased in a separate bag. Bake in hot oven, 400 degrees, for 10 minutes. 6 servings.

Baked Red Snapper

Mrs. R. P. Jones, St. Augustine, Florida

1 (6-pound) red snapper
Soft butter and salt
½ cup chopped green pepper
½ cup chopped celery
6 thin slices lemon

½ cup butter
1 large onion, chopped
¼ cup flour
4 cups canned tomatoes

Cut snapper into halves and fillet. Rub with soft butter and season with salt. Lay one fillet in bottom of baking dish, and over it spread the green pepper, celery, and lemon slices. Top with second fillet.

In a skillet heat ½ cup butter and sauté onion. Stir in flour, then tomatoes; simmer until thickened. Pour this sauce over the snapper and bake at 350 degrees for 15 minutes per pound. Baste occasionally. Serve the sauce over hot rice along with fish. 4 to 6 servings.

Cashew-stuffed Red Snapper

A Pensacola, Florida, favorite

1 (3½- to 4-pound) snapper
Lime juice
Dry sherry
Salt
1 green onion, chopped
½ cup diced celery
½ clove garlic
6 tablespoons butter

2 cups day-old bread crumbs
1½ cups chopped cashew nuts
Dash nutmeg
¼ cup minced parsley
½ teaspoon grated lemon rind
⅛ teaspoon thyme
1 cup dry white wine

Sprinkle fish with lime juice, brush with sherry, and salt. Place in refrigerator for 2 to 3 hours. Sauté onion, celery, and garlic in butter until onion is transparent, about 5 minutes. Mix remaining ingredients except wine, with the vegetables. Stuff fish and place in baking pan. Pour wine over fish. Bake at 350 degrees for 45 minutes. Baste often. 6 servings.

Mrs. Fendig gave me this recipe years ago with the promise I would use it as is. The Fendigs were among the first settlers on the island and she has had the opportunity to collect and concoct a great variety of seafood dishes. All of them good!

Baked Shad
Mrs. Edwin Fendig, Sr., St. Simons Island, Georgia

Shad is a fish of such delicious flavor, but has so many bones to discourage preparing or eating it. Cook in the following manner and it is a joy to serve; *all* bones disintegrate and disappear.

Always choose a roe shad, never a buck. Carefully clean and gut fish, saving the roe for another meal. Season with salt and pepper inside and out.

Lay shad on trivet in a roasting pan. Pour in enough hot water just to cover fish, add ½ cup tarragon vinegar to water. Bring to boil and simmer 3 or 4 minutes. Carefully lift out fish and rinse roasting pan.

Wrap shad in a double layer of foil, close tight but leave loose space inside for fish. Put several cups of hot water under trivet and lay shad on trivet. Do not cover pan. Put in 200-degree oven and let cook 6 hours, replenishing water if it evaporates.

Carefully loosen foil and fold back to expose one flat side of fish. Lay slices of white bacon on top of fish. Set roaster well down in oven and turn on broiler heat. Watch carefully. Bacon should get done and crisp, and fish should be browned nicely. If this is being done too rapidly, turn off top heat and let radiant hot oven brown it.

Lift shad from foil and carefully place on serving platter. Cut through fish crosswise, in serving pieces. All bones are gone except backbone.

Spread on the exposed side of fish a good coating of cold basic white wine sauce before laying on bacon slices, if you prefer. This is a fish stock sauce with wonderful flavors which it imparts to the shad and makes it brown beautifully, too.

Baked Shad and Wine Sauce

Mrs. Charlie Russo, Savannah, Georgia

1 (4-pound) shad	*1½ cups hot water*
1 cup bread or cracker crumbs	*1 tablespoon catsup*
4 tablespoons melted butter or	*1 tablespoon browned flour*
margarine	*Juice of 1 lemon*
Salt and pepper	*⅓ cup sherry or madeira*
1 tablespoon finely minced	*2 tablespoons cold water*
parsley	
Pinch of crushed, dried	
tarragon	

Wipe and dry the cleaned fish, leaving the head and tail on. Prepare a stuffing by combining the crumbs, 2 tablespoons melted butter, salt and pepper, parsley, and tarragon and use to fill the cavity of the shad. Skewer or sew the edges together. Place on a rack in a baking pan and pour around the fish 1 cup hot water. Bake about 10 minutes in a 400-degree oven, then reduce heat to 325 degrees and cook about 30 minutes longer. Baste with butter frequently while cooking. Transfer fish to serving dish and keep hot.

Add ½ cup of water and the catsup to gravy in pan and thicken with the flour moistened with 2 tablespoons cold water. Stir until boiling. Cook 5 minutes and add the lemon juice and wine. Do not allow gravy to boil again. Sauce may be poured over fish or served separately. Garnish with lemon and watercress or parsley. 4 servings.

Shad Roe and Bacon

Mrs. R. P. Jones, St. Augustine, Florida

1½ pounds shad roe or other	*Dash pepper*
fish roe, fresh or frozen	*12 slices bacon*
½ teaspoon salt	

Thaw roe if frozen. Drain on absorbent paper. Sprinkle with salt and pepper. Fry bacon until crisp in a 10-inch fry pan; drain bacon. Fry roe in hot bacon fat over moderate heat for 3 to 5 minutes or until brown. Turn carefully and fry 3 to 5 minutes longer. Drain. Serve with bacon. 6 servings.

Fresh Trout à la Bryant

Chef George Bryant
The William Hilton Inn, Hilton Head Island, South Carolina

Broil trout until tender, baste with lemon butter (melted butter and lemon juice), and run back under broiler for light glaze. In the meantime, score cucumber, slice thin, and sauté in butter until tender. Surround trout with cucumber slices, top with sliced ripe olives, and serve. 1 serving.

A great treat from Kingwood Country Club, Clayton, Georgia.

Pan-fried Mountain Rainbow Trout

1 (10- to 12-ounce) whole rainbow trout with head and tail, cleaned	*½ tablespoon salt*
	⅓ teaspoon black pepper
	¼ teaspoon paprika
½ cup flour	*Cooking oil for frying*

Wash and drain trout. Combine flour, salt, pepper, and paprika. Roll fish in mixture and press on firmly. Heat cooking oil to smoking point, add trout, and reduce heat to medium. Fry fish about 4 minutes on each side or until golden brown and done. 1 serving.

Serve with hot biscuits, sourwood honey, and hot coffee.

Stuffed Trout

Mrs. Jerry Cope, Betty's Creek, Dillard, Georgia

1 cup chopped carrots	*1 tablespoon lemon juice*
¾ cup chopped celery	*Salt and pepper*
½ cup chopped onion	*½ teaspoon ground thyme*
1 small potato, diced (optional)	*6 (1 to 1½ pounds each)*
¼ cup butter	*rainbow trout*
1½ cups white bread crumbs	*6 slices bacon*
½ cup corn bread or hush puppy crumbs	*Paprika*

Chop vegetables in blender; cut in ¼ cup butter. Add crumbs, lemon juice, 1 teaspoon salt, ½ teaspoon pepper, and thyme. Grease baking pan. Salt and pepper the fish inside and out and fill cavity with stuffing. Fasten.

Over top of each fish place one slice bacon cut in three pieces. Sprinkle liberally with paprika and bake at 350 degrees for 25 to 30 minutes or until fish flakes when tested with a fork. 6 servings.

SHELLFISH

Clams and Crab Meat à la Hart
Hart's Restaurant, Atlanta, Georgia

Open 3 dozen cherrystone clams. Loosen the clams and set the shells firmly on a layer of rock salt in a shallow baking pan.

Cook 12 hard-shelled crabs in boiling salted water for 15 minutes. Flake the meat and carefully remove the tendons.

Add ½ cup fine soft bread crumbs to ½ cup cream sauce, along with 2 tablespoons each of finely chopped green pepper and onion, 1 tablespoon each of chopped chives and prepared mustard, a few drops of Tabasco, and salt to taste.

Combine this with flaked crab meat and place about 1 teaspoon on each clam. Broil about 3 inches from heat for 8 to 10 minutes. Serve in the shell garnished with watercress. 6 servings.

Virginia's Deviled Crab
Mrs. Joe Savard, Brunswick, Georgia

Salt	*4 slices dry toast*
2 tablespoons crab boil spice	*Worcestershire sauce*
mix	*Tabasco*
18 fresh live crabs	*Paprika*
½ green pepper, chopped	*Cayenne pepper*
1 medium onion, chopped	*¼ teaspoon crushed red pepper*
¾ cup butter or margarine	*½ teaspoon dry mustard*

Bring large container of salted water to boil and add crab boil spice mix. Add crabs and boil 20 minutes. Crack crabs and remove meat from claws and body. Clean and save 12 of the backs.

Sauté green pepper and onion in ½ cup of the butter. Add to crab meat. Moisten 2 slices of toast with water, then squeeze out water; crumble into crab meat. Add several dashes Worcestershire and Tabasco. Sprinkle with paprika and cayenne. Add crushed red pepper and dry mustard.

Combine ingredients well and fill crab shell backs. Add remaining toast, crumbled and mixed with remaining butter, melted. Sprinkle over tops of crab and add additional paprika. Bake at 350 degrees for about 30 minutes. 6 servings.

NOTE: This may be prepared in advance and frozen prior to baking.

One of Mr. Lewis' great recipes which he prepares for special occasions.

Crab Mornay
W. B. Lewis, Brunswick, Georgia

½ cup butter
3 tablespoons flour
1 teaspoon salt
1½ teaspoons white pepper

1½ cups milk
1 pound lump crab meat
½ pound grated sharp cheese

Make cream sauce of butter, flour, salt, pepper, and milk. In a casserole, place layer of crab meat, then layer of cheese; add the cream sauce. Bake in 325-degree oven for 25 to 30 minutes. 4 servings.

Spaghetti with Buttered Crab Sauce

1 pound spaghetti
1 cup butter
1 small onion, minced
⅛ teaspoon nutmeg
½ teaspoon freshly ground
*   black pepper*

Dash cayenne pepper
1 pound lump crab meat
½ cup coarsely chopped parsley

Cook spaghetti according to package directions. Melt butter and add onion. Cook over low heat until onion is soft and golden. Add nutmeg, pepper, cayenne, and crab meat. Stir to blend and heat gently until crab is piping hot.

Stir in parsley and salt to taste, and cook 1 minute more. Pour spaghetti into colander and shake until all the water is drained off. Place in a serving dish, pour sauce over hot spaghetti, and serve immediately. 8 servings.

Crab Stew

Mrs. Sam Lewis, Raccoon Keys Island, Georgia

1 dozen crabs
2 quarts salted water
4 tablespoons fat, for seasoning
1 (6½-ounce) can crab meat or
  equivalent in fresh crab meat
Flour and corn meal for
  thickening

Wash crabs and place in salted water with bacon fat; cook 20 minutes. Add crab meat. Heat thoroughly and thicken with flour and corn meal. Serve in soup bowls; eat crabs with fingers.

Other ingredients such as corn, tomatoes, onion, celery and potatoes may be added to the stew if desired.

Crisp Fried Oysters

36 double crisp crackers
½ teaspoon salt
¼ teaspoon paprika
¼ teaspoon dried dill weed
2 eggs
2 tablespoons water
1 pint frying oysters, well
  drained
Fat or oil for frying

With rolling pin crush crackers into medium fine crumbs between two pieces of waxed paper; there should be about 2 cups. Mix well with salt, paprika, and dill weed; divide into two flat plates. Beat eggs well and beat in water. Dip each oyster on both sides into first plate of crumbs, then into egg mixture, and finally into second plate of crumbs.

Let stand at least 30 minutes to "set" crumbs. (If desired, oysters can be prepared early in the day and refrigerated until needed.)

Fry in moderately hot fat (365 degrees) until crusty and golden. Do not overcook. Drain on paper towels on warm platter. Garnish with lemon wedges and parsley. Serve with tartar sauce. 4 servings.

Serve these oysters as appetizers or a late-supper delicacy.

Stuffed Oysters

12 fresh oysters on half shell
(canned or frozen may be
used)
1 (7½-ounce) can crab meat
2 tablespoons chopped celery
1 tablespoon minced green
pepper

¼ cup mayonnaise
½ teaspoon salt
¼ teaspoon Tabasco sauce
¼ teaspoon dry mustard
¼ cup bread crumbs

Have shells opened at market. Remove any bits of shell and loosen oyster from shell. Combine crab meat, celery, and pepper; add mayonnaise, salt, Tabasco, and dry mustard; toss lightly. Just before placing stuffing in shells, toss in bread crumbs. Spoon a heaping tablespoonful of crab mixture on top of each oyster.

Place in shallow baking dish or on cookie sheet. Bake in 425-degree oven about 12 or 15 minutes, or until moisture around edge of shell is bubbly. Do not overcook. Serve immediately. 2 dinner servings or 6 appetizer servings.

Oyster Fritters

Mrs. W. W. Anderson, St. Simons Island, Georgia

1 cup milk
1 tablespoon butter or
margarine, melted
2 eggs
2 cups flour
1 tablespoon baking powder

⅛ teaspoon nutmeg
1 teaspoon salt
White pepper to taste
1 pint shucked oysters, drained
and chopped
Fat or oil for deep frying

Beat milk and melted butter with eggs. Sift flour, baking powder, and seasonings together. Add slowly to the milk mixture, stirring until blended and smooth. Add the oysters and stir gently into the batter.

Heat fat in deep fryer to hot but not smoking, 350 to 375 degrees. Deep fryer should not be more than half full. Drop fritter batter into the hot fat by the teaspoon or tablespoon, depending on size desired, and fry to golden brown about 3 to 5 minutes. Remove fritters with a slotted spoon and drain on absorbent paper before serving. Do not fry too many fritters at one time. 6 servings.

Hangtown Scramble

6 slices bacon, cut in ½-inch
  pieces
1 (8-ounce) can oysters, well
  drained (clams or shrimp
  may be substituted)
½ cup cracker crumbs
3 tablespoons chopped green
  onions

6 eggs
⅓ cup milk
½ teaspoon salt
Dash pepper
1 (8-ounce) can tomato sauce

Fry diced bacon in skillet. Coat oysters with cracker crumbs. Sauté oysters and green onions in bacon fat. Combine eggs, milk, salt, and pepper; pour over bacon-oyster mixture.

Cover and cook slowly until eggs are set. Pour heated tomato sauce over. Cover and heat through. 4 to 5 servings.

Oyster Patties

Salvatori Cimino, Atlanta, Georgia

1 onion, chopped
1½ sticks butter
2 cloves garlic, chopped
12 sprigs fresh parsley
1 small bunch green onions
1 teaspoon thyme

1½ pints fresh oysters
1 cup milk
½ cup flour
Salt and pepper
12 pastry shells or timbales

Sauté chopped onion in butter, adding garlic, parsley, green onions, and thyme. Then add oysters, milk, and flour, stirring carefully until creamy. Salt and pepper to taste, and simmer for 30 minutes. Fill pastry shells with mixture and bake on cookie sheet in 250-degree oven for 25 minutes. 6 servings.

We like oyster stew at many times during the year, but it is a must at our house on Christmas Eve.

Oyster Stew

1 pint oysters
6 tablespoons butter or
   margarine

1 quart milk
1½ teaspoons salt
⅛ teaspoon pepper

Carefully clean oysters. Melt butter or margarine in saucepan; add drained oysters and cook just until edges curl, about 1 or 2 minutes. Add milk, salt, and pepper and bring almost to boiling point—but do not boil. 4 servings.

Mills B. Lane, Jr., president of Citizens and Southern National Bank—now chairman of the board—gave us this recipe as is. He enjoys good food and likes to fix it his own way. The reason this is a good and unusual dish is that the shrimp know how to make their own gravy.

Alligator Creek Shrimp

Mills B. Lane, Jr., Atlanta, Georgia

Use small shrimp, if possible, preferably fresh but thawed ones will do. Peel and clean. Use as many as you need to go 'round (at least ½ pound per serving).

Place shrimp in a bowl and sprinkle with soy sauce—gives them a nice color all over. Set the bowl in a corner and go have a real cold beer. Take about ½ to 1 hour and give the bowl a stir whenever you feel like it.

Now take a frying pan, no cover, and warm up some cooking oil. Peanut oil best, corn oil next, then any other oil you may have. Put in chopped onion and cook until you have a sort of oil-onion soup, about 5 minutes.

Next dump in the shrimp and soy sauce marinade. Give it a good dash of pepper—no salt needed. Gently toss and cook no more than 3 minutes, maybe less.

Now, you have really got something! Just have the hominy grits ready and some hot biscuits and you're in business!

Boiled Shrimp

2 pounds raw shrimp
10 peppercorns
1 clove garlic, peeled and cut in
   half

½ teaspoon powdered thyme
2 cloves
1 bay leaf, chopped
2 teaspoons salt

Put shrimp and seasonings in a saucepan and add enough water to cover. Bring to a boil and simmer gently from 3 to 5 minutes—no more—just until shrimp turn pink. Remove from heat immediately and drain. Let cool. Peel off shells and remove the black vein down the back with point of a knife. Rinse shrimp and chill until wanted. 4 to 6 servings.

Paella Valenciana

Chef Manuel Filotis
The William Hilton Inn, Hilton Head Island, South Carolina

½ cup oil or butter
2 cloves garlic, minced
4 medium-size onions, chopped
3 green bell peppers, diced
2 pounds chicken, cut into
   small pieces
½ pound pork, diced
1 pound fresh tomatoes, peeled
   and cut into 8 pieces
1 Maine lobster, cut into small
   pieces with shell on
1 pound unpeeled shrimp
1 pound cubed cooked chicken
1 pound cubed cooked pork

1 Spanish sausage, sliced
6 cups broth made with
   bouillon cubes
½ teaspoon saffron, soaked in a
   little chicken bouillon
4 cups uncooked rice
15 mussels or clams
12 ounces artichoke hearts
1 cup green peas
8 ounces pimiento, chopped
⅓ ounce freeze-dried chives
Salt and pepper
1 pound crab claws

Heat oil in a deep frying pan with garlic and onions. Add green pepper, chicken, and pork; sauté. Add tomatoes and cook for 15 minutes.

In another frying pan sauté lobster pieces for 5 minutes and add the shrimp. Cook for 2 minutes; reserve.

In a special paella pan put cooked chicken and pork, Spanish sausage, and broth. Add saffron and rice. Bring to a boil, stirring occasionally. Add lobster, shrimp, mussels or clams, artichoke hearts, peas, pimiento, and chives. Season with salt and pepper. Add crab claws and place in 350-degree oven for 20 minutes. Before serving arrange ingredients so that seafood will show. Serve hot. 15 servings.

Shrimp Creole

Chef Eilyses Maxmillian Baldwin
Sea Island Yacht Club, Sea Island, Georgia

½ pound white bacon
2 bell peppers, cut in large
  pieces
2 large onions, cut in large
  pieces
2 cloves garlic, chopped
2 stalks celery, chopped
½ pound okra, sliced

1 (1-pound) can tomatoes
1 (8-ounce) can tomato paste
2 bay leaves
1 teaspoon rosemary
1 teaspoon coarsely ground
  black pepper
Salt to taste
1½ pounds shrimp, cleaned

Sauté bacon until brown. Add bell peppers, onions, garlic, and celery. Cook until tender—but do not brown. Add okra, tomatoes, and tomato paste; the bay leaves, rosemary, pepper, salt, and shrimp. Cook 10 minutes longer. Serve with hot fluffy rice. 6 servings.

Hurry Shrimp Curry

Mrs. Joreka Loomis, Atlanta, Georgia

1 teaspoon curry powder
½ cup chopped onion
2 tablespoons butter

1 (10¾-ounce) can shrimp
  soup
1 cup sour cream
1 pound cooked shrimp

Preheat electric skillet to 250 degrees. Add curry powder, onion, and butter. Sauté until onion is tender but not brown. Add the shrimp soup. Stir until smooth. Turn temperature control to 200 degrees. Add sour cream and shrimp. Heat until hot. Cover until ready for serving. Serve on hot fluffy rice with a variety of curry accompaniments such as chopped peanuts, bacon, olives, egg yolks, sweet pickles, coconut, kumquats, chutney, raisins, and tart jelly. 4 servings.

Shrimp Jambalaya

1 cup chopped onion
¼ cup chopped celery
¼ cup chopped green pepper
1 clove garlic, crushed
3 cups canned tomatoes
1 bay leaf, crushed
1¼ teaspoons salt
½ teaspoon powdered thyme

1 cup diced cooked ham
1 tablespoon chopped parsley
1¼ cups raw rice
1 tablespoon grated lemon rind
1½ cups water
2 (7 ounces each) packages
   frozen green shrimp

Put all ingredients except shrimp into 10½-inch skillet. Stir enough to distribute ingredients evenly. Place shrimp in border around edge of skillet. Cover and cook at low temperature for 30 minutes. 6 servings.

Shrimp Mull

John Chalfa, Executive Steward
The Cloister, Sea Island, Georgia

½ cup bacon fat
1 cup finely chopped onion
1 cup diced, green pepper
4 cloves garlic, finely chopped
4 bay leaves
½ cup sugar
2 tablespoons chili powder
¼ cup flour
1 cup water
Salt and Tabasco to taste
1 (8-ounce) can tomato paste

2 tablespoons Worcestershire
   sauce
4 pounds raw peeled cleaned
   shrimp, cut in halves
1 cup dry white wine
½ cup vinegar
1 cup chili sauce
1 cup catsup
½ cup prepared mustard
Cornstarch (optional)

In a pot put bacon fat, onions, green pepper, garlic, bay leaves, sugar, and chili powder. Cook until all juices are gone and vegetables are light brown.

Add flour, mixing and cooking at low heat for 5 minutes. Add remaining ingredients except cornstarch. Bring to boil; cook for 15 minutes. If too thin, thicken the mull with a little cornstarch. 16 servings.

Shrimp and Lobster Thermidor

Mrs. George Brumley, St. Mary's, Georgia

3 pounds fresh shrimp (2 cups
    when cooked, peeled, and
    deveined)
3 (7 ounces each) packages
    frozen lobster tails (2 cups
    when cooked)
3 lemons
2 tablespoons salt
1 small onion, sliced
Celery leaves
Parsley
4 to 5 tablespoons butter

6 tablespoons flour
1 pint half and half
1 cup heavy cream
1 cup milk
½ cup dry sherry
1 teaspoon salt
⅓ teaspoon white pepper
4 to 5 tablespoons cracker
    crumbs to thicken, if needed
1 (14-ounce) package
    quick-cooking rice (optional)

Cook shrimp and lobster the day before.

To cook shrimp, wash in colander, put in heavy saucepan, and squeeze lemon juice over shrimp. Add 2 tablespoons salt, onion, celery leaves, and parsley to flavor. Bring to full boil, stirring. Cook 8 to 10 minutes and let cool in liquid. You may use shrimp seasoning or crab boil and follow directions on package.

Peel and devein shrimp. If shrimp are large, cut in half.

Cook lobster according to package directions and remove meat; cut into bite-size pieces. Store shrimp and lobster in covered container in refrigerator overnight.

On morning of the meal make the sauce. Cook over medium heat in heavy pot.

Melt butter, add flour, and stir to blend; gradually add half and half, cream, and milk, stirring constantly until it thickens. Do not let boil. Add sherry, 1 teaspoon salt, and pepper. Add seafood. Add cracker crumbs if sauce needs thickening. It should be the consistency of medium white sauce.

If sauce must be kept for several hours, refrigerate, then reheat over low heat. The sauce may be frozen for 1 month. Thaw in top of double boiler and serve immediately.

Cook rice according to package directions. Keep warm in top of double boiler.

Serve thermidor over hot rice or toast or noodles. 8 servings.

Carolina Deviled Seafood

Chef Manuel Filotis
The William Hilton Inn, Hilton Head Island, South Carolina

½ cup butter	1 pint small oysters
1 medium-size onion, minced	Salt, red pepper, Worcestershire
1 cup chopped celery	sauce
1 cup chopped green pepper	1 cup chopped pimientos
1 pound shrimp	2 eggs
½ pound fresh flaked crab meat	1 cup saltine cracker crumbs

Melt butter and add onions, celery, green pepper and cook until tender. Combine with seafood and seasonings. Cook for 5 minutes. Add pimientos, continue cooking, and add the beaten eggs with sufficient cracker crumbs to make the right consistency to fill crab shells that have been buttered. Fill shells and bake about 10 minutes at 400 degrees. Serve with a lemon garnish. 4 servings.

Sea Island Seafood Newburgh

The Cloister, Sea Island, Georgia

5 ounces cooked lobster meat, in chunks	2 tablespoons flour
	2 tablespoons paprika
5 ounces cooked and cleaned shrimp	1 pint light cream
	2 teaspoons leaf tarragon
5 ounces lump crab meat	1 tablespoon salt
1 cup poached bay scallops	¼ teaspoon Tabasco sauce
1 cup poached oysters or mussels	3 egg yolks
	½ cup dry sherry wine
½ cup butter	¼ cup brandy
1 tablespoon chopped shallots	2 tablespoons heavy cream

All the seafood should be cooked in a well-seasoned, strong court bouillon. (A 1½-pound lobster takes about 22 minutes at a slow boil.)

In half the butter sauté the shallots until golden. Add flour and stir. To remaining butter add paprika and seafood. Sauté until well mixed.

To shallot butter add the light cream. Bring to boil; stir with wire whip until smooth. Combine the two mixtures; add tarragon, salt, Tabasco, and while stirring, bring to a boil.

Beat together egg yolks, sherry, brandy, and heavy cream. Fold into the above mixture. Do not boil. Reduce heat to simmer and mix well for a few minutes. Serve in casserole with melba toast. 8 servings.

Frogs' Legs Poulette

1½ pounds frozen frogs' legs
Salt and white pepper
3 tablespoons butter or
  margarine
¼ cup minced onion
1 clove garlic, minced

1 tablespoon flour
½ cup dry white wine
1 tablespoon lemon juice
½ cup light cream
¼ pound fresh mushrooms,
  sliced

Thaw frogs' legs and sprinkle with salt and pepper. Melt butter in a large skillet. Add onion and garlic and cook until tender but not brown. Sprinkle flour into pan and mix to blend.

Gradually add white wine, stirring to keep mixture smooth. Add lemon juice and light cream; stir to blend. Add frogs' legs and mushroom slices. Cover pan and cook over medium heat, stirring occasionally, until legs are tender, 5 to 8 minutes for medium legs and 10 to 12 minutes for large legs.

If needed, thin sauce with a little extra cream. Before serving, sprinkle with chopped parsley or tiny bouquets of parsley. Serve on toast. 4 to 6 servings.

STUFFINGS

Fish Dressing
Mrs. L. A. Corbitt, Nashville, Georgia

⅔ cup chopped celery
1 small onion, chopped
4 tablespoons butter
6 slices bread in coarse crumbs
⅓ cup corn meal
½ teaspoon seasoned salt

1 teaspoon salt
Pepper to taste
4 eggs
1 (10¾-ounce) can cream of
  chicken soup
1 cup milk

Sauté celery and onions in butter until soft. To crumbs, add corn meal and seasonings and toss until blended. Then add sautéed vegetables and eggs. Combine with soup and milk and toss again to blend. Bake at 375 degrees until brown, about 30 to 40 minutes. About 3 cups—enough for 4- to 5-pound fish.

Savory Pimiento Stuffing for Fish

½ cup thinly sliced celery
1 small onion, minced
½ cup butter or margarine
1 cup hot chicken broth or
  water
1 (4-ounce) jar pimientos,
  chopped

¼ teaspoon sage
1 teaspoon salt
⅛ teaspoon pepper
4 cups diced day-old bread

Sauté celery and onion in hot butter or margarine. Stir in broth or water and bring to a boil. Combine all ingredients and mix lightly. Taste and adjust seasoning, if needed.

(If other seasoning is preferred, try thyme, poultry seasoning, or marjoram in place of sage. Use one seasoning only, not all, as excessive seasoning will kill the delicate flavor of the fish.) About 5 cups —enough for 5-pound fish.

9

VEGETABLES

Vegetables are reliable passports to a wealth of healthy and flavorful dining, and we are fortunate to live in an area where fresh vegetables are always available and where the supermarkets are filled with those of fine quality both canned and frozen. We are still rural enough for many people to have excellent home gardens from which they eat of plenty during the season of growth and can or freeze the surplus.

In my younger days it was quite the usual thing to have from six to twelve vegetables on the table at one meal. When we lived on the farm, Mama never had less than five or six vegetables, both cooked and raw. Grandma insisted on eight or more. Yes—the vegetables were usually cooked with fat back or streak-o'-lean pork. And the beans were cooked in an iron pot sometimes up to three hours. My —how good they were! And still are.

Another thing I learned and continue to this day: add a pinch of sugar to the pot when cooking nearly all vegetables, especially if they are not fresh from the garden.

I do not think most people overcook vegetables today. We like them tender but crisp, well seasoned but not greasy, and we do not flood them with liquid. Seasonings range from pork and bacon drippings, ham hocks, margarine or butter, to sour cream or sauces.

Stuffed Artichokes

6 artichokes
1½ pounds ground lamb
¾ cup cracked wheat*
1 large onion, chopped
2 tablespoons pine nuts
   (optional)
3 cups hot vegetable bouillon

⅓ cup chopped fresh mint or
   2½ teaspoons dried mint
1 teaspoon seasoned salt
¼ teaspoon pepper
1 teaspoon grated lemon peel
2 tablespoons lemon juice

While artichokes are cooking, brown lamb in large skillet, stirring frequently. Drain off excess fat. Add remaining ingredients. Cover and cook over low heat, stirring occasionally, until wheat and onion are tender and liquid is almost all absorbed.

Fill artichokes with lamb mixture. Arrange in oiled baking dish. Cover and bake in 350-degree oven 10 to 15 minutes or until heated through. Sprinkle with additional pine nuts. 6 servings.

* Or substitute ¾ cup brown rice for cracked wheat. Before adding to recipe, cook until rice is tender and liquid is absorbed, about 1 hour.

Asparagus with Nut Butter Sauce

1½ pounds asparagus
¼ cup butter
½ teaspoon grated onion
½ teaspoon lemon juice

¼ teaspoon salt
½ cup coarsely chopped pecans
Lemon twist

Cook asparagus in small amount salted water. Meanwhile, in a small skillet, melt butter; stir in onion, lemon juice, and salt. Add pecans and sauté 5 minutes. Serve over asparagus with a lemon twist for garnish. 4 to 6 servings.

Savory Pole Beans

1 pound green pole beans
2 tablespoons cooking oil
1 clove garlic
½ cup diced green pepper
3 slices onion

1 teaspoon salt
1 teaspoon basil leaves
½ teaspoon sugar
¼ cup boiling water
Grated Parmesan cheese

Remove tips from beans and cut them into 1-inch pieces. Set aside. Heat oil in a saucepan. Peel garlic, cut in half, and cook in hot oil until golden. Remove and discard garlic. Add green pepper and onion. Cook slowly 3 minutes or until pepper and onion are limp. Add beans, salt, basil, sugar, and water. Cover and cook slowly 15 minutes or until beans are crisp tender. Serve hot topped with Parmesan cheese. 6 servings.

Special Baked Beans

2 cups navy beans	1 green pepper
½ pound salt pork	2 sweet red peppers
6 sprigs parsley	2 tablespoons maple syrup
1 large onion	6 tablespoons catsup
1 clove garlic	

Wash beans and soak overnight in cold water. Drain and save liquid. Cover with fresh water and simmer 2 hours. Use medium blade and put pork through the food chopper along with parsley, onion, garlic, and green and red peppers. Mix with beans. Add syrup and catsup.

Put bean mixture into 2-quart bean pot. Add just enough bean liquid to cover beans. Cover. Bake at 300 degrees for 2¼ hours. Uncover and bake 1½ hours longer. Serve hot with steamed bread. 6 servings.

Dry Pea Beans

2 cups dry pea beans	1¼ cups molasses
1½ quarts water	½ teaspoon dry mustard or 1
1 teaspoon salt	teaspoon prepared mustard
¼ pound salt pork	

Wash and sort beans. Add water, boil 2 minutes. Remove from heat, cover, and soak for 1 hour. Add salt, cover, and boil gently 45 minutes. Cut salt pork into pieces about ½ inch thick. Add salt pork to beans and cook 30 minutes longer or until beans are tender. Mix molasses and mustard and stir into beans. Put beans into a bean pot or 2-quart baking dish and arrange pork on top. Bake at 350 degrees for 1 hour or until beans are done and lightly brown on top. 6 servings.

The late Dr. Thomas Stewart of Lithonia, Georgia, had one cooking specialty—border beans. He never remembered where the name came from, he just knew they were good. He and his wife Ellen often served a large crowd of friends border beans, black bread, and beer. They cooked the beans outdoors in a big iron "wash pot."

Border Beans
Dr. and Mrs. Thomas Stewart, Lithonia, Georgia

2 pounds pinto beans
½ pound streak o' lean or fat
   back
2 tablespoons oregano
5 cloves garlic, pressed
5 to 8 chili piquins, chopped
2 tablespoons salt

Use a large bean pot or preferably a tall pot with straight sides. Keep a kettle of water boiling on another unit.

Rinse and pick over beans if necessary. Cover beans with water and bring to boil; reduce to simmer. Keep adding water as needed just to cover beans. After first hour of simmering, add the meat, scored. Do not stir—just push down.

After the second hour, add oregano and garlic. After third hour add the chili piquins according to how hot you want the beans to be. During the fourth hour add the salt. Then continue cooking at simmer another hour. Keep adding hot water as needed to keep beans covered.

Serve hot in bowls and eat with spoon. 12 servings.

Texas Ranch House Beans
Mrs. Robert Mouk, Atlanta, Georgia

12 cups cooked pinto beans or
   6 (1 pound, 4 ounces each)
   cans
2 onions, sliced
½ pound bacon, cut into 1-inch
   cubes
1 cup chili sauce
1 clove garlic, chopped
2 tablespoons firmly packed
   dark brown sugar
1 quart beer
Salt and pepper

Drain beans and mix with onion, bacon, chili sauce, garlic, brown sugar, and beer. Simmer, uncovered, stirring occasionally, for 1 hour or until liquid is absorbed. Season to taste with salt and pepper. 12 generous servings.

Glazed Lima Beans

1 (10-ounce) package frozen   2 tablespoons butter
  lima beans   3 tablespoons brown sugar
1 small red onion, sliced
1 medium-size tart apple, cored
  and sliced

Cook beans as directed on package. Drain well. In skillet sauté
onion and apple in butter until tender. Add brown sugar and beans.
Toss lightly and heat through. 4 servings.

Buttered Beets

2 cups diced pared raw beets   2 tablespoons vinegar
2 tablespoons cornstarch   2 tablespoons butter
¼ cup sugar

Cook beets in covered pan with enough water to cover, until tender. Drain, reserving ¼ cup liquid. Mix cornstarch and sugar. Add
liquid slowly, stirring to smooth paste. Cook until slightly thickened.
Add vinegar and butter; stir to blend and pour over beets. 4 servings.

Broccoli Ring
Mrs. Frank L. Middleton, Blue Ridge, Georgia

2 cups very finely chopped   ½ pint light cream
  cooked broccoli   ½ teaspoon salt
1 cup mayonnaise   1 tablespoon flour
1 tablespoon melted butter   3 eggs, well beaten

Line a 4-cup ring mold with waxed paper. Arrange broccoli in
mold. Mix remaining ingredients and pour over broccoli. Set mold in
pan of water and bake 30 minutes at 350 degrees. Turn onto serving
plate and fill center with spiced crab apples or pickled peaches. 4
servings.

Brussels Sprouts with Mustard Sauce

2 pounds Brussels sprouts,
washed and trimmed
Salt
¼ cup chopped onion
3 tablespoons butter or
margarine

3 tablespoons flour
2 cups chicken bouillon
1½ teaspoons dry mustard
2 tablespoons tarragon vinegar

Cook Brussels sprouts until just tender, covered in a small amount of boiling salted water. In separate pan, sauté onion in butter. Add remaining ingredients and cook until smooth and thickened. Serve with drained Brussels sprouts. 6 servings.

Easy Supper Cabbage

3 tablespoons oil or butter
1 slice onion, separate rings
½ pound cabbage (about 3
cups), shredded

¼ teaspoon dry mustard
3 to 4 frankfurters
½ teaspoon salt

Heat fat in skillet with onion rings (electric skillet at 300 degrees). Add cabbage and mustard. Cover and shake skillet occasionally. Cut frankfurters in slices on the bias and add to cabbage along with salt after 3 minutes. Complete steaming, about 5 minutes. 3 to 4 servings.

Swamp Cabbage
Leslie Hatchett, Lamont, Florida

4 quarts cleaned swamp
cabbage
¾ cup smoked bacon drippings

4 or 5 pieces bacon
Salt to taste

Cut swamp cabbage into pieces and place with other ingredients in large pot with water to cover. Cook on medium heat about 2 hours or until cabbage is tender. 12 servings.

NOTE: Swamp cabbage is the heart of the swamp palm. The palm should be at least 3 feet high when cut. The bud is cut out and trimmed until it "rings." The bud should be about 5 inches in diameter for best flavor and tenderness.

This is a German recipe.

Shredded Red Cabbage

Mrs. Klaus P. Jurende, Doraville, Georgia

2 pounds red cabbage	1 clove
4 strips bacon	1 apple, shredded
1 onion, chopped fine	1 tablespoon flour
½ cup water	2 tablespoons vinegar
2 teaspoons salt	2 teaspoons sugar
2 peppercorns	

Shred cabbage. Cut bacon into 1-inch pieces and fry. Sauté onion in bacon fat. Add shredded cabbage; cook 5 minutes. Add ½ cup water, salt, peppercorns, clove, and apple. Cook on medium heat until tender. Sprinkle flour over and turn under. Add vinegar and sugar, more or less to taste. 6 servings.

Company Carrots

1 pound carrots	¼ cup honey
½ teaspoon salt	2 teaspoons grated orange rind
¾ cup water	¼ cup slivered toasted blanched
¼ cup butter	almonds

Pare carrots. Slice diagonally into very thin crosswise ovals. Cook carrots in a covered 10-inch skillet with boiling salted water until tender crisp, about 5 minutes. Drain.

Push carrots to one side of skillet. Add butter, honey, and orange rind to other side of skillet and mix over low heat. Mix with carrots. Sprinkle with almonds. 6 servings.

Dilled Carrots

4 medium-size fresh carrots, sliced	¼ cup milk
1 chicken bouillon cube	2 egg yolks, beaten
1½ cups boiling water	1 tablespoon fresh lemon juice
2 tablespoons butter or margarine	1 tablespoon chopped fresh dill
1 tablespoon flour	¼ teaspoon salt
	$\frac{1}{16}$ teaspoon black pepper

Place carrots in saucepan with bouillon cube and boiling water. Cover. Cook until crisp tender, about 15 minutes. Drain carrots. Reserve ¼ cup cooking water. Keep carrots warm until serving time. In small pan melt butter. Stir in flour and gradually add milk and reserved carrot cooking water. Cook sauce to medium thickness over low heat. Combine egg yolks with lemon juice. Blend into sauce. Add dill, salt, and black pepper. Cook 1 minute, stirring constantly. Pour over carrots in serving dish. 4 servings.

Sweet and Sour Cauliflower

1 medium head cauliflower
Salt, plus ¼ teaspoon salt
4 tablespoons butter
½ green pepper, sliced
1 teaspoon cornstarch

1 teaspoon powdered ginger
½ cup water
3 tablespoons grapefruit juice
⅔ teaspoon soy sauce

Remove outer leaves and stalks of cauliflower. Wash well. Leave whole and place in boiling salted water in saucepan. Cook about 20 minutes or until tender. While cauliflower is cooking, measure other ingredients. Drain cauliflower; place on warm dish while preparing sauce. Melt butter in saucepan; add green pepper and sauté until tender.

Combine cornstarch, ginger, and ¼ teaspoon salt; stir in water, grapefruit juice, and soy sauce. Add to green pepper and cook, stirring constantly, until sauce comes to a boil and is thickened. Pour sauce over cauliflower and serve. 3 to 4 servings.

Fresh Creamed Corn

Mrs. Lamar Hall, Paupers Club, Jekyll Island, Georgia

10 ears fresh corn
1 cup half and half
1 teaspoon salt

1 tablespoon sugar
2 tablespoons butter

Clean and wash corn. Just tip the corn with a sharp knife or corn cutter, then scrape. Add milk, salt, and sugar and heat until thickened, in heavy saucepan, stirring well. Add butter and reduce heat to simmer for 30 minutes. 4 to 6 servings.

Corn Oysters

2 eggs, separated
½ cup milk
1 cup pancake mix

2 cups fresh whole kernel corn
Fat for frying

Blend egg yolks and milk. Add pancake mix and stir until smooth. Fold in corn. Beat egg whites until stiff peaks form. Fold into the corn mixture. Drop by teaspoonfuls into hot fat, ½ to 1 inch deep. Cook 4 to 5 minutes or until golden brown. Serve with warm buttered syrup. 8 servings.

Corn Pudding

2 cups fresh whole kernel corn
1 cup milk
2 tablespoons butter or
   margarine
2 tablespoons flour

2 teaspoons salt
1 tablespoon sugar
Red or white pepper to taste
3 eggs

To corn, add milk, butter, flour, and seasonings. Beat eggs until light. Add to mixture. Pour into buttered baking dish and bake at 350 degrees for 1 hour or until firm like a custard. 4 to 6 servings.

Baked Stuffed Cucumbers

4 medium-size cucumbers
1 tablespoon butter
1 tablespoon flour
1 cup milk
½ cup chopped cooked meat
2 hard-cooked eggs, chopped

1 teaspoon chopped parsley
1 teaspoon chopped chives
1 teaspoon grated onion
½ cup finely diced celery
Salt, pepper, and nutmeg
½ cup buttered bread crumbs

Cut cucumbers in half lengthwise and remove seeds. Place in cold water for 15 minutes. Drain and parboil about 5 minutes in small amount of boiling water.

Make a cream sauce of butter, flour, and milk, and combine with other ingredients except bread crumbs. Fill cucumbers with this mixture and top with buttered crumbs. Bake at 375 degrees about 20 minutes or until crumbs are browned. Serve very hot. 4 servings.

Eggplant Creole

Coreen Bradford, Atlanta, Georgia

1 medium eggplant	*1 small onion, chopped*
Salt, plus ½ teaspoon salt	*1 tablespoon brown sugar*
4 tablespoons butter	*½ bay leaf (optional)*
3 tablespoons flour	*2 cloves (optional)*
3 large tomatoes, peeled and	*½ cup bread crumbs*
chopped	*2 tablespoons grated Cheddar*
1 small green pepper, chopped	*cheese*

Peel, cut, and dice eggplant. Cook for 10 minutes in boiling salted water. Drain and place in greased baking dish.

Melt 3 tablespoons butter and stir in flour until blended. Add tomatoes, green pepper, onion, ½ teaspoon salt, sugar, bay leaf, and cloves. Cook for 5 minutes. Pour over eggplant.

Cover top with bread crumbs. Dot lightly with remaining butter and grated cheese. Bake in moderate oven, 350 degrees, for 30 minutes. 4 servings.

Shrimp-stuffed Eggplant

Mrs. W. W. Anderson, St. Simons Island, Georgia

1 pound shrimp	*Salt and pepper*
¾ cup liquor from the cooked	*½ medium onion, chopped*
shrimp	*1 clove garlic, finely chopped*
1 large eggplant	*⅓ cup butter or margarine*
1 cup canned tomato purée	*¾ cup dry bread crumbs*
½ teaspoon crushed thyme	

Shell and devein shrimp and simmer gently in water to cover until they turn pink, about 3 minutes. Drain and reserve liquid.

Cut eggplant in half lengthwise. Scoop out pulp, leaving a ½-inch-thick shell. Turn shells upside down in a pan of cold water. Chop pulp and combine with ¾ cup shrimp liquor, tomato pureé, thyme, salt, and pepper. Simmer about 10 minutes or until eggplant is tender. Remove from water and drain.

Cook onion and garlic in butter until soft, stir in bread crumbs. Add shrimp to tomato mixture; fill eggplant shells with alternate layers of mixture and buttered crumbs, topping with crumbs. Bake in 400-degree oven for 30 to 40 minutes or until crumbs are brown. 6 servings.

Stuffed Mushrooms

1 pound large fresh mushrooms
2 tablespoons butter or
  margarine
¼ cup diced onion
½ pound ground raw steak

1 clove garlic, minced
1 teaspoon celery salt
1 teaspoon freshly ground black
  pepper

Clean mushrooms; remove and chop stems. Melt butter or margarine in skillet. Add mushroom stems, onion, and meat. Brown lightly. Stir in garlic and seasonings. Fill mushroom caps. Place in greased shallow baking dish. Bake 25 minutes at 350 degrees.

In the meantime make sauce:

2 tablespoons butter or
  margarine
¼ cup diced onion
1 clove garlic, minced
2 tablespoons flour
½ teaspoon dry mustard

½ teaspoon marjoram
½ teaspoon celery salt
1 tablespoon lemon juice
1 cup white wine
1 cup dairy sour cream

Melt butter, add onion and garlic; brown lightly. Blend in flour, seasonings, lemon juice, and wine. Cook and stir over low heat until thickened. Add sour cream just before serving. Spoon sauce over the stuffed mushroom caps. 4 to 6 servings.

Mustard Greens

1 bunch (about 1 pound)
  mustard greens
2 tablespoons meat drippings
  (pork or bacon)

1 teaspoon sugar
Salt
Butter
Pepper

Wash greens. Remove stems. Place in frying pan with meat drippings. Add sugar and ½ teaspoon salt. Cook at low heat, stirring frequently until tender. Place in serving dish. Add butter, salt, and pepper to taste. 4 servings.

Buttered Okra

1 pound small okra pods
Salt
3 tablespoons melted butter

Wash okra well and trim stem ends, leaving enough on the pod to
keep the juice in. Cover with boiling water and boil gently until tender, about 15 minutes. When half done, season with salt. To serve,
drain and pour okra into a hot dish and add melted butter. 4 to 6
servings.

Fried Okra

¼ pound white bacon
3 pounds fresh okra
Salt and pepper

Into a heavy frying pan cut bacon in small pieces and fry until
crisp. Wash and slice okra crosswise. Put into hot bacon. Cook, uncovered, for about 40 minutes on low heat. Occasionally stir carefully. Then cover and continue cooking until done. Season with salt
and pepper. 8 servings.

Southern Stuffed Onions

6 large onions
1 cup sliced mushrooms
1 tablespoon butter or
* margarine*
2 tablespoons fat
2 tablespoons flour
1 cup chicken broth

¼ teaspoon salt
Dash pepper
½ cup chopped pecans
Additional pecans, halved
* (optional)*
12 toast triangles

Cook onions 30 minutes or until tender. Drain and remove centers. Sauté mushrooms in butter about 3 minutes.

Meanwhile make cream sauce of fat, flour, chicken broth, salt, and
pepper. When thickened stir in mushrooms and chopped pecans. Fill
centers of onions with mushroom and pecan sauce. Top with half
pecans if desired. Set on triangles of toast. Garnish with parsley. 6
servings.

Onion Custard Pie

1 (9-inch) pie shell
1/4 cup butter
4 cups thinly sliced sweet
    Spanish onions
3 eggs
1 teaspoon salt

1/8 teaspoon each thyme, nutmeg
    and pepper
1 1/4 cups half and half
4 slices bacon, cut into 1-inch
    strips

Prepare dough for pie shell. Place in pie plate and flute edges. Chill.

To prepare filling, heat butter in fry pan, add onions, and cook until transparent but not brown. Remove from heat and cool.

Whip eggs until well blended. Add seasonings and half and half. Carefully fold in onions and set aside while frying bacon. Cook bacon until lightly brown. Drain.

Pour onion-custard into pie shell. Scatter bacon over the top. Bake in 400-degree oven 30 minutes or until filling is firm. Do not overcook. Serve hot. 6 servings.

Dill Onion Rings

Kerry Ann Strong, Perry, Georgia

1 large Bermuda onion
1/2 cup white vinegar
1/4 cup water
2 teaspoons salt

1/4 teaspoon dill weed
Liquid no-calorie sweetener,
    equivalent of 1/2 cup sugar

Peel and cut onion into thin crosswise slices. Separate into rings. Place in small bowl. Combine vinegar, water, salt, dill weed, and your favorite no-calorie sweetener in small saucepan. Heat to boiling, pour over onion rings, cover tightly, and chill at least 1 hour to blend flavors. 4 servings.

We like to serve blackeye peas quite often—but always on New Year's Day. Of course, they are supposed to bring good luck for the year, so we always add a dish of turnip greens or collard greens, too (that's for folding money). However, we think the reason this down-to-earth food is so good is that we are just fed up with the rich foods of the Christmas season.

Hog Jowl and Blackeye Peas

1 pound blackeye peas   *3 cups boiling water*
3 pounds hog jowl   *1 teaspoon salt*

Cover peas with cold water and soak overnight. Cook hog jowl in boiling water for 1 hour, add drained peas and salt, and simmer for 2 hours longer. 6 to 8 servings.

We don't know how this dish was named, but the story goes there was a man so fond of this combination that when his wife called him to eat she would yell out, "Come a-hoppin', John." So the word got around, and the dish was dubbed Hoppin' John.

Hoppin' John

1 cup dried blackeye peas   *3 cups cooked rice*
¼ pound smoked bacon or salt   *Cayenne, salt, and black pepper*
  pork, cut into small pieces   *to taste*
1 pod red pepper

Soak peas overnight in water to cover. Cook in same water with bacon and pepper pod until peas are tender (not overdone—keep the peas whole). Add cooked rice and mix well. Season with cayenne, salt, and pepper to taste. Place in covered casserole and cook until liquid is absorbed and dish is hot through. 8 to 10 servings.

English Peas and Dumplings

Mrs. Emory Rogers, Manassas, Georgia

About 3 cups water   *Salt and pepper to taste*
1 small piece ham   *Dumplings*
1 pint frozen English peas

In water in a saucepan put ham and cook for short period. Add frozen peas, salt, and pepper. Boil about 30 minutes or until peas are just about done. Then add dumplings a few at a time. Keep water boiling continuously. Cover pot tightly and cook about 15 minutes longer. Time will vary with tenderness of peas. 4 servings.

DUMPLINGS

1 egg
3 cups self-rising flour, sifted

Break egg in measuring cup and fill cup with water. Beat well with a fork to blend. Put flour in mixing bowl and make well in center. Pour water-egg mixture in the well. Blend with fork to make soft dough. Roll thin on pastry cloth and cut into short strips.

Stuffed Pimientos

2 (7 ounces each) cans whole
  pimientos
2 (3 ounces each) packages
  cream cheese
¼ pound Cheddar cheese,
  grated
1 teaspoon flour

2 teaspoons milk
1 egg
1 teaspoon salt
½ teaspoon paprika
¼ teaspoon prepared mustard
Tabasco sauce and black
  pepper to taste

Drain pimientos. Mash cream cheese and mix well with cheddar. Stir in flour, milk, slightly beaten egg, and seasonings. Stuff pimiento with mixture and place in greased muffin pans. Bake 30 minutes at 375 degrees. Serve at once with the following sauce: Heat 1 (10¾ ounce) can mushroom soup, undiluted; pour over baked pimiento and top with 3 strips crisp bacon. 8 to 10 servings.

Baked Potato Supreme

Mrs. James E. Deadwyler, Atlanta, Georgia

2 large baking potatoes,
  scrubbed
4 strips bacon, quartered
¼ cup chopped green onion
2 tablespoons grated Parmesan
  cheese

½ cup sour cream
½ teaspoon white pepper
½ teaspoon salt
Melted butter
Paprika

Bake potatoes in 400-degree oven for 1 hour. While potato is cooling, grill bacon slices until crisp. Drain off all except 3 table-spoons fat. Add onion and sauté. Remove skillet from heat. Cut shallow lengthwise slice from each potato and carefully spoon out inside. Add to skillet with cheese, cream, crumbled bacon, pepper, and salt. Mix and mash to blend well. Return to heat and heat through. Stuff mixture into potato shells. Drizzle with butter and sprinkle with paprika. Bake at 350 degrees for 15 to 20 minutes. 2 servings.

New Potatoes with Bacon

2 pounds new potatoes　　　　　*3 strips bacon*
1 teaspoon salt　　　　　　　　*⅛ teaspoon black pepper*

Wash and scrape potatoes. Place in saucepan with 1 inch boiling water and salt. Cover and bring to boiling point and continue cooking 15 to 20 minutes. Cooking time depends on size of potatoes. Drain if necessary. Cook bacon until crisp.

Remove bacon from fat and drain on paper towel. Add potatoes to hot fat and brown on all sides. Place on a serving dish. Crumble crisp bacon over top and sprinkle with pepper. Serve at once. 6 to 8 servings.

Scalloped Potatoes Supreme

1 (10¾-ounce) can mushroom　　*Grated Cheddar cheese*
*　soup*　　　　　　　　　　　　*4 tablespoons butter or*
¾ cup milk　　　　　　　　　　*　margarine*
3 or 4 medium potatoes, thinly　*Paprika*
*　sliced*　　　　　　　　　　　　*Salt and pepper to taste*
1 medium-size onion, thinly
*　sliced*

Blend mushroom soup and milk together. Arrange potatoes, onions, and mushroom sauce in layers, ending with the sauce. Cover with cheese. Dot with butter or margarine and sprinkle with paprika and salt and pepper. Cover and bake at 375 degrees for 1 hour. Remove cover and bake 10 to 15 minutes longer or until slightly browned. 4 servings.

NOTE: A small can of garden peas may be added along with the potatoes and onion if desired.

Cheese Whipped Potatoes

6 medium potatoes
1½ teaspoons salt
1 to 2 tablespoons milk
3 tablespoons butter or
  margarine

⅛ teaspoon ground white
  pepper
⅓ cup grated sharp Cheddar
  cheese

Wash potatoes and cook covered in 1 inch boiling water and ½ teaspoon of the salt until tender. Drain and peel. Add milk, butter or margarine, remaining salt, and white pepper. Mash until fluffy. Blend in grated cheese. Turn into a casserole and heat in hot oven, 400 degrees, only until very hot, about 5 minutes. 6 servings.

Fishermen's Fries

1 tablespoon salt, plus 1
  teaspoon
2 quarts cold water
8 medium-size scrubbed
  potatoes, sliced ⅛ inch thick

⅓ cup cooking oil or more
2 tablespoons butter
⅛ teaspoon black pepper

Add the 1 tablespoon salt to cold water. As unpeeled potatoes are sliced, drop into the water to prevent discoloration. Drain and shake off excess moisture before placing in a hot heavy ironware skillet with hot oil and butter. Put in one layer of potatoes at a time. Cook over high heat, turning only once.

Set aside nicely browned pieces and continue cooking remainder, one layer at a time. More oil may be needed.

When all potatoes are browned, replace them in skillet. Cover top with aluminum foil or another skillet inverted and cook at low heat about 10 minutes or until fork tender. Sprinkle with 1 teaspoon salt and the black pepper. 6 to 8 servings.

Sweet Potato Boats

Mrs. Roscoe A. Stallings, Nashville, Georgia

8 medium-size sweet potatoes
1 (1-pound) can sliced cling
  peaches
3 tablespoons margarine
5 tablespoons brown sugar

1 tablespoon grated lemon rind
½ teaspoon ground ginger
½ teaspoon cinnamon
1 teaspoon lemon juice
½ teaspoon salt

Bake potatoes until tender, about 35 minutes at 425 degrees. Save 8 peach slices, dice remainder. Slice top off each potato when cool. Scoop out insides; save shells. Combine potato with remaining ingredients and fill potato shell. Bake at 425 degrees for 10 minutes. Top each with peach slice. 8 servings.

Sweet Potatoes in Orange Shells

Mrs. Annie Keith, cook for 25 years
for Mrs. Jack Mazier, Atlanta Georgia

2 pounds sweet potatoes	*1 teaspoon nutmeg*
½ cup margarine	*1 teaspoon vanilla flavoring*
3 eggs, slightly beaten	*1 cup orange juice*
1 teaspoon cinnamon	*3 oranges, halved and inside*
1 cup brown sugar	*removed*
¾ cup granulated sugar	*6 marshmallows*

Wash potatoes and boil in skins. Cook until done. Peel and mash, add melted margarine and eggs, mashing and combining thoroughly. Add cinnamon, sugar, nutmeg, vanilla, and orange juice. Bake in casserole in 350-degree oven 20 minutes or until about half done. Fill orange shells with partially baked sweet potato mixture and finish baking. Top each orange half with marshmallow and let brown lightly. 6 servings.

Candied Yams and Apples

Mrs. A. N. Holbrook, Jr., Mableton, Georgia

6 medium-size sweet potatoes, peeled	*Sprinkling of ginger, nutmeg, or allspice (optional)*
4 to 6 red-skinned cooking apples	*¾ cup water*
	Shredded coconut (optional)
1 cup brown sugar	
6 to 8 tablespoons butter or margarine	

In casserole lay slices of sweet potato, slices or wedges of apple (unpeeled), and layer of sugar and dots of butter. Repeat. Add seasoning and water. Bake at 350 degrees for 35 to 45 minutes. If coconut is used sprinkle over top last 5 minutes of baking period. 6 to 8 servings.

Special Sauerkraut

Mrs. J. C. Steinmetz, Niskey Lake, Ben Hill, Georgia

> 2 pounds ham hocks
> 2 cups water
> 2 (14 ounces each) cans
>   sauerkraut
> 2 carrots, grated
> 1 large potato, grated
>
> 1 large apple (grated on
>   medium grater)
> 1 medium-size onion, chopped
> 2 tablespoons brown sugar
> 6 bacon slices, cooked and
>   crumbled

A day in advance cook ham hocks in 2 cups water until tender. Refrigerate. On day of preparation skim off fat, save broth (about 2 cups). Cut lean ham in small cubes (4 cups).

In large casserole combine sauerkraut, carrots, potato, apple, onion, and the brown sugar. Heat ham and broth and add to mixture; cover. Cook 1½ hours at 350 degrees. Then uncover and sprinkle top with crisp bacon bits; cook 15 minutes longer. Serve hot. This may be refrigerated and served later, reheated. 8 servings.

Sour Cream Fluff Top Spinach

> 6 strips bacon, cut in 1-inch
>   pieces
> 3 tablespoons chopped onion
> 2 tablespoons flour
> ¼ cup vinegar
> 2 teaspoons sugar
> 1 teaspoon salt
> 1 egg, beaten
>
> 1 cup sour cream
> 1½ pounds fresh spinach or 2
>   (10 ounces each) packages
>   frozen spinach, cooked and
>   drained
> 1 hard-cooked egg, sliced
>   (optional)

Fry bacon in skillet until crisp. Remove. In drippings lightly brown onion. Remove. Pour off all but about 2 tablespoons drippings. Blend flour into drippings and remove from heat. Stir in vinegar, sugar, and salt. Fold egg into sour cream. Add to mixture in skillet. Add bacon and onion. Return to low heat and cook, stirring constantly, until smooth and thickened. Serve immediately over hot spinach. Garnish with sliced egg if desired. 6 to 8 servings.

Stuffed Acorn Squash

3 acorn squash
Butter, salt, and pepper
¾ pound ground beef
¼ pound bulk sausage
½ cup chopped celery

⅓ cup chopped onion
1 (10½-ounce) can condensed
    cream of mushroom soup
Buttered bread crumbs

Split squash. Remove seeds and fibers. Brush inside and edge with butter. Sprinkle with salt and pepper. Bake cut side down in shallow baking dish at 400 degrees for 35 minutes. Meanwhile, in skillet, cook beef, sausage, celery, and onion until meat is browned and celery tender. Stir in soup. Fill squash with mixture. Top with bread crumbs. Bake for an additional 20 minutes or until tender. 6 servings.

Baked Zucchini and Tomatoes

2 medium-size zucchini
2 medium-size tomatoes
2 medium-size mild onions

Salt and pepper
Butter or margarine
1 cup buttered crumbs

Wash zucchini but do not peel it unless the skin is hard. Peel tomatoes and onions. Slice the vegetables into very thin crosswise slices.

In a greased baking dish make alternate layers of zucchini, tomatoes, and onions, sprinkling each layer with a little salt and pepper and dotting with butter or margarine. Spread the top layer with buttered crumbs. Bake in a moderate oven, 350 degrees, until vegetables are tender. 4 servings.

Fried Green Tomatoes and Gravy

Salt, pepper, and flour slices of 4 green tomatoes. Fry in ¼ cup butter. Remove all except one slice and continue cooking it until it will mush up in gravy.

Make gravy as for fried chicken cream gravy—about 1 tablespoon flour stirred into the butter and 1 cup milk. Simmer to thicken. Pour over fried green tomato slices, sprinkle lightly with brown sugar and a little chopped parsley. Serve hot. 1 serving per medium-size tomato.

Hearty Cheese Tomatoes

Mr. and Mrs. William T. Shuler
Garden Valley Farm, Cobb County, Georgia

4 large firm ripe tomatoes	1 teaspoon parsley flakes
2 cups toasted bread cubes	½ cup chopped cashew nuts
½ teaspoon nutmeg	2 tablespoons melted butter
1 cup shredded Cheddar cheese	4 green onions, chopped

Cut off tops of tomatoes, scoop out insides. Combine bread, to-mato pulp, and remaining ingredients and fill tomato cups with mix-ture. Wrap cups three fourths of depth in aluminum foil. Bake in 375-degree oven about 15 minutes or until cheese melts and tomato is heated through. Serve piping hot. 4 servings.

Tomato Pie

4 to 5 large tomatoes	1 teaspoon sugar
1 tablespoon minced parsley	Salt and pepper
1 small onion, chopped	2 cups hot mashed potatoes
1 small cucumber, sliced	3 tablespoons grated American
1 tablespoon butter or	cheese
margarine	

Peel and slice tomatoes. Place in casserole and sprinkle with minced parsley, onion, cucumber, butter or margarine, sugar, salt and pepper to taste. Spread well-seasoned hot mashed potatoes over tomatoes. Sprinkle cheese over top. Bake in 375-degree oven until nicely browned. 4 servings.

Scalloped Tomatoes Supreme

6 slices bacon	Salt and pepper to taste
1 small onion, chopped	1½ cups cooked rice (½ cup
2 tablespoons chopped green	raw)
pepper	6 hard-cooked eggs
3 cups (about 8 medium)	Grated Cheddar cheese
cooked tomatoes	

Chop bacon and fry until crisp. Remove bacon and brown onion and green pepper in fat. Add tomatoes and bacon and season with salt and pepper. Arrange layers of rice, sliced hard-cooked eggs, tomatoes, and cheese in buttered casserole. Bake at 325 degrees until hot and cheese is melted. 6 servings.

Vegetable Goulash

Mrs. Bernard C. Mote, McDonough, Georgia

4 chopped tomatoes
2 cups sliced okra
1 cup chopped onion

1 cup cut corn
Salt and pepper

Combine all ingredients in saucepan. Cover and bring to a boil. Keep covered and cook until vegetables are about half done (15 minutes). Remove cover, reduce heat to low, and cook until thickened, about 15 minutes. 4 to 6 servings.

10

><><><><><><><><><><><><><><><><><><><><><><><><><

SAUCES AND
SALAD DRESSINGS

Very often a sauce can make the difference between an elegant and a run-of-the-mill dish. A sauce should be a complement to a dish, not an overpowering addition. "Just enough" is the right phrase. Too much can mean an unsightly dish, reducing not only the eye appeal but the appetite appeal.

Sauce making is one of the cook's finest arts. This is recognized in all the best restaurants. Many of our great sauces have been developed by excellent chefs, and some have been handed down through decades of usage.

Sauces have thousands of variations. They can be of many consistencies, range in taste from sour to sweet, and are used with anything from soups, through vegetables, meats, salads, and desserts.

The following recipes do not claim to be originals, but our readers use them and like them. Perhaps each of you will find something here that will add interest to your own menus.

Barbecue Sauce Piquante

Mrs. C. E. Gadlike, Brunswick, Georgia

4 pounds onions, chopped fine
1 bell pepper, chopped fine
1 stalk celery, chopped fine
½ to 1 clove garlic, chopped
  fine
1 (6-ounce) jar prepared
  mustard
1 tablespoon vinegar
1 tablespoon sugar

3 tablespoons Worcestershire
  sauce
2 tablespoons Tabasco
1 (14-ounce) bottle catsup
2 (16 ounces each) cans
  tomato sauce
1 pint salad oil
1 tablespoon salt
1 tablespoon pepper

Combine all ingredients, cover and cook at a simmer, stirring often, for several hours. 9 cups.

Great over green beans or cauliflower.

Cheese Onion Sauce

3 tablespoons butter
¼ cup chopped onion
2 tablespoons flour

1¼ cups milk
1 cup (4 ounces) shredded
  Cheddar cheese

In a 1-quart saucepan melt butter; add onion and sauté 5 minutes. Blend in flour. Remove from heat; gradually add milk. Return to heat and cook, stirring constantly, until mixture thickens. Cook 2 additional minutes. Remove from heat and stir in cheese until melted. If necessary, return to low heat to finish melting cheese. (Do not boil). Serve immediately over cooked cauliflower or green beans. 1¾ cups.

Gingered Sauce

1 (1-pound) can crushed pineapple
1 tablespoon cornstarch
¼ teaspoon ground ginger
½ cup chopped red maraschino cherries

Drain pineapple, reserving juice. Add cornstarch to juice and cook slowly until sauce thickens. Stir in ginger. Add crushed pineapple and cherries. Stir until well mixed and heated through. Serve with ham. 2 cups.

Quick Hollandaise Sauce
Mrs. Hansel A. Parks, Atlanta, Georgia

4 egg yolks	*Dash of cayenne pepper*
1 tablespoon lemon juice	*⅔ cup melted butter*

Place yolks, juice, and pepper in blender. Cover. Blend 10 seconds (or mix at high speed 30 seconds in electric mixer).

Heat butter over low heat until bubbling. Turn blender to high and slowly pour thin stream of hot butter into egg mixture. Blend 30 seconds, until mixture becomes thick and fluffy. (In electric mixer, add butter a few drops at a time and beat until fluffy.) About 1 cup.

Creamed Horseradish Sauce

8 tablespoons butter	*4 tablespoons freshly grated*
4 tablespoons flour	*horseradish (or to taste)*
2 cups light cream	*Salt to taste*

Melt butter. Blend in flour smoothly. Heat the cream and pour in gradually, stirring constantly until thickened. Add horseradish and season with salt to taste. Do not let sauce boil after this point. Pour over meat and serve at once. About 2 cups.

Herbed Lemon Butter

¼ cup butter or margarine	*1 tablespoon freshly squeezed*
1 teaspoon freshly grated lemon	*lemon juice*
peel	*½ teaspoon crushed marjoram*

Heat butter in small saucepan; blend in remaining ingredients. Serve with fish. 4 servings.

Mustard Sauce

Jean Peruzzi, Atlanta, Georgia

1½ cups prepared mustard	1 teaspoon salt
½ cup dry white wine	2 tablespoons flour
2 tablespoons sugar	¼ cup water

Combine mustard, wine, sugar, and salt in a saucepan. Bring to boil over moderate heat, stirring constantly. Mix flour in water and stir into mustard mixture. Reduce heat and simmer 10 minutes or until thickened, stirring constantly. Serve hot or cold. About 2 cups.

Raisin Sauce

Mrs. A. Jude Robinson, Auburn, Alabama

½ cup brown sugar	3 tablespoons lemon juice
1 teaspoon dry mustard	¼ teaspoon grated lemon rind
2 tablespoons cornstarch	1½ cups water
1 tablespoon vinegar	¾ cup seedless raisins

Combine all ingredients in saucepan. Bring to a boil; reduce heat and simmer for about 5 minutes. Good with baked ham. 1½ cups sauce.

Here's a sour cream sauce to make fish dishes melt in your mouth.

Sour Cream Sauce

3 tablespoons butter	1 cup dairy sour cream
¼ cup sliced scallions	1 teaspoon lemon juice
¼ cup diced green pepper	½ teaspoon bottled browning
½ teaspoon salt	sauce
⅛ teaspoon pepper	

Melt butter in small saucepan. Add scallions and green pepper. Cook over moderate heat about 3 minutes. Add seasonings, sour cream, lemon juice, and browning sauce. Bring to boil and let simmer a couple of minutes. Pour over broiled fish. If desired, return under broiler until lightly browned. About 1⅓ cups.

Steak Marinade

½ cup salad oil
¼ cup lime or lemon juice
½ teaspoon Tabasco sauce

½ cup dry red wine
1 teaspoon dry mustard
½ teaspoon salt

Blend salad oil, lime juice, and Tabasco in shallow dish. Stir in wine, dry mustard, and salt. Put steak in marinade, let stand 5 hours, turning once. About 1½ cups—enough for 1 four-pound steak.

Sweet and Sour Sauce for Vegetables

4 cups shredded cabbage
Salt
½ cup diced bacon
3 tablespoons flour

¼ cup honey
¼ cup vinegar
½ cup water
1 teaspoon chopped onion

Cook shredded cabbage in boiling salted water until tender; drain. Dice bacon. Cook until well done. Remove bacon and place on cabbage. Blend bacon fat with flour. Add honey, vinegar, water, and onion. Cook until thickened. Pour over cabbage and bacon. Season to taste. Heat thoroughly. Serve hot. 6 servings.

This same recipe may be used with cooked potatoes.

Spaghetti Sauce à la Carissimo

Paul Carissimo, Atlanta Georgia

½ pound salt pork, finely diced
¼ cup olive oil or vegetable oil
¼ cup butter
¾ pound onions, finely diced
1 pound lean beef (preferably chuck), cubed
½ pound lean pork shoulder, cubed
2 bay leaves, crumbled (optional)
Basil (optional)

5 cloves garlic
1 teaspoon freshly ground black pepper
3 (28 ounces each) cans tomatoes
1 (16-ounce) can tomato purée
8 fresh parsley sprigs, leaves only
½ tablespoon salt (or to taste)
2 (16 ounces each) cans tomato paste

Combine salt pork, olive oil, and butter in a large saucepan; heat. Add onions and sauté to medium brown. Add beef, pork, bay leaves, and basil. Stir. Cook slowly, uncovered for 30 minutes. Mash garlic and add to sauce with black pepper. Stir well and continue to cook over low heat for 20 minutes. Take time out to inhale the aroma!

Add tomatoes, tomato purée, parsley, and salt. Simmer slowly for 1½ hours, stirring occasionally. *Do not hurry the cooking.*

Remove from heat and allow to cool for 10 minutes. Strain sauce. Put whatever remains in the strainer through a food mill and return to the sauce. Add the tomato paste. *Stir well.* Bring to boil, and simmer gently for 1 hour. Check to see if more salt is needed. About 1 gallon (16 cups).

NOTE: Sauce may be frozen for later use. Water can be added before final cooking if one desires a thinner sauce.

Chicken may be added—cut in small pieces and browned in skillet.

Joe's Spaghetti Sauce
Joe Savard, Brunswick, Georgia

4 cloves garlic, chopped fine	2 whole red peppers (hot)
6 tablespoons cooking oil	2 (6 ounces each) cans tomato
1 pound ground beef	paste
1 teaspoon allspice	2 (No. 303) cans tomatoes
1 teaspoon cloves	1 (6-ounce) can tomato sauce
1 teaspoon cinnamon	2 sauce cans water
1 teaspoon oregano	Salt to taste
2 teaspoons celery flakes	

In an iron skillet brown garlic in the oil, add ground beef, spices, and crushed red peppers. Cook over medium heat until meat browns, stirring occasionally. Add tomato paste, canned tomatoes, tomato sauce, and water. Season to taste. Cover skillet, reduce heat to low, and simmer 3 hours. 8 cups—enough for 4 servings.

NOTE: This sauce improves with age. It may be refrigerated or frozen for future use. Serve over spaghetti and sprinkle generously with finely grated Romano cheese.

Homemade Tartar Sauce

*1 cup mayonnaise (not salad
dressing)*
*1 hard-cooked egg, finely
chopped*
*2 teaspoons freshly grated
lemon peel*
*2 tablespoons freshly squeezed
lemon juice*

*2 tablespoons finely minced or
grated onion*
*2 tablespoons sweet pickle
relish or finely minced sweet
pickle*
*1 tablespoon finely snipped
fresh parsley*
¼ teaspoon salt

Thoroughly combine all ingredients; chill. 1¼ cups.

Mrs. Treadwell's Chocolate Sauce

*Mrs. E. E. Treadwell
Clairmont Elementary School Lunch Room, Decatur, Georgia*

*½ cup cocoa
1 cup sugar
¼ cup sifted flour*

*¼ teaspoon salt
1½ cups hot water
1 teaspoon vanilla*

Mix dry ingredients. Gradually stir in hot water. Cook over low heat, stirring constantly until it boils. Remove from heat and add vanilla. Serve over plain cake, doughnuts, or pudding. 2 cups.

White Raisin Sauce for Ice Cream

*1 cup sugar
¾ cup water
½ cup white corn syrup
Few grains salt
1 cup chopped seedless white
raisins*

*1 to 2 teaspoons chopped
crystallized ginger
2 tablespoons lemon juice
1½ teaspoons grated lemon rind
½ cup coarsely chopped walnuts*

Combine sugar, water, corn syrup, and salt, and cook over medium heat, stirring until mixture boils. As soon as sugar is dissolved add raisins, ginger, lemon juice and rind. Cook until mixture thickens slightly, about 5 to 7 minutes. Add nuts and blend thoroughly. Serve hot or cold with ice cream. 1½ cups.

Peanut Caramel Sauce

1 cup firmly packed light brown   *1 cup water*
  sugar   *½ cup peanut butter*
1 tablespoon flour   *1 teaspoon vanilla*
⅛ teaspoon salt

Mix sugar, flour, and salt. Stir in water. Cook and stir over low heat until mixture comes to a full rolling boil. Add peanut butter and bring again to a boil, stirring constantly to make a smooth mixture. Remove from heat. Add vanilla. Serve hot or cold over ice cream. 1½ cups.

This dressing is especially good with vegetable salads. Great with potato salad.

Cooked Salad Dressing

2 tablespoons flour   *1 egg, well beaten*
1½ teaspoons salt   *1¼ cups scalded milk*
½ teaspoon dry mustard   *⅓ cup vinegar*
1 tablespoon sugar   *2 tablespoons melted margarine*
Dash paprika

Combine flour, salt, mustard, sugar, and paprika in top of double boiler; add egg and mix well. Stir in milk gradually, place over hot water, and cook 7 to 10 minutes or until thickened, stirring constantly. Remove from heat and stir in vinegar and margarine; chill. Thin with milk if necessary before using. About 1⅔ cups.

Cranberry Salad Dressing

⅔ cup cranberry juice cocktail   *½ teaspoon salt*
¼ cup lime juice   *¼ teaspoon white pepper*
⅔ cup salad oil   *¼ teaspoon dry mustard*
½ teaspoon sugar   *Few drops Tabasco sauce*

Combine all ingredients in a jar with a tight-fitting lid. Shake until well blended. Serve with crisp salad greens or with fruit salads. About 1½ cups.

Honey French Dressing

½ cup honey
1 cup salad oil
½ teaspoon salt
⅓ cup chili sauce

½ cup (scant) vinegar
1 small onion, grated
1 tablespoon Worcestershire
sauce

Place all ingredients in quart jar, cover, and shake well. Use on favorite tossed salad or other salads. 2½ cups.

Herb Salad Dressing

Mrs. Carl Sanders, wife of Georgia's former governor, Atlanta, Georgia

1 cup vinegar
2 tablespoons sugar
1 teaspoon salt
1 teaspoon paprika
1 tablespoon Worcestershire
sauce

1 tablespoon salad herbs
½ cup salad oil
3 cloves garlic

Blend first six ingredients in a heavy saucepan. Simmer for 8 minutes. Cool and add salad oil and garlic. About 1½ cups.

Homemade Mayonnaise

Mrs. C. A. McCravy, Atlanta, Georgia

1 egg yolk
1½ teaspoons salt
½ teaspoon dry mustard
¼ teaspoon paprika

Dash cayenne
2 tablespoons vinegar or lemon
juice
1 cup salad oil

Put egg yolk and seasonings in small bowl and beat thoroughly. Add 1 tablespoon vinegar and beat again. Gradually beat in oil, adding ½ teaspoon at a time, until ¼ cup is used, then add 1 to 2 tablespoons at a time. As mixture thickens, add remaining vinegar. If oil is added too rapidly, mayonnaise will curdle. To remedy this at once beat curdled mixture gradually into a second egg yolk and continue as above. Keep in moderately cold place. Too much heat or freezing will cause oil to separate and come to top. If this happens, skim off oil. About 1¼ cups.

Garlic Mayonnaise

2 to 4 cloves garlic (according
   to taste)
2 egg yolks

2 cups olive oil
Pinch salt
Pepper to taste

Crush garlic and mix well with egg yolks. Beat until thick. Add oil gradually, as for mayonnaise, beating constantly until the mixture thickens. Add salt and pepper. Mix well. Chill. 2¼ cups.

Strawberry Peanut Mayonnaise

½ cup peanut butter
¼ cup mayonnaise
½ cup strawberry jam

3 tablespoons lemon juice
Dash salt

Combine all ingredients, mixing lightly to blend. Chill. Serve as dressing with fruit salad. 1½ cups.

Especially good with fish or vegetable salads.

Cucumber Dressing

1½ cups sour cream
1 cucumber, diced
3 tablespoons wine vinegar
2 tablespoons finely chopped
   fresh parsley

2 tablespoons finely chopped
   green pepper
½ teaspoon salt
Dash pepper

Place all ingredients in quart jar, cover, and shake well. Chill. 2¼ cups.

Fruit Salad Dressing

Juice ½ lemon
1 cup mayonnaise
2 tablespoons heavy cream,
   whipped

1 teaspoon grated lemon peel

Add lemon juice to mayonnaise. (For sweeter dressing, add 1 teaspoon honey). Fold in cream and lemon peel. About 1¼ cups.

NOTE: This is also good on avocado and vegetable combinations.

Poppy Seed Dressing

Mrs. Olen A. Bell, Sylva, North Carolina

2 teaspoons poppy seed	⅓ cup honey
½ cup sugar	6 tablespoons tarragon vinegar
1 teaspoon dry mustard	1 teaspoon onion
1 teaspoon paprika	3 tablespoons lemon juice
¼ teaspoon salt	1 cup salad oil

Soak poppy seed 2 hours in water; drain through cheesecloth. Mix dry ingredients; add honey, vinegar, onion, and lemon juice. Pour oil in very slowly, beating constantly; add drained poppy seed. This dressing is best made with the electric mixer. 1¾ cups.

Roquefort Dressing

Mrs. John K. O'Quinn, Decatur, Georgia

1 cup oil	¼ cup lemon juice
1 tablespoon minced onion	1 teaspoon paprika
1 clove garlic, cut in half	1 teaspoon sugar
⅓ cup crumbled Roquefort cheese	1 teaspoon salt
¼ cup vinegar	Dash ground pepper

Combine the oil, onion, and garlic and allow to stand for 1 hour. Remove the garlic, cream the cheese, and gradually add the oil mixture. Pour into a glass jar with a tight fitting cover. Add the remaining ingredients. Shake until thoroughly blended. Chill. Shake well before serving. 1¾ cups.

11

DESSERTS

Americans have a sweet tooth. They like to end the dinner meal with "a little something" sweet.

A good homemade pie or pudding can light up the eyes and tantalize the appetite. And you don't have to be an expert to bake them.

One of our favorite family desserts has always been egg custard. Its rich creamy texture combined with a flaky pastry is just right. Another we like to remember is dried fruit pie, made with dried apples or other fruit in an egg custard base, baked in pastry, and topped with "mile-high" meringue.

Banana pudding must have originated in the South. It has been a favorite since I can remember and the young generation today still "eat it up." I have a great-nephew, David, though, who adores the pudding if you leave out the bananas.

Cakes bring back memories of special occasions, exciting events, and, yes, just everyday experiences. They are reminders of birthdays, weddings, anniversaries, graduations, picnics, holidays, and Sunday dinners. It doesn't have to be a special kind of cake to fit into any of these occasions, although some have more association than others.

Baking a cake can be an exciting experience, and every young cook looks with pride at her success or cries over her failure. The first thing I ever cooked was a cake, with the help of a very under-standing neighbor. Many inexperienced cooks start with cakes.

In all of the forty years of my being a newspaper food editor the requests for cake recipes or the desire to share them has ranked near the top of the list. One of the most used recipes I recall is the 1-2-3-4 cake, basic and easy to remember. Mama used it for everything—from coconut, chocolate, caramel, lemon cheese, and even as a fruit cake base. It also made a quick sheet cake which she called "a little puddin'," served with fruit or sauce.

The best fruit cake in the world (I am sure it is because of my nostalgia for it) was made with homemade preserves and jams with oodles of home-grown black walnuts, hickory nuts, and pecans. Al-ways so moist and utterly elegant! My oldest brother, William, could just about do away with half a cake at a time, if it wasn't put out of sight.

Several cakes at a time on the side table or sideboard at Grandma's house was a common sight. You helped yourself to one or all. And with the family, grandchildren, and numerous other rela-tives and friends, they didn't last too long.

These recipes for cakes are memorable. We have shared them to-gether for many years. Some are heirlooms, some are modern. They range from simple to elegant and all are a joy to eat.

We have several ice cream suggestions. Since many people do not have a hand-cranked ice cream freezer, most of these recipes are de-signed so they can be frozen in the home freezer.

There is nothing tastier than a fruit cobbler or soufflé. Several of our favorites have been sent to us over and over again. Among them are blackberry, peach, and apple cobbler.

There is something for all in this section, enough to satisfy most ev-eryone's sweet tooth.

PIES AND PUDDINGS

Apple Cream Pie

Hazel Douglas, Monteagle, Tennessee

3 cups chopped tart apples
½ cup sugar
1 (9-inch) unbaked pie shell
1 tablespoon flour

¼ teaspoon mace
2 tablespoons butter
Cream Filling

Combine apples, sugar, flour, and mace. Spread apple mixture in pastry shell. Dot with butter and bake in very hot, 450-degree oven for 10 minutes. Reduce temperature to moderate, 350 degrees, and bake 35 minutes longer, or until apples are tender.

Cool and then cover with Cream Filling.

CREAM FILLING

1½ cups milk
¼ cup sugar
¼ teaspoon salt
3 tablespoons flour

1 egg, beaten
1 tablespoon butter
½ teaspoon vanilla

To make filling, scald 1 cup milk over boiling water. Mix sugar, salt, flour, and remaining milk together. Stir into hot milk and cook slowly until thickened, stirring constantly. Cover and cook over boiling water for 4 minutes.

Add egg slowly to mixture and cook 1 minute longer. Add butter and vanilla. Cool. Pour over apples in pastry shell. 6 servings.

Cantaloupe Pie

Stone Mountain Inn, Stone Mountain, Georgia

1 cantaloupe, peeled and diced
1 cup sugar
Cornstarch

1 tablespoon vanilla
1 (8-inch) baked pie shell

Heat cantaloupe in top of double boiler over boiling water until very hot. Drain off excess liquid. Add sugar and enough cornstarch to thicken. Stir in vanilla and pour into pie shell. Cool. Garnish with whipped cream to serve. 6 servings.

This pie is hard to resist. It is so handsome and so good. It is one of the wonderful desserts served at this unique restaurant owned by Herb Fraub.

Black-bottom Pie

The Pirate's House, Savannah, Georgia

2 cups milk	1¼ tablespoons plain gelatin
½ cup plus 4 tablespoons sugar	soaked in ¼ cup cold water
1¼ tablespoons cornstarch	4 tablespoons rum
4 eggs, separated	Whipped cream
1¼ ounces chocolate	Shaved chocolate
1 teaspoon vanilla	
1 (9-inch) Chocolate Cracker	
Crust	

Put milk in top of double boiler. Combine ½ cup sugar, cornstarch, and egg yolks. Add to milk. Stir over boiling water until custard coats the spoon. Remove 1 cup of custard and add to it the chocolate and vanilla. Pour into chocolate crust. Add gelatin to remaining custard. Cool; add rum. Beat the egg whites, gradually adding the 4 tablespoons sugar. When stiff, but not dry, fold into custard. Pile on top of chocolate custard. Refrigerate for 8 to 10 hours. Decorate with whipped cream and shaved chocolate. 6 servings.

CHOCOLATE CRACKER CRUST

Combine 4 tablespoons melted butter with 1¼ cups ground chocolate crackers. Press into 9-inch pie pan. Chill.

Mrs. Hansen sent this authentic recipe to us. She says corn meal was not used in the custard mix at that time.

Williamsburg Chess Pie

Mrs. E. L. Hansen, Atlanta, Georgia

3 eggs, separated	Vanilla or lemon flavoring
1 cup sugar, plus 3 tablespoons	1 (8-inch) unbaked pie shell
¼ cup butter	
3 tablespoons light cream	
(evaporated milk can be	
used)	

Beat yolks very light. Beat in 1 cup sugar. Melt butter and beat in. Add cream and flavoring. Pour into uncooked pastry and bake 25 to 30 minutes at 350 degrees. Let settle.

Beat egg whites, gradually adding remaining sugar, until soft peaks are formed. Spread over baked pie and bake at 375 degrees 10 to 12 minutes or until golden brown. 6 servings.

Chocolate Angel Pie

Mrs. Robert A. Reeves, Millen, Georgia

2 egg whites	½ cup finely chopped walnuts
⅛ teaspoon salt	or pecans
⅛ teaspoon cream of tartar	½ teaspoon vanilla
½ cup sugar	Filling

Combine egg whites, salt, and cream of tartar and beat until foamy. Add sugar 2 tablespoons at a time, beating well after each addition. Continue beating until very stiff peaks form. Fold in nuts and ½ teaspoon vanilla. Spoon into lightly greased 8-inch pie pan and make a nestlike shell, building up sides to about ½ inch above the pan. Bake in a slow oven, 300 degrees, 50 to 55 minutes. Cool.

FILLING

1 (4-ounce) package German	1 teaspoon vanilla
sweet chocolate	1 cup whipping cream
3 tablespoons water	

Melt chocolate in water over low heat, stirring constantly. Cool until thickened. Add 1 teaspoon vanilla. Then whip cream and fold into the chocolate mixture. Pile into meringue shell. Chill for about 2 hours. 6 to 8 servings.

Coconut Caramel Pie

Mrs. W. W. Cardwell, Marietta, Georgia

¾ cup sugar, plus ⅓ cup	½ teaspoon vanilla
5 tablespoons flour	1 (9-inch) baked pie shell
¼ teaspoon salt	½ cup heavy cream, whipped
2 cups milk	and sweetened
3 egg yolks, slightly beaten	½ cup flaked coconut
1 tablespoon butter	

Combine ¾ cup sugar, flour, and salt in top of double boiler. Add milk and egg yolks, mixing thoroughly. Place over rapidly boiling water and cook 10 minutes, stirring constantly. Remove from heat but allow to remain over hot water.

Caramelize remaining ⅓ cup sugar by placing in iron skillet over medium and stirring constantly until melted and straw-colored. Add at once to thickened mixture, stirring until blended. Add butter and vanilla and cool. Turn ino 9-inch baked pie shell. Garnish with a ring of whipped cream and sprinkle cream with coconut. 6 to 8 servings.

This is a long-time family favorite of the Kaley family. Several generations have used it.

Corn Meal Pie

Frank M. Kaley, Headmaster, Pace Academy, Atlanta, Georgia

½ cup margarine
1 cup sugar
1 egg, separated

½ cup milk
3 tablespoons corn meal
1 (8-inch) unbaked pie shell

Melt margarine and blend in sugar. Beat egg yolk, add milk, and blend well. Beat egg white until stiff and fold into margarine mixture, then fold in corn meal quickly. Pour into unbaked pastry shell and bake at 350 degrees for 30 minutes. 6 servings.

Many requests have come in through the years for this unusual and interesting pie.

Cracker Pie

3 egg whites
1 cup sugar
1 cup unsalted cracker crumbs
1 teaspoon baking powder

1 teaspoon vanilla
1 cup chopped pecans or
  walnuts
1 cup heavy cream, whipped

Grease 8-inch pie plate. In mixing bowl beat egg whites until foamy. Gradually add sugar; beat until stiff and glossy. Fold in crumbs, baking powder, vanilla, and nuts. Turn into pie plate. Bake in 350 degree oven for 35 minutes. Cool. Cover with whipped cream, refrigerate for 2 hours. 6 servings.

Old-fashioned Custard Pie

4 egg yolks
1¼ cups sugar
2 cups milk, scalded
¼ teaspoon salt

1 teaspoon vanilla
1 (9-inch) unbaked pie shell
4 egg whites

Beat egg yolks well. Combine with ¾ cup sugar and beat until lemon-colored. Pour hot, but not boiling milk slowly over this mixture, stirring constantly. Add salt and vanilla flavoring. Bake pastry shell 3 minutes before pouring in egg mixture. Bake 15 minutes at 400 degrees or until firm.

For meringue beat egg whites until stiff but not dry. Beat in remaining ½ cup sugar. Place on custard and bake to a golden brown at 350 degrees. 6 to 8 servings.

Simple Egg Pie

Pastry for 1 9-inch crust pie
3 eggs
1½ cups sugar

½ cup butter
½ cup buttermilk

Line pan with pastry and partially cook. Beat eggs well, add sugar, melted butter, and buttermilk. Pour into crust. Bake until golden brown at 350 degrees about 45 minutes or until set. 2 to 4 servings.

Years ago, when travel was more of a problem, people often traveled long distances to attend funerals, so a hearty meal was served before they started the long journey back. Since raisins were readily available, raisin pie was served so often it came to be called "Funeral Pie."

Funeral Pie or Raisin Pie

1 2-cup recipe plain pastry
1 cup seeded raisins
2 cups water
1½ cups sugar
4 tablespoons flour

¼ teaspoon salt
3 tablespoons lemon juice
2 tablespoons grated lemon rind
1 egg, well beaten

With half the pastry line an 8-inch pie pan. Save remaining pastry for top of pie.

Wash raisins and soak in cold water for 3 hours. Drain. Combine raisins, water, sugar, flour, salt, lemon juice and rind, and egg. Mix thoroughly and cook over hot water for 15 minutes, stirring occasionally. Cool. Pour into pastry shell. Cover with narrow strips of remaining pastry crisscrossed. Bake in a hot oven, 450 degrees, for 10 minutes. Reduce heat to moderate, 350 degrees, and bake 30 minutes longer. 6 servings.

Key Lime Pie

Mrs. Harry A. Ray III, Atlanta, Georgia

1 (3-ounce) package
   lime-flavored gelatin
1 cup boiling water
1 or 2 teaspoons grated lemon
   rind
½ cup lime juice
1 egg yolk
1⅓ cups sweetened condensed
   milk
1 teaspoon aromatic bitters
1 egg white
Few drops green food coloring
   (optional)
1 (9-inch) baked pie shell,
   cooled

Dissolve gelatin in boiling water. Add lime rind and juice. Beat egg yolk slightly. Slowly add gelatin, stirring constantly. Add milk and bitters, stirring until blended. Chill until slightly thickened. Beat egg white until stiff peaks form. Then fold into gelatin mixture. Add food coloring. Pour into pastry shell. Chill until firm. Garnish with whipped cream or prepared whipped topping and lime slices, if desired. 6 to 8 servings.

Lemon Pie

Mrs. John F. McMullan, Hartwell, Georgia

2¼ cups sugar
½ cup flour
Grated rind of 2 lemons
2 cups boiling water
8 eggs, separated
⅓ cup lemon juice
2 (8-inch) baked pie shells

Combine 1½ cups sugar, flour, lemon rind, and water. Cook until thick and clear, about 5 minutes. Add slightly beaten egg yolks and lemon juice; cook 5 minutes longer.

During this cooking time beat egg whites. Add remaining ¾ cup sugar gradually after egg whites become slightly stiff. Continue beating meringue until stiff. Fold half into cooked mixture and put into two pie shells. Cover with remaining meringue and bake about 10 minutes at 325 degrees or until meringue is golden brown. 12 servings.

Macaroon Pie

Mrs. William L. Jones, Jackson, Georgia

1 (9-inch) unbaked pie shell	*2 tablespoons butter*
¼ teaspoon salt	*1 teaspoon lemon juice*
3 eggs, separated	*¼ teaspoon almond extract*
1½ cups sugar	*1½ cups flaked coconut*
¼ cup milk	

Add salt to egg yolks. Beat until thick and lemon-colored. Add sugar, half a cup at a time, beating well after each addition. Add milk, butter, lemon juice, and almond extract. Blend well.

Fold in coconut and stiffly beaten egg whites. Turn into pie shell. Bake at 375 degrees, 50 minutes or until knife inserted comes out clean. 6 servings.

This is a real family favorite. We always had plenty of home-dried fruits and stewed fruit custard pie was ever in demand.

Dried Peach Custard Pie

1 (9-inch) unbaked pie shell	*¼ cup sugar*
2 cups mashed and sweetened	*2 cups milk*
cooked dried peaches	*2 tablespoons margarine*
4 egg yolks	*2 tablespoons water*
4 egg whites	*4 tablespoons sugar*

Spread the peaches in pie shell. Beat 4 egg yolks and 2 egg whites together with sugar. Add milk. Pour over peaches. Dot with margarine. Bake in 350-degree oven until custard is set and lightly browned, 20 to 25 minutes.

Add 2 tablespoons water to remaining 2 egg whites and beat until peaks form. Add 4 tablespoons sugar, slowly beating until smooth and glossy. Spread over custard. Lower heat and bake until meringue is browned, about 8 minutes. 6 servings.

An old-fashioned delight. We used to carry these in our school lunch box.

Fried Peach Pies

Mrs. Zack Corley, Thomaston, Georgia

> *1½ cups dried peaches*
> *4 cups water*
> *½ to ¾ cup sugar*

Simmer peaches in water until tender and easily broken with a fork. Stir in sugar to taste. The pies turn out better if the peach filling sets overnight.

TO MAKE PASTRY

> *3 cups self-rising flour*
> *3 tablespoons softened shortening*
> *¾ cup ice water*
> *Fat for baking*

Set aside ¼ cup flour. To rest of flour blend in shortening with fork. Gradually work in ice water a little at a time. Work in the ¼ cup of flour while rolling dough on waxed paper.

Roll dough to ⅛-inch thickness. Cut in circles using a saucer for pattern. Place 2 tablespoons peach filling on half of circle. Fold other half over and seal edges with fork. Prick top of pies three or four times with fork.

Put fat ¼ inch deep in baking pan and place pies in it one layer deep. Bake at 450 degrees about 12 minutes until brown on bottom. Carefully turn pies over and brown other side. Remove from pan and drain on absorbent paper. Serve warm with ice cream or let cool and serve at room temperature. 8 servings.

Georgia Peanut Pie

20 round buttery crackers, rolled fine
1 cup sugar
1 cup chopped husked roasted peanuts

3 egg whites
¼ teaspoon cream of tartar
1 teaspoon vanilla
Flour

Mix crackers with ½ cup sugar and peanuts. Beat egg whites until stiff, add cream of tartar, remaining ½ cup sugar, and vanilla.

Fold in peanut-cracker mixture. Pour into a greased 9-inch pan sprinkled with flour, and bake 25 minutes at 350 degrees.

Garnish with whipped cream and grated bitter chocolate or chopped roasted peanuts. 6 to 8 servings.

Peanut Butter Chiffon Pie

Mrs. Vivian Webb, for
Georgia School Food Service Training Program

1 envelope plain gelatin
1 cup cold water
2 egg yolks, well beaten
½ cup sugar or light corn syrup
½ teaspoon salt

½ cup peanut butter
½ teaspoon vanilla
2 egg whites
1 (8-inch) baked pie shell or Crumb piecrust

Soften gelatin in ¼ cup cold water. Combine egg yolks, half of the sugar or corn syrup, ¼ cup water, and salt in top of a double boiler. Blend. Place over boiling water and beat constantly with rotary beater until thick and fluffy. Add softened gelatin. Cool. Place peanut butter in a bowl. Beat in remaining water gradually. Add egg-yolk mixture and vanilla. Blend with beater. Chill until slightly thickened. Beat egg whites until foamy. Add remaining sugar or syrup slowly. Beat until stiff. Fold in peanut mixture. Turn into baked pie shell. Chill until firm. 6 servings.

CRUMB PIECRUST

1¼ cups bread crumbs
5 tablespoons margarine, softened
2 tablespoons (about) milk

Mix crumbs and margarine. Add enough milk to form ball and hold crumbs together. Press into greased 8-inch pie pan and bake 10 minutes at 350 degrees.

This resembles graham cracker crust but does not crumble when cut. Enough for 1 (8-inch) piecrust.

In our state, where peaches and pecans grow in abundance, this recipe was assured of immediate success.

Peach-pecan Pie

¼ cup soft butter
½ cup sugar
2 tablespoons flour
½ cup corn syrup
¼ teaspoon salt

3 eggs
1½ cups diced peaches
1 (9-inch) unbaked pie shell
Nut Crumb Topping

Cream together butter, sugar, and flour. Stir in syrup and salt. Mix well. Beat in eggs one at a time. Add peaches.

Pour into pie shell and sprinkle with topping. Bake at 375 degrees for 35 minutes or until firm in center. 6 servings.

NUT CRUMB TOPPING

Combine ¼ cup flour and ¼ cup brown sugar. Work in 2 tablespoons soft butter until crumbly. Add ½ cup coarsely chopped pecans.

Grandma's Pumpkin Pie

1 (9-inch) unbaked pie shell
1½ cups pumpkin
¾ cup sugar
½ teaspoon salt
½ teaspoon ginger
1 teaspoon cinnamon

½ teaspoon nutmeg
¼ teaspoon cloves
3 eggs, slightly beaten
1¼ cups milk
1 (6-ounce) can evaporated
   milk

Make sure edges of pastry shell are crimped high because of generous amount of filling.

Blend all ingredients together thoroughly. Bake in 400-degree oven for 50 minutes. 6 servings.

So very rich and sinfully good.

Sour Cream Pecan Pie

4 egg yolks
2 cups granulated sugar
2 cups sour cream
½ cup sifted flour
½ teaspoon lemon extract
¼ teaspoon salt
2 (9-inch) unbaked pie shells
4 egg whites
2 cups brown sugar
2 cups broken pecan meats

Combine egg yolks, granulated sugar, sour cream, flour, lemon extract, and salt. Cook over boiling water until thickened, about 45 minutes. Spoon mixture into pie shells.

Beat egg whites and brown sugar. Stir in pecan meats. Spread over pie filling and bake at 325 degrees until brown, about 15 minutes. 12 servings.

Ice-box Persimmon Pie

Mrs. A. M. Moon, Mableton, Georgia

4 cups persimmon pulp
½ teaspoon cinnamon
1 teaspoon nutmeg
1½ teaspoons lemon rind
1 package unflavored gelatin
½ cup water
½ cup orange juice
1 (9-inch) graham cracker
crust
Whipped cream (optional)

Mash persimmons through colander. Measure and have 1 quart of pulp. Add spices, lemon rind, and gelatin that has been dissolved in the water. Add orange juice and pour into graham cracker crust. May be served with whipped cream. 6 servings.

Strawberry Cream Pie

4 cups hulled strawberries
3 tablespoons cornstarch
1 cup sugar
2 tablespoons lemon juice
⅛ teaspoon salt
1 (9-inch) baked pie shell
Whipped cream

Crush half of berries with potato masher or fork. Stir in corn-starch, sugar, lemon juice, and salt. Cook over medium heat until mixture is thickened and clear. Cool.

Cut remaining 2 cups of berries in halves, reserving 6 whole ber-ries. Fold berry halves into the cooked mixture. Pour into pie shell and chill.

To serve, garnish with puffs of whipped cream and a few choice berries. 6 servings.

An old, old favorite dating back several generations and still being enjoyed.

Vinegar Pie
Mrs. Sam Carithers, Dalton, Georgia

2 egg yolks	¼ cup flour
2 cups water	1½ cups sugar
½ cup vinegar	½ teaspoon lemon flavoring
1 tablespoon butter, melted	1 (8-inch) unbaked pie shell

Combine egg yolks, water, vinegar, and butter. Mix flour and sugar and stir into vinegar mixture. Add lemon flavoring and pour mixture into pie shell.

Bake in very hot 450-degree oven for 10 minutes. Then reduce heat to 350 degrees and bake 20 to 30 minutes longer. Cool. 6 serv-ings.

Apple Date Pudding
Mrs. W. R. Mercier, Blue Ridge, Georgia

3 cups peeled cored apples	1 cup sugar
⅔ cup chopped dates	⅔ cup water
⅔ cup chopped pecans	Dash cinnamon and nutmeg

Cook above ingredients together until apples are just tender. Set aside to cool.

1½ cups flour	1 cup brown sugar
½ teaspoon soda	1 tablespoon vanilla
½ teaspoon salt	¾ cup shortening
1½ cups rolled oats	1 cup whipped cream

Sift flour, soda, and salt together. Add rolled oats, brown sugar, and vanilla. Cut in shortening as for pastry. Press half of mixture in greased 8×10-inch baking dish. Arrange apple mixture over this, top with remaining crumb mixture. Bake at 350 degrees for about 30 minutes or until browned. Top with whipped cream. 8 servings.

Banana Pudding
Mrs. L. L. Phillips, Soperton, Georgia

1 cup sugar, plus 2 tablespoons	*1 teaspoon vanilla*
½ cup flour	*Dash of salt*
2 cups boiling water	*Vanilla wafers*
2 eggs, separated	*Bananas*
1 tablespoon butter	

Mix 1 cup sugar and flour well. Slowly add boiling water, stirring constantly. Over low heat cook until mixture begins to thicken. Stir in beaten egg yolks. Continue to cook until thick. Add butter, vanilla, and salt. Cool.

In a quart-size casserole place a layer of vanilla wafers. Cover with a layer of bananas, then a layer of sauce. Repeat. Beat egg whites until stiff, add remaining 2 tablespoons sugar. Spread over pudding top and bake in 325-degree oven until golden brown. 6 servings.

Baked Egg Custard

3 cups milk	*1 teaspoon vanilla*
6 tablespoons sugar	*1 tablespoon butter or*
¼ teaspoon salt	*margarine*
3 eggs, slightly beaten	*Ground nutmeg or cinnamon*

Scald milk with sugar and salt. Stir slowly into eggs and add vanilla. Strain into custard cups or large baking dish, dot with butter or margarine. Add a dash or two of nutmeg or cinnamon. Set cups in a shallow pan of hot water almost to top of cups. Set on center rack of oven and bake at 325 degrees until done, about 30 minutes. To test for doneness insert knife in center of custard. When knife comes out clean custard is done. 6 servings.

Chocolate Bread Pudding
Mrs. A. L. Kenyon, Morrow, Georgia

5 cups diced fresh bread or 3⅓   3 eggs, separated
  cups stale bread   ½ cup sugar, plus 6 tablespoons
3 cups warm milk   1½ teaspoons vanilla
1½ ounces chocolate, melted   ½ teaspoon nutmeg, optional
¼ teaspoon salt, plus ⅛   ¼ cup raisins or nutmeats,
  teaspoon   optional

Soak bread 15 minutes in warm milk to which melted chocolate has been added. Add ¼ teaspoon salt. Combine and beat well the egg yolks, ½ cup sugar, 1 teaspoon vanilla, and nutmeg. Add raisins or nutmeats. Pour these ingredients over soaked bread. Stir lightly with a fork until well blended. Place in a baking dish set in a pan of hot water in a moderate 350-degree oven for 45 minutes. Cool pudding. Cover with a meringue made of 3 egg whites, ⅛ teaspoon salt, 6 tablespoons sugar, and ½ teaspoon vanilla. Bake in a slow oven, 300 degrees, until meringue is set, about 15 minutes. Serve hot with a chocolate or vanilla sauce if desired. 8 servings.

NOTE: Vary the pudding by substituting brown sugar for white sugar and by using maple flavoring instead of vanilla, omitting nutmeg, raisins, and chocolate. Another variation: Use coconut and lemon flavoring.

This recipe dates back to our early settlers. It is still used and enjoyed regularly in many sections.

Syrup Custard

4 tablespoons (½ stick) butter   ½ cup milk
2 tablespoons flour   1 teaspoon vanilla
3 eggs   1 (8-inch) unbaked pie shell
1 cup cane syrup

Melt butter, stir flour into melted butter. Combine butter mixture with beaten eggs, syrup, milk, and vanilla. Beat all together with rotary beater. Pour into unbaked pie shell. Bake 10 minutes at 450 degrees, then reduce heat to 375 degrees and bake 15 to 20 minutes longer or until set. Sprinkle top with nutmeg if desired. 6 servings.

This recipe is so simple it's unbelievable how delicious it is. Mrs. Robinson says, "It's been in our family longer than I care to admit." If there is any left over, it's just as delicious cold served with or without whipped cream.

Robinson's Date Pudding
Mrs. William M. Robinson, Atlanta, Georgia

2 cups boiling water
1 cup packed brown sugar
About 2 tablespoons butter
1½ cups flour
1 cup white sugar
2 teaspoons baking powder

Pinch of salt
¾ cup milk
1 cup cut-up dates
½ cup nuts, if desired
Whipped cream

Mix water, brown sugar, and butter. Heat to boiling. Combine remaining ingredients to make batter. Spread in greased baking dish about 7×22 inches and pour syrup mixture over top. Bake at 350 degrees for 25 to 30 minutes, until light brown and syrup mixture is thick and bubbly. Top with whipped cream. 6 to 8 servings.

Persimmon Pudding
J. Howard Hinshaw, Newnan, Georgia

3 cups persimmon pulp
2 eggs
1 cup milk
2 cups self-rising flour

¼ cup sorghum molasses
¼ teaspoon almond or vanilla
    flavoring
¼ cup melted butter

Combine all ingredients, beating until lumps are gone. Divide batter into two small baking dishes, and bake for about 40 minutes at 425 to 450 degrees.

Pudding is done when it rises like cornbread and crusts over. Remove from oven and allow to cool. Cut into squares and serve as a dessert with ice cream or whipped cream or eat it with vegetables. 8 servings.

Coconut may be added to the batter to give a different flavor. Omit other flavorings when coconut is added. The sorghum molasses also may be omitted. With the molasses omitted the pudding has a distinctive country flavor.

Lemon Fluff

Mrs. Carl Sanders, Former First Lady of Georgia, Atlanta, Georgia

3 (3 ounces each) packages
   ladyfingers
1 cup lemon juice
1 cup sugar
6 eggs, separated

2 envelopes unflavored gelatin
½ cup water
1 pint whipping cream
12 lemon peel twists

Line bottom and sides of springform pan with lady fingers. Mix lemon juice, sugar, and egg yolks in top of double boiler. Cook over boiling water until mixture coats spoon. Soak gelatin in water and add to egg mixture. Stir until gelatin dissolves. Whip egg whites; fold into cooled custard. Whip cream. Fold into egg mixture and pour into mold. Refrigerate until set. Garnish with twisted lemon peel. May be made a day in advance of serving. 12 servings.

A favorite in the peach states.

Peach Crisp

6 or 7 large peaches
Juice 1 lemon
½ cup sifted flour
¾ cup rolled oats

½ cup packed brown sugar
⅓ cup margarine
Hard Sauce

Put peeled, sliced peaches in shallow baking dish and sprinkle with lemon juice. Mix flour, oats, and brown sugar. Cut in margarine with pastry blender. Press over peaches. Bake in 325-degree oven for 30 minutes or until peaches are tender. Serve warm with Hard Sauce. 8 to 10 servings.

HARD SAUCE

¼ cup butter
¾ cup confectioners' sugar

½ teaspoon vanilla
1 tablespoon hot water

Rub butter with back of spoon until very creamy. Stir in sugar gradually. Add vanilla. Stir in hot water a few drops at a time. Chill thoroughly.

Viennese Strawberry Mold

*Mrs. Robert M. Bunzl, wife of
Austrian consul general, Atlanta, Georgia*

1¼ tablespoons unflavored
  gelatin
½ cup cold water
2 cups heavy cream
¾ cup sifted confectioner's
  sugar

¾ cup small pieces fresh
  strawberries
3 teaspoons vanilla extract
¼ teaspoon almond extract

Soften gelatin in water 5 minutes. Then dissolve in top of double boiler over boiling water. Chill until it begins to thicken. Whip cream and fold in sugar, strawberries, vanilla and almond extract, and gelatin. Pour into 4-cup mold and chill until firm. Decorate, if desired, with additional strawberries and whipped cream.

Soft Boiled Custard

6 egg yolks
½ cup sugar
4 cups milk, scalded

Beat egg yolks lightly and add sugar. Pour milk over egg yolks a little at a time in top of double boiler. Cook over boiling water until mixture coats spoon. Remove from heat and cool. 4 cups.

The Pink House is a historic place in the heart of Savannah. It is said to be built of stone brought over from England as ballast when the ships came to pick up cotton.

Carolina Trifle

The Pink House, Savannah, Georgia

1 pint heavy cream, whipped
1 quart soft boiled custard
Almond or brandy flavoring or
  sherry wine

1 (1 pound) lemon-flavored
  sponge or pound cake

Flavor both the whipped cream and boiled custard with either almond or brandy flavoring or sherry. Slice cake very thin and place a slice on dish. Cover it with layer of custard, then thin layer of whipped cream. Repeat, using all cake slices. Top with layer of whipped cream. Chill and serve. 6 to 8 servings.

CAKES

We think of this as a real country-style cake, for we always had plenty of home-dried apples. This cake went to many an all-day meeting or family reunion.

Old-fashioned Stack Cake

2 cups sugar	6 cups sifted flour
1 cup butter or shortening	1 teaspoon salt
2 eggs	½ cup buttermilk
1 teaspoon soda	1 teaspoon vanilla
3 teaspoons baking powder	

Cream sugar and butter. Add eggs, one at a time, beating well after each addition. Combine dry ingredients and add alternately to batter with buttermilk and vanilla; mix. Divide batter into six equal portions.

Put batter into six greased 9-inch pans. Bake at 450 degrees for 10 to 15 minutes. Cool.

APPLE FILLING

1 pound dry apples	2 teaspoons cinnamon
1 cup brown sugar	½ teaspoon cloves
½ cup granulated sugar	½ teaspoon allspice

Cover apples with water and cook until tender; mash. Add remaining ingredients; mix. Spread each of the layers except the top one with apple filling. Stack layers. Let cake stand for 12 hours before cutting. 12 to 14 servings.

Mr. Wingate is one of north Georgia's apple growers.

Fresh Apple Cake

Mrs. William G. Wingate, Ellijay, Georgia

3 cups plain flour	2 cups sugar
1½ teaspoons soda	1¼ cups salad oil
½ teaspoon salt	2 teaspoons vanilla
1 teaspoon cinnamon	5 cups chopped apples
2 eggs	1 cup chopped nuts

Sift together twice, the flour, soda, salt, and cinnamon. Beat eggs and sugar until creamy; add oil and vanilla and beat until smooth. Add sifted flour mixture and mix to form stiff dough. Stir in apples and nuts. Pour into greased and floured 10-inch tube pan. Bake at 350 degrees for 1 hour or until done and browned. 12 to 14 servings.

Banana Cake

Mrs. Ralph C. Bunn, Atlanta, Georgia

½ cup shortening	½ teaspoon soda
1½ cups sugar	4 tablespoons sour milk
1 teaspoon vanilla	1 cup banana pulp
2 eggs, well beaten	Seven-minute Frosting
2 cups cake flour	12 Brazil nuts, chopped
½ teaspoon salt	

Thoroughly cream shortening and sugar; add vanilla and eggs. Beat until fluffy. Add sifted dry ingredients alternately with milk and banana pulp, beating well after each addition. Bake in greased, 8-inch square pan in moderate oven, 350 degrees. Makes 2 layers. When cake is cool, frost with Seven-minute Frosting to which Brazil nuts have been added. 12 servings.

Seven-minute Frosting

2 egg whites	⅓ cup water
1½ cups sugar	2 teaspoons light corn syrup
Dash salt	1 teaspoon vanilla

Combine egg whites, sugar, salt, water, and corn syrup in top of double boiler. Beat about 1 minute, or until thoroughly mixed. Then place over boiling water and beat constantly with rotary beater or at high speed of electric mixer 7 minutes, or until frosting stands in stiff peaks, stirring frosting up from bottom and sides of pan occasionally with rubber scraper, spatula, or spoon.

Remove from boiling water. For a very smooth and satiny frosting, pour at once into a large bowl for final beating. Then add vanilla and beat 1 minute, or until thick enough to spread. 4½ cups frosting.

My husband's very favorite cake. On his birthday he always gets a lemon cheese cake.

Lemon Cheese Cake

1 cup butter
2 cups sugar
4 eggs, separated
1 cup milk

3 cups cake flour
1 teaspoon vanilla
½ teaspoon soda, dissolved in 1 tablespoon water

Cream butter and sugar. Add two of the egg yolks, one at a time, beating well after each addition. (Other two yolks are used in filling.)

Add milk and flour, alternately; then vanilla and soda-water. Fold in four well-beaten egg whites and bake in three 8-inch layers at 350 degrees for about 30 minutes.

FILLING

2 cups sugar
2 grated peeled apples
2 tablespoons butter
Juice 2 lemons
Grated rind 1 lemon (be sure not to grate the white pulp under the rind or filling will be bitter—grate only the outer yellow part)

Fresh grated coconut (optional)

Mix all ingredients plus 2 remaining egg yolks and cook about 5 minutes, stirring constantly. Cool, spread between layers, on top and sides of cake. A little fresh, grated coconut added to filling just before spreading on cake adds a delicious flavor.

We don't know why this is called lemon cheese—except for its color. There is no cheese in it—but there's no cheese in the moon either—so to us in the Southeast this is lemon cheese cake. 12 to 14 servings.

Sour Cream Bundt Cake

Mrs. J. C. Steinmetz, Niskey Lake, Ben Hill, Georgia

1 cup butter	*½ teaspoon vanilla extract*
3 cups granulated sugar	*¼ teaspoon almond extract*
6 eggs	*¼ teaspoon mace*
3 cups flour	*2 tablespoons cocoa*
½ teaspoon salt	*¼ cup confectioners' sugar*
¼ teaspoon soda	*⅓ cup ground almonds*
1 (8-ounce) carton commercial sour cream	

Cream butter and granulated sugar, add eggs one at a time, beating well after each. Combine flour, salt, and soda and sift together. Add to butter mixture in three parts alternately with sour cream, beginning and ending with dry ingredients. Add vanilla, almond extract, and mace. Combine cocoa, powdered sugar, and almonds and when spooning batter into bundt pan fold mixture in with cutting strokes. Bake at 325 degrees for 1½ hours. 12 servings.

The Original Bourbon Cake

From The Bourbon Institute, New York

2 cups red candied cherries	*6 eggs, separated*
1½ cups seedless raisins	*5 cups sifted cake flour*
2 cups Bourbon	*2 teaspoons nutmeg*
1½ cups butter or margarine	*1 teaspoon baking powder*
2⅓ cups granulated sugar	*4 cups (about 1 pound)*
2⅓ cups brown sugar	*chopped pecans*

Combine cherries, raisins, and Bourbon. Cover and let stand overnight. Drain fruits; reserve Bourbon. Cream butter or margarine and sugar together until light. Add egg yolks and beat well. Combine ½ cup flour, nutmeg, baking powder, and pecans. Add remaining flour and Bourbon alternately to butter mixture, beating well after each addition. Beat egg whites stiff but not dry, fold into batter mixture, then fold in the soaked fruits and pecan-flour mixture. Turn into greased 10-inch tube pan lined with greased paper or foil. Bake in slow oven, 275 degrees, for 3½ hours. Cool. Remove from pan.

Chiffon Cake

Mrs. Woodrow W. Hendrix, Nahunta, Georgia

2 cups sifted self-rising flour	*½ teaspoon lemon extract*
1½ cups sugar	*1 teaspoon vanilla extract*
½ cup vegetable oil	*½ teaspoon cream of tartar*
7 or 8 eggs, separated	*Lemon Glaze*
¾ cup cold water	

Sift flour again with sugar. Add oil, egg yolks, water, and extracts and beat until smooth. In large mixer bowl place egg whites and cream of tartar and beat until very stiff. Pour flour mixture over beaten egg whites, and *fold* gently until blended. *Do not stir.*

Pour into ungreased 10-inch tube pan and bake 55 minutes at 325 degrees. Increase temperature to 350 degrees and bake 10 to 15 minutes longer or until top springs back when lightly touched. Turn upside down over neck of bottle, if pan doesn't have supports, and leave until cool. Gently loosen from sides of pan and pour Lemon Glaze over cake. 12 servings.

LEMON GLAZE

Combine 1 cup confectioners' sugar with grated rind and juice of one lemon. Makes enough to glaze a 10-inch cake.

Spicy Chiffon Cake

Use recipe for Chiffon Cake, omitting lemon and vanilla extracts, and sift the following with the flour and sugar: ¼ teaspoon powdered cloves, 1 teaspoon cinnamon, ½ teaspoon nutmeg, and ½ teaspoon allspice. Spread Creamy Nut Icing over inverted cooled cake. 12 servings.

CREAMY NUT ICING

½ cup butter or margarine
2½ tablespoons flour
½ cup milk
½ cup brown sugar

2 cups confectioners' sugar
½ teaspoon vanilla
½ cup chopped pecans

Melt butter, blend in flour, and add milk slowly; stirring, bring to boil and boil 1 minute. Add brown sugar and stir until dissolved. Remove from heat, add confectioners' sugar, vanilla, and pecans. Makes enough icing for a 10-inch cake.

So moist and delightfully good.

Carrot Cake

Mrs. Robert Christian, Atlanta, Georgia

2 cups sugar
1½ cups salad oil
4 eggs
3 cups grated carrots
2 cups self-rising flour

1 cup chopped nuts
1 teaspoon cinnamon
1 tablespoon vanilla
Glaze

Cream sugar and oil. Add eggs one at a time. Add carrots, flour, nuts which have been floured, cinnamon, and vanilla. Bake in a 10-inch tube pan at 325 to 350 degrees for about 1 hour. Spread glaze on cake while both are still hot. 12 to 14 servings.

GLAZE

1 cup sugar
½ cup buttermilk
1 teaspoon soda

1 tablespoon corn syrup
Dash of salt

Put all ingredients in saucepan. Cook until thick, about 2 or 3 minutes. ¾ cup glaze.

A much requested recipe—a delightful cake.

Black Forest Cake

1½ cups (about 10) egg whites
¼ teaspoon salt
1½ cups granulated sugar, plus
    2 tablespoons
½ pound blanched almonds,
    finely grated or ground
2 tablespoons flour

5 squares semi-sweet chocolate
1½ teaspoons plain gelatin
6 tablespoons cold water
3 cups heavy cream
2 to 3 tablespoons
    confectioners' sugar

Beat egg whites with salt until creamy; gradually add ½ cup plus 2 tablespoons sugar, beating until soft peaks form. Fold in almonds and flour. Pour into three 9-inch cake pans lined with brown paper. Bake at 250 degrees for 1½ hours. Turn off heat. One at a time, remove cake layers from the oven, turn out on rack, and peel off paper at once.

Cool thoroughly. Melt 4 squares chocolate and brush or spread chocolate on top of layers. Let stand until chocolate is firm.

In top of double boiler soften gelatin in cold water, put over hot water, and stir until gelatin is dissolved; cool; add gelatin to cream and whip until almost stiff. Gradually add remaining 1 cup sugar and beat until stiff. Spread cream between cake layers and spread over top and sides. Shave remaining square of chocolate and sprinkle on top of cake. Sift the confectioners' sugar lightly on cake. Keep in refrigerator. 16 servings.

Recipes for chocolate cake are among the most popular. This one is especially good and easy to make.

Chocolate Cake

Mrs. L. H. Gillespie, Athens, Georgia

3 squares chocolate
½ cup hot water
½ cup soft shortening
1⅔ cups sugar
3 eggs
2⅛ cups sifted flour

¼ teaspoon soda
2¼ teaspoons baking powder
1 teaspoon salt
1 cup buttermilk
Chocolate Butter Icing

Grease and flour two 9-inch layer cake pans. Combine chocolate and hot water, stir until thick. Cool. Cream shortening and sugar together. Add eggs and beat thoroughly; blend in cooled chocolate mixture. Sift dry ingredients together and stir into creamed mixture alternately with the buttermilk. Pour into prepared pans and bake at 350 degrees for 30 to 35 minutes. Cool and frost with Chocolate Butter Icing. 12 to 14 servings.

Chocolate Butter Icing

6 tablespoons butter
¼ teaspoon salt
1 pound confectioners' sugar, sifted

5 tablespoons cocoa, sifted
2 teaspoons vanilla
6 tablespoons milk

Have butter at room temperature and cream well. Add salt, a little of the sugar, and all of the cocoa and combine well. Add vanilla, more sugar, and part of the milk. Add remaining sugar and milk alternately in small portions, mixing thoroughly after each addition. Spread between cake layers and on top and sides of cake. Makes enough to frost one 9-inch 2-layer cake.

I love this cake. It is rich and yummy. Frost with chocolate caramel or coffee icings. It's a big cake—but so good it won't last long.

Chocolate "Dump" Cake

3½ cups sifted cake flour
2½ teaspoons baking powder
1 teaspoon soda
2 teaspoons salt
3 cups sugar

¾ cup cocoa
1⅓ cups butter or shortening
2 cups buttermilk
4 eggs
2 teaspoons vanilla

Measure and sift together the dry ingredients. Add butter or shortening, softened to room temperature, and the buttermilk. Beat 2 minutes. Add eggs and beat again for 2 minutes. Add vanilla.

Grease and dust with flour two 10-inch-square layer cake pans that are 2 inches deep. Divide cake batter between pans and bake at 350 degrees for 1 hour. Frost as desired. 12 servings.

Sour Cream Fudge Cake

Mrs. J. H. Bradley, Hapeville, Georgia

3 eggs
1¼ cups sugar
1 teaspoon vanilla
1¼ cups cake flour
¾ teaspoon salt

1 teaspoon soda
1 cup commercial sour cream
2 ounces unsweetened chocolate
 (melted)

Beat egg yolks until thick and lemon-colored. Add ½ cup sugar gradually, beating until very thick. Add vanilla and mix well. Sift the flour, salt, and baking soda together. Add dry ingredients slowly to the mixture, alternating with sour cream and melted chocolate. Beat batter smooth. Add remaining sugar by spoonfuls to the beaten egg whites, beating after each addition.

Fold egg whites lightly but thoroughly into the batter. Pour into two waxed-paper-lined 8-inch layer cake pans. Bake in moderately hot oven, 375 degrees, for 30 minutes. Remove from pans and pull off paper. Cool and frost. 8 servings.

Crumb Cake

Mrs. Harry Luttrell, Atlanta, Georgia

½ pound butter or margarine
2 cups sugar
5 eggs
2 teaspoons baking powder
1 (13-ounce) package graham
 cracker crumbs

½ cup milk
1 (4-ounce) can flake coconut
1 cup chopped pecans
1 teaspoon vanilla
Filling

Cream butter and sugar. Add eggs one at a time, beating after each. Add baking powder, crumbs, milk, coconut, pecans, and vanilla. Mix well. Bake in three greased and floured 9-inch layer pans at 350 degrees about 30 minutes, or until done. Cool. Spread filling between layers and on top of cake. 12 servings.

FILLING

½ cup butter or margarine
1 (1-pound) box confectioners'
 sugar

1 (9½-ounce) can crushed
 pineapple
1 teaspoon vanilla

Cream softened butter with sugar; add drained pineapple and vanilla and beat well. Spread between layers and on top of cake. (Filling will be thin.) Makes enough filling for one 9-inch 3-layer cake.

Mrs. Murray's husband was an executive with Atlanta Newspapers. She gave us this recipe years ago and it is requested over and over.

Mrs. Murray's Dark Fruit Cake

Mrs. J. C. Murray, Atlanta, Georgia

1 pound citron, chopped
1 pound cherries, chopped
1 pound pineapple, chopped
1 (8-ounce) package dates, chopped
1 pound raisins
3 tablespoons each lemon and orange peel
Flour for dredging
⅚ cup sugar
⅓ pound butter

5 eggs
1 teaspoon allspice
1 teaspoon mace and nutmeg
⅓ teaspoon ground cloves
1⅔ cups plain flour
⅓ cup wine
1 teaspoon soda, dissolved in 1 tablespoon cold water
¼ cup cane syrup
1 teaspoon vanilla
5 cups shelled nuts, chopped

Dredge fruit and lemon and orange peel with flour. Cream sugar and butter, add eggs one at a time, beating in. Sift spices with flour. Add flour alternately with wine to butter-egg mixture. Add soda and water to syrup and stir into batter. Add vanilla, fruits, and nuts. Place in well-greased pan and bake slowly at 250 degrees for about 5 hours. 10 pounds. 40 servings.

Cola Cake

Mrs. Roy Peak, Anderson, South Carolina

2 cups unsifted flour
2 cups sugar
2 tablespoons cocoa
1 teaspoon soda
1 teaspoon salt
1 cup butter or margarine

1 cup cola beverage
½ cup buttermilk
2 eggs
1½ cups miniature marshmallows
Cola Frosting

Combine flour, sugar, cocoa, soda, and salt. Bring the butter and cola to a boil and add to the dry mixture. Add the buttermilk, eggs, and marshmallows. This will be a very thin batter with the marshmallows floating on top. Bake in a greased 13×9½×2 inch pan at 350 degrees for 45 to 60 minutes. Spread Cola Frosting over cake while hot. 12 servings.

COLA FROSTING

½ cup butter
2 tablespoons cocoa
6 tablespoons cola
1 (1-pound) box confectioners'
   sugar

1 cup chopped nuts
1 teaspoon vanilla

Combine butter, cocoa, and cola and bring to a boil. Pour over confectioners' sugar and mix well. Add nuts and vanilla. About 2 cups.

This recipe was always a must in the food section of the *Atlanta Journal*.

White Fruit Cake

½ pound (2 sticks) butter
2 cups sugar
4½ cups cake flour
2 teaspoons baking powder
1 cup (scant) water
8 egg whites, stiffly beaten
1 teaspoon lemon extract
1 teaspoon vanilla
2 pounds white raisins

½ pound light color citron,
   sliced fine
½ pound red crystallized
   cherries, cut in half
½ pound crystallized pineapple,
   cut up
1 pound almonds, blanched and
   chopped

Cream butter and sugar. Sift flour and use ½ cup for dusting fruit and nuts. Sift baking powder with remaining flour. Add water and flour alternately to the creamed mixture. Fold in beaten egg whites, add flavoring, and then the floured fruit and nuts. Bake in a greased pan lined with greased brown paper. Bake at 275 degrees for 2½ to 3 hours or until done. 20 servings.

Gingerbread

Chef Joe Clayton, Saddle Rock Inn, Rock City, Tennessee

1 cup sugar	*3 cups flour*
1 cup shortening	*½ teaspoon allspice*
1 cup sorghum syrup	*1 teaspoon ginger*
1 teaspoon soda, dissolved in 1	*½ teaspoon cinnamon*
cup boiling water	*½ teaspoon nutmeg*
3 eggs	

Cream sugar and shortening together, then add sorghum syrup and hot water with the soda dissolved in it. Add eggs and combine well. Mix flour and spices and add to first mixture until well blended. Bake in greased (13×9½×2-inch) pan at 350 degrees for about 30 minutes or until springy to the touch. 15 servings.

A long-time southern favorite.

Lane Cake

2 cups sugar	*1 cup milk*
1 cup butter or shortening	*1 tablespoon vanilla*
3¼ cups cake flour	*8 egg whites, stiffly beaten*
2 tablespoons baking powder	*Filling*

Cream sugar and butter. Sift flour and baking powder together. Add flour mixture alternately with milk to the creamed mixture. Add vanilla and beat. Fold in egg whites slowly. Bake in three 9-inch layer pans at 350 degrees for 25 to 30 minutes or until done. When cool spread filling between layers. 12 servings.

FILLING

8 egg yolks	*1 cup chopped nuts*
1 cup sugar	*2-ounces wine or grape juice*
½ cup butter	*1 teaspoon vanilla*
1 cup raisins	
1 (3½-ounce) can flake	
coconut	

Beat egg yolks, add sugar and butter. Cook until thick, stirring constantly. Add remaining ingredients.

This has been a family favorite. Mama used to bake two or more every Christmas when we were children. But she used fresh coconut.

Japanese Fruit Cake

1 cup butter or margarine	1 teaspoon cloves
2 cups sugar	1 teaspoon nutmeg
4 eggs	1 teaspoon soda
3 cups flour	1 cup buttermilk
½ teaspoon salt	1 cup chopped raisins
1 teaspoon cinnamon	1 cup chopped nutmeats
1 teaspoon allspice	Filling

Cream butter and sugar together, add eggs one at a time, beating well after each addition. Sift dry ingredients together, add alternately with buttermilk. Flour raisins and nutmeats and add to above mixture. Pour into three 9-inch greased and floured layer pans and bake in slow oven, 300 degrees, about 1 hour or until cake leaves side of pan. Put filling between layers and on top of cake. 12 to 14 servings.

FILLING

2 (3½ to 4 ounces each) boxes coconut	2 tablespoons flour
	2 lemons, grated rind and juice
2½ cups sugar	1½ cups hot water

Combine all ingredients, cook until thick. Cool slightly. Makes enough for one 9-inch 3-layer cake.

Lemon Tea Loaf

Mrs. Emmett Reece, Woodstock, Georgia

3 cups sifted flour	¼ cup firmly packed brown sugar
½ cup granulated sugar	
3 teaspoons baking powder	2 tablespoons grated lemon rind
1 teaspoon salt	1 egg
¼ teaspoon soda	1¼ cups milk
¼ teaspoon nutmeg	4 tablespoons melted butter
½ cup chopped English walnuts	

Sift flour, granulated sugar, baking powder, salt, soda, and nutmeg together into a bowl; add walnuts, brown sugar, and lemon rind. Beat egg slightly with milk in a bowl. Stir in melted butter. Pour all at once into flour mixture. Stir about 30 strokes, or just until evenly moist. Spoon into a well-greased 9×5×3-inch loaf pan, let stand 20 minutes. Bake at 350 degrees for 1 hour, 15 minutes. 12 to 14 servings.

Lord and Lady Baltimore cakes are just as elegant as the names imply. They are a handsome pair and most often are baked together since one uses the whites of the eggs and the other makes use of the yolks. These have graced many an elegant board here in the South.

Lord Baltimore Cake

2½ cups sifted cake flour
4 teaspoons baking powder
¾ cup butter or shortening
1¼ cups sugar

8 egg yolks, well beaten
¾ cup milk
½ teaspoon lemon extract
Lord Baltimore Filling

Sift flour and baking powder together three times. Cream shortening and sugar together until light and fluffy. Add egg yolks and beat well. Add flour alternately with milk, beating well after each addition. Add extract. Bake in three greased 9-inch pans (can use two) at 350 degrees for about 25 minutes.

Put layers together and cover cake with Lord Baltimore filling or put layers together with filling and cover top and sides with Boiled Frosting. 12 servings.

LORD BALTIMORE FILLING

1½ cups sugar
¼ teaspoon cream of tartar
½ cup water
2 egg whites, stiffly beaten
¼ teaspoon orange juice
2 teaspoons lemon juice

12 candied cherries, cut in
quarters
½ cup macaroon crumbs
½ cup chopped pecans
½ cup chopped blanched
almonds (optional)

Dissolve sugar and cream of tartar in water and boil until syrup forms a soft ball in cold water or spins a thread (238 degrees). Pour syrup over beaten egg whites. Continue to beat.

Add orange and lemon juice to cherries, macaroon crumbs, and nuts. Combine the two mixtures. Cool and spread between cake layers.

Lady Baltimore Cake

3 cups sifted cake flour
3½ teaspoons baking powder
¾ teaspoon salt
¾ cup butter or other fat
2 cups powdered sugar

½ teaspoon rose or almond
  extract
½ cup milk
½ cup water
6 egg whites, stiffly beaten

Sift together flour, baking powder, and salt. Cream butter until soft and smooth and gradually add sugar, beating until very fluffy. Add flavoring. Add flour alternately with combined milk and water, beating until smooth after each addition; fold in thoroughly the stiffly beaten egg whites. Turn into three greased and floured or paper-lined, 8-inch pans and bake in moderate oven, 375 degrees, for 30 to 35 minutes. Spread Boiled Frosting between layers and on top of cake. 12 servings.

BOILED FROSTING

1½ cups sugar
½ cup water
1 tablespoon light corn syrup
2 egg whites

¼ teaspoon cream of tartar
Dash salt
1 teaspoon vanilla

Put sugar, water, and corn syrup in saucepan and stir over low heat until sugar is dissolved: boil, covered, about 3 minutes; then boil uncovered and without stirring until a small amount of syrup forms a soft ball when dropped into cold water. Remove syrup from heat; quickly beat egg whites with the cream of tartar until stiff but not dry, then pour syrup in fine stream over egg whites, beating constantly; add salt and flavoring and continue beating until frosting is cool and of proper consistency to spread. If frosting hardens before spreading, beat in a few drops of hot water. Enough to frost one 9-inch 3-layer cake.

LADY BALTIMORE FROSTING

1 recipe Boiled Frosting
½ cup chopped seeded raisins
½ cup chopped figs

¼ cup chopped blanched
  almonds
¼ cup chopped walnuts

Prepare boiled frosting, flavoring with ¼ teaspoon vanilla and ⅛ teaspoon almond extract. When of proper consistency to spread, add fruits and nuts. If preferred, add just enough frosting to fruits and nuts to make mixture that will spread easily and use as filling between layers. Spread remaining frosting over top and sides of cake. Enough to frost one 9-inch 3-layer cake.

Southern Nut Cake
Mrs. Karl Ekmark, Sandy Springs, Georgia

½ pound butter	2 pounds seedless raisins
1 pound sugar	1 quart chopped pecans
1 pound flour	2-ounces Bourbon
2 teaspoons cinnamon	2 teaspoons soda, dissolved in a
2 teaspoons nutmeg	little water
6 eggs, separated	

Cream butter and sugar. Sift flour and spices together. Beat egg yolks and whites separately and mix yolks with butter and sugar. Add flour and spices to raisins and nuts, then to yolk mixture, alternating with whiskey and soda. Then fold in stiffly beaten egg whites. Pour into four greased 9×5×3-inch loaf pans and bake 3½ to 4 hours in 250-degree oven. 4 loaves.

An all-time good basic cake recipe. It's easy to remember and can be used in many different ways. Bake it in layers, loaves, tube pans or in sheets. Frost as desired.

1, 2, 3, 4 Cake

1 cup butter	½ teaspoon salt
2 cups sugar	2 teaspoons baking powder
3 cups cake flour	1 cup milk
4 eggs	1 teaspoon vanilla

Cream butter and sugar. Add eggs one at a time, beating well after each addition. Sift flour with salt and baking powder. Add alternately with milk to the creamed mixture. Add vanilla. Bake in four greased and floured 8- or 9-inch layer pans at 350 degrees for 25 to 30 minutes. Frost as desired.

A southern specialty you will surely enjoy. This is served at Pitty Pat's Porch in downtown Atlanta, A. J. Anthony, owner.

Pecan Cake

1 cup sugar
10 eggs, separated
1 teaspoon vanilla extract
2 cups finely ground pecan
   meats
½ teaspoon salt
1 tablespoon rum

Dash allspice
3 tablespoons fine dry bread
   crumbs
1 cup heavy cream
1 teaspoon coffee extract
2 teaspoons ground pecan
   meats

Beat sugar gradually into well-beaten egg yolks. Add vanilla, pecans, salt, rum, and allspice. Stir to blend thoroughly. Beat egg whites until stiff, fold in 1 tablespoon fine dry bread crumbs. Then fold into the sugar-egg yolk mixture. Grease a springform pan, sprinkle with remaining fine dry bread crumbs, and pour in the batter. Bake in 350-degree oven 40 to 50 minutes.

Whip cream with coffee extract and fold in pecan meats. When cake is cool, split and fill with whipped cream mixture. Top with a little whipped cream. 12 servings.

Pineapple Upside-down Cake

Mrs. Patricia Maxey, Decatur, Georgia

½ cup shortening
½ cup brown sugar
1½ cups drained crushed
   pineapple
¾ cup granulated sugar
1½ cups sifted rye or wheat
   flour

¼ cup cornstarch
3 teaspoons baking powder
½ teaspoon salt
1 cup milk

Melt ¼ cup shortening in 9-inch layer pan. Add brown sugar and stir until it melts. Spread mixture evenly, remove from heat, spread pineapple, and set aside.

Cream remaining ¼ cup shortening and gradually beat in sugar. Combine sifted flour, cornstarch, baking powder, and salt. To creamed mixture add flour mixture alternately with milk. Blend well.

Pour in pan. Bake at 350 degrees for 45 to 50 minutes. Turn cake pan upside down and let stand a few minutes before removing pan. 8 servings.

Pork Cake

C. C. Hamby, Atlanta, Georgia—brought this to us many years ago

1 pound salt pork, ground
   through a food chopper
1 pound currants
1 pound raisins
¼ pound citron
2 cups brown sugar
1 cup any kind of nuts
1 heaping teaspoon soda

2 tablespoons cinnamon,
   dissolved in 2 cups boiling
   water
1 teaspoon cloves
1 teaspoon nutmeg
½ teaspoon salt
2 pounds (about 6½ cups)
   flour

Mix all ingredients well. Bake in greased and floured large tube pan at 350 degrees until done, about 45 minutes to 1 hour. About 18 servings.

From the restored Bedingfield Inn, Lumpkin, Georgia.

Martha Fort's Real Pound Cake

8 medium-size eggs, separated
2⅔ cups sugar
1 pound butter (sweet is best,
   but not necessary)

1 tablespoon vanilla flavoring
3½ cups sifted cake flour
8 tablespoons coffee cream

Whip the egg whites and add 6 level tablespoons sugar while beating; put in refrigerator until cake is mixed. Cream butter and remaining sugar; whip until light. Add egg yolks about two at a time, beating well each time. Beat in vanilla. Add flour and cream alternately; whip until mixture is light, using low speed. Remove bowl from mixer and fold in whites by hand, just enough to mix. Pour batter into lightly greased tube pan 10-inches in diameter and 4 inches deep. Start baking at 250 degrees. After about 15 minutes increase temperature to 275 or 300 degrees and continue baking another 45 minutes. Let cake stand in pan to cool before turning out. 12 servings.

This cake keeps exceptionally well—if you hide it!

Pound Cake Delight

Miss Emma Carter, Covington, Georgia

3½ cups flour, sifted	*½ cup solid vegetable*
½ cup granulated sugar	*shortening*
1 teaspoon baking powder	*6 large eggs*
1 (3-ounce) package	*½ cup evaporated milk*
lemon-flavored gelatin	*½ cup water*
1 (1-pound) box confectioners'	*1 teaspoon lemon extract*
sugar, sifted	*1 teaspoon coconut flavoring*
1 cup margarine	*1 teaspoon orange extract*

Sift together three times the flour, sugar, baking powder, and lemon-flavored gelatin. Cream confectioners' sugar, margarine, and shortening. Add eggs, one at a time, cream thoroughly. Add dry ingredients to egg mixture alternately with the evaporated milk, which has been diluted with the water, beginning and ending with the flour mixture. Add the flavorings just before the last addition of flour.

Bake in a large tube pan that has been slightly greased and lined with waxed paper on the bottom.

Bake at 325 degrees for 1½ hours or until cake is done. Let the cake cool in the pan about 15 minutes, then remove to rack.

This is a very moist cake that will keep at least two weeks wrapped in waxed paper. 12 servings.

NOTE: For variety, use orange-flavored gelatin, 1½ teaspoons coconut flavoring, and 1½ teaspoons orange flavoring.

Mrs. Dorothy Clark, Altanta, Georgia, found this recipe in an old southern cookbook.

Palm Beach Poinciana Cake

1 pound butter	*2 cups chopped blanched*
1 pound sugar	*almonds*
9 eggs, separated	*Juice and grated rind of 1*
3¼ cups flour	*lemon*
½ pound citron, chopped fine	*Filling*
½ pound raisins, chopped fine	

Cream butter and sugar and add to well-beaten egg yolks. Then add alternately the flour and the whites, beaten stiff. Dredge the fruits and nuts with flour and add to the batter. Add lemon juice and rind. Bake in four 9-inch layer pans, which have been greased and floured, in a slow oven (300 degrees) from 40 to 50 minutes. Spread filling between layers and on top of cake. 12 to 14 servings.

FILLING

2 cups sugar	*1 tablespoon cornstarch*
1 cup boiling water	*2 cups grated coconut*
Juice and grated rind of 2	
lemons	

Boil the first three ingredients and add the cornstarch, which you have dissolved in a little cold water. Cook until it spins a thread and then beat until creamy; add coconut. Enough to frost four 9-inch layers.

Raspberry Torte

Mrs. W. E. Harris, Milledgeville, Georgia

1 cup butter	*1 teaspoon baking powder*
1½ cups sugar	*2 cups sifted plain flour*
5 eggs, separated	*1 cup raspberry preserves*
2 tablespoons milk	*1⅓ cups flake coconut*
1 teaspoon vanilla	*1 teaspoon vanilla*
1¼ teaspoon salt	*2 cups sour cream*

Cream together butter, 1 cup sugar, and egg yolks. Blend in milk, vanilla, 1 teaspoon salt, and baking powder. Beat well. Stir in flour. Spread in three 9-inch well-greased round pans. Spread ⅓ cup preserves on each layer to within 1 inch of edge.

Beat egg whites and remaining salt. Gradually add remaining sugar beating until stiff peaks form. Fold in flaked coconut and vanilla. Spread over preserves. Bake at 350 degrees for 35 to 40 minutes. Cool 15 minutes. Remove from pans.

Spread 2 cups sour cream between layers. Garnish top with sour cream or raspberry preserves or dust with confectioners' sugar. Chill several hours before serving. 10 to 12 servings.

Mrs. Frank Robertson, Lewisport, Kentucky, uses either canned or fresh frozen pumpkin to make this luscious cake.

Pumpkin Spice Cake

½ cup shortening	2 teaspoons cinnamon
1¼ cups sugar	½ teaspoon ginger
2 eggs, well beaten	½ teaspoon nutmeg
2¼ cups sifted all-purpose flour	1 cup pumpkin
2½ teaspoons baking powder	¾ cup milk
½ teaspoon soda	½ cup finely chopped nuts
1 teaspoon salt	

Cream shortening; add sugar gradually. Cream until light and fluffy. Blend in eggs. Sift flour, baking powder, soda, salt, and spices together. Combine pumpkin and milk. Add dry ingredients alternately with pumpkin mixture, beginning and ending with dry ingredients. Stir in chopped nuts. Spread batter in two 9-inch layer pans which have been greased and lined with waxed paper. Bake in a moderate oven, 350 degrees for about 30 minutes. Cool. Frost with your favorite butter cream icing, using orange juice and grated orange rind for color and flavor. 10 to 12 servings.

Prune Cake

Mrs. C. T. Swann, Doraville, Georgia

3 eggs	1 teaspoon allspice
1½ cups sugar	½ teaspoon salt
1 cup cooking oil	1 cup buttermilk
1 teaspoon soda	1 cup mashed cooked prunes
2 cups flour	1 cup nuts, chopped
1 teaspoon cinnamon	1 teaspoon vanilla
1 teaspoon nutmeg	Topping

Beat eggs until light. Add sugar, beat well. Add oil. Sift together dry ingredients. Add alternately with buttermilk. Add prunes, nuts, and vanilla.

Bake in a greased, floured 9-inch tube pan for 1 hour at 375 degrees.

Remove cake from pan while still warm, punch holes in top with toothpick. Pour hot topping over cake. 10 servings.

TOPPING

1 cup sugar	*1 tablespoon corn syrup*
½ cup buttermilk	*¼ cup butter*
½ teaspoon soda	*1 teaspoon vanilla*

Combine ingredients and simmer for 30 minutes. 1½ cups.

Sponge Cake

Mrs. Hollis Kezar, Elko, Georgia
A great cake baker!

⅛ teaspoon salt	*Juice of ½ lemon*
6 eggs, separated	*1¼ cups sifted plain flour*
½ teaspoon cream of tartar	*Butter Sauce*
1¼ cups sifted sugar	

Add salt to egg whites and beat until foamy; then add cream of tartar and continue beating until stiff. Gradually add sugar, beating all the time until egg whites stand in peaks. Let stand while beating egg yolks until light and creamy; add lemon juice. Add to beaten whites gradually, beating all the time. Fold flour in slowly and well. Pour into ungreased 10-inch tube pan. Bake 50 minutes at 300 degrees. Invert on cake rack until cake cools. Cut with cake breaker or two forks. When ready to serve, pour Butter Sauce on pieces of sponge cake. 8 to 10 servings.

BUTTER SAUCE

2½ cups sugar	*1 teaspoon vanilla*
2 cups water	*Salt*
½ cup (1 stick) butter	

Combine sugar, water, and butter and cook until mixture begins to thicken. Add 1 teaspoon vanilla and a dash of salt. Keep sauce warm. About 3 cups sauce.

Snow White Cake

Mrs. Luther Smith, Atlanta, Georgia

6 egg whites	3 cups plain flour
1½ cups sugar	2 teaspoons baking powder
1 cup vegetable shortening	Dash salt
¼ teaspoon soda	1 teaspoon vanilla flavoring
1 cup buttermilk	1 teaspoon lemon flavoring

First, beat egg whites with ½ cup cold water; set aside. Cream sugar and shortening. Add soda to buttermilk; combine this along with rest of ingredients with the creamed mixture. Beat until smooth. Fold in beaten egg whites. Bake in three 9-inch layers at 325 degrees 30 to 35 minutes. 10 to 12 servings.

Wedding Cake

Mrs. J. O. Steele, Rome, Georgia

5½ cups soft plain flour	2½ cups milk
3½ cups sugar	1 cup (about 10) egg whites
8 teaspoons baking powder	1 teaspoon vanilla extract
2 teaspoons salt	½ teaspoon almond extract
1½ cups pure vegetable	½ teaspoon coconut flavoring
shortening	Wedding Cake Frosting

Sift flour, sugar, baking powder, and salt together. Add shortening and milk and turn mixer on low speed until it is well mixed. Then add egg whites and set mixer on cream setting until well blended, about 4 to 5 minutes. Add flavorings and mix. Pour into well-greased and floured cake pan; this will fill a 15-inch round pan. Bake at 350 degrees until done, approximately 2 hours.

Prepare the same recipe and when cool the layers are put together with frosting, then iced all over. This makes the bottom tier.

For the second tier make two recipes and bake the two layers in two 10-inch pans. Ice between layers and cover with frosting.

For the top tier fill two 7-inch pans one-half full. This will require about half the recipe. Frost this layer as others. Trim crust from cake layers before frosting. 80 to 100 servings, depending on size.

WEDDING CAKE FROSTING

Beat until very stiff, 4 egg whites to which is added ⅛ teaspoon salt.

In a saucepan place 2 cups sugar, ½ cup water, 2 tablespoons white corn syrup, and ½ teaspoon white vinegar. Boil mixture until it spins a thread, then add twelve marshmallows; stir well.

Pour syrup slowly into beaten egg whites, beating constantly. Then add 1 teaspoon vanilla extract, ¼ teaspoon almond extract, and ¼ teaspoon coconut flavoring. Spread between layers and on top of cake.

This recipe should be made three times, to finish up the three tiers of wedding cake.

Wine Cake

Mrs. J. Stewart Tuten, Brunswick, Georgia

2 cups candied cherries	*6 eggs, separated*
2 cups seedless raisins	*5 cups cake flour*
2 cups dry wine	*1 teaspoon nutmeg*
1½ cups butter or margarine	*1 teaspoon cinnamon*
2⅓ cups granulated sugar	*1 teaspoon baking powder*
2⅓ cups brown sugar	*4 cups chopped pecans*

Combine cherries, raisins, and wine and let stand overnight. Cream butter or margarine and sugar until light. Add egg yolks and beat well. Combine ½ cup flour, spices, baking powder, and chopped pecans. Drain wine off fruits; add remaining flour and wine to butter mixture, beating well after each addition.

Beat egg whites stiff and fold into butter mixture. Then fold in the soaked fruits and pecan-flour mixture. Bake in a 10-inch tube pan lined with greased paper or foil.

Bake at 275 degrees for 3½ hours. 16 servings.

ICINGS

Caramel Cake Filling

2 cups sugar
½ cup brown sugar
½ teaspoon soda

½ cup butter
1 cup buttermilk
1 tablespoon vanilla flavoring

Mix sugar, soda, butter, and milk. Cook until it forms soft ball when tested in cold water. Cool; add flavoring and beat until creamy. Nuts may be added if desired. Enough filling for one 2-layer cake, sides and top.

Chocolate Fudge Topping

2 cups sugar
½ cup cocoa
Dash salt

1¼ cups milk
½ cup butter or margarine
1 teaspoon vanilla

Mix dry ingredients. Then add milk and butter. Bring to full boil, then boil 2½ to 3 minutes. Remove from heat. Add vanilla. Beat for 2 minutes. Ready to use. Enough topping for one 8-inch 2-layer cake.

Old-fashioned Coconut Icing

1 (8-ounce) package coconut
2 cups sugar
2 tablespoons flour

¾ cup milk
¼ cup margarine

Combine all ingredients and boil until thick enough to spread (about 3 minutes). Enough frosting for one 8-inch 2-layer cake.

Orange Icing

2 cups sugar
1 heaping tablespoon self-rising flour
1 cup fresh squeezed orange juice

Grated rind of 1 orange
2 tablespoons butter

Combine sugar and flour in fairly shallow saucepan. Stir in orange juice and grated rind. Place on medium heat and stir constantly. Boil until it reaches soft ball stage, remove from heat and add butter.

This icing is thin and should be placed on layers while they are still warm. Prick layers with toothpick so icing will soak in more. As icing cools, it will thicken more. Cover sides and top of cake. When cold the icing will form a glaze over the top and will be moist underneath. Use this with a basic 1, 2, 3, 4 three-layer cake. Enough icing for one 8- or 9-inch 2-layer cake.

Ornamental Frosting

½ cup butter or margarine
½ teaspoon salt
12 cups sifted confectioners'
sugar

5 egg whites
½ cup (about) light cream
2 teaspoons vanilla

Cream butter or margarine. Add salt and part of the sugar gradually, blending after each addition. Add remaining sugar alternately with the egg whites first, then with the cream, until of right consistency to spread. Beat after each addition until smooth. Add vanilla; blend. (While frosting cake, keep bowl of frosting covered with a damp cloth, to prevent excessive evaporation.) Enough frosting for large wedding cake.

ASSORTED DESSERTS

Blueberry Ice Cream
Mrs. Lee Carpenter, Palmetto, Georgia

3 cups fresh blueberries
½ cup water
2 pints half and half cream

1 quart whole milk
3 cups sugar

Crush blueberries, place in saucepan with water, and boil until berries are soft, stirring to prevent scorching. Strain to remove hulls. This makes about 2½ cups purée.

Put fruit purée into 1-gallon freezer churn, add remaining ingredients; stir to dissolve. Freeze. 3 quarts.

NOTE: This recipe may be used with blackberries, raspberries, strawberries, or muscadines.

Chocolate Ripple Ice Cream

1½ squares unsweetened
chocolate
⅓ cup water
¼ cup sugar, plus ⅔ cup
Dash salt
¼ cup light corn syrup

¼ teaspoon vanilla, plus 1
tablespoon
2 (3 ounces each) packages
cream cheese
2 cups light cream

Place chocolate and water in a saucepan. Cook and stir over low heat until thick and blended. Add ¼ cup sugar, salt, and corn syrup. Bring to boil and boil gently 4 minutes, stirring constantly. Remove from heat and add ¼ teaspoon vanilla. Cool sauce; then chill.

Meanwhile cream the cheese and remaining sugar together until thoroughly mixed. Add remaining vanilla and light cream gradually, mixing well. Pour into freezing tray of refrigerator and set control to coldest. Freeze until mixture is firm about 1 inch around edges (1½ to 2 hours). Spoon into chilled bowl and beat until smooth, but not melted. Return half of mixture to tray and cover with half the chocolate sauce. Spoon on remaining ice cream and top with remaining sauce in a swirled pattern. With knife or spatula, cut through ice cream in zigzag course. Freeze until firm, 2 to 3 hours. About 1 quart.

Custard Ice Cream

Mrs. E. F. Horne, Thomasville, Georgia

4 eggs
12 tablespoons sugar
¼ teaspoon salt
4 cups milk, scalded

2 teaspoons vanilla
3 cups half and half or
whipping cream

Beat eggs until well blended. Add sugar and salt. Mix well. Add milk slowly, stirring constantly. Cook over hot water until mixture thickens and will coat a spoon. Remove from heat at once. Chill. Add flavoring and cream. Freeze. 16 servings, or 1 gallon.

NOTE: For variation, leave out vanilla and add 2 to 3 cups mashed peaches just before freezing.

Before this hotel was demolished their famous ice cream was always a Sunday specialty.

Forrest's Famous Vanilla Ice Cream
General Forrest Hotel, Rome, Georgia

12 eggs	*6 quarts whipping cream*
2 quarts milk	*¼ cup pure vanilla extract*
10 cups sugar	

Make custard of eggs and milk; cook at low temperature, stir constantly until thickened. Combine with sugar. Cool. Whip cream, but not stiff. Add the custard and whip again. Add vanilla, mix, and freeze in 5-gallon churn.

Apple Nut Dessert
Mrs. A. N. Holbrook, Jr., Mableton, Georgia

1 cup sugar	*1 tablespoon vanilla*
¾ cup sifted flour	*½ cup broken nutmeats*
2 teaspoons baking powder	*3 cups cut-up peeled apples*
3 tablespoons soft butter	*2 tablespoons brown sugar*
1 cup evaporated milk	*⅓ cup flour*

Mix with fork in bowl, sugar, ¾ cup sifted flour, baking powder, 1 tablespoon butter; stir in milk and vanilla. Add nuts and apple and stir until mixed well. Spread in buttered casserole or pan.

Mix until crumbly, brown sugar, ⅓ cup flour, and remaining butter. Sprinkle over apple mixture. Bake at 400 degrees for 30 to 35 minutes, or until golden brown. Serve warm or cold with Lively Lemon Sauce. 8 servings.

Lively Lemon Sauce

⅓ cup butter
1 cup sugar
½ cup light corn syrup
¼ teaspoon salt

1 cup evaporated milk
¼ cup fresh lemon juice
1 teaspoon grated lemon rind

In saucepan melt butter. Add sugar, corn syrup, and salt. Cook over low heat, stirring constantly for 3 to 4 minutes. Remove from heat, gradually stir in milk; add lemon juice and rind, beat vigorously. Serve as topping for desserts. If sauce separates while stored in refrigerator, beat hard to combine. 2½ cups.

New Orleans Calas

Mrs. Warren Franklin, Stone Mountain, Georgia

3 cups cooked rice
3 eggs, well beaten
¼ teaspoon each vanilla,
　nutmeg, cinnamon, and
　grated lemon rind
½ cup sifted flour

½ cup granulated sugar
3½ teaspoons baking powder
½ teaspoon salt
Fat for frying
Confectioners' sugar

Mix rice, eggs, vanilla, spices, and lemon rind. Sift flour with granulated sugar, baking powder, and salt. Stir into the rice mixture. Blend well. Drop from tablespoon into deep hot fat (360 degrees) and fry until golden brown on all sides, about 2 minutes. Drain on absorbent paper. Sprinkle with confectioners' sugar and serve hot. About 12 calas.

Mrs. Dorsey's Apple Cobbler

Mrs. Ralph Dorsey, Berryville, Virginia

3 tablespoons vegetable
　shortening
1¼ cups sugar
½ cup milk
1 teaspoon baking powder
1 cup flour

½ teaspoon flour
Peeled and sliced apples (about
　4)
½ teaspoon cornstarch
1 cup boiling water
¼ cup brandy

Cream shortening, add ¾ cup sugar, then milk. Stir in the baking powder, flour, and salt. Grease an 8-inch square baking dish and put in a thick layer of peeled and sliced apples. Spread batter over top.

Combine remaining ½ cup sugar, cornstarch, boiling water, and brandy. Gently pour over top of batter. Bake at 350 degrees for 1 hour. Serve warm or cold, with cream or ice cream, if desired. 6 servings.

Blackberry Cobbler

Mrs. Jerry Cope, Betty's Creek, Dillard, Georgia

½ cup (*1 stick*) *margarine*
¾ cup self-rising flour
¾ cup sugar

¾ cup milk
4 cups sweetened blackberries

Put margarine in casserole or baking dish and melt. Combine flour, sugar, and milk; pour over melted margarine and add berries. Do not stir. Bake at 350 degrees for about 30 minutes. 6 to 8 servings.

Fort Valley Peach Cobbler

Mrs. W. G. Little, Marietta, Georgia

Combine ¾ cup flour, 1 cup sugar, 2 teaspoons baking powder, dash of salt, and ½ cup milk into a batter.

In a deep casserole melt ¾ stick of butter. Pour batter into center of melted butter and do not stir. Add 2 cups sliced peaches mixed with 1 cup sugar. Do not stir.

Bake 1 hour at 350 degrees. Serve warm or cold with or without cream. Sweetened frozen peaches may be substituted for fresh peaches successfully. 6 servings.

Cream Tart

Mrs. Paul Keeler, Athens, Georgia

1½ cups sugar
¼ cup butter
4 eggs, separated
1½ teaspoons vanilla
1 cup cake flour

1 teaspoon baking powder
¼ teaspoon salt, plus ⅛
    teaspoon
5 tablespoons light cream
⅓ cup almond slivers

Sift ½ cup sugar and cream with butter; add egg yolks one at a time, then ½ teaspoon vanilla. Sift together flour and baking powder and ¼ teaspoon salt and add alternately with cream, ending with dry ingredients. Beat batter until smooth and spread in bottom of two 9-inch layer pans lined with brown paper.

Whip egg whites until stiff with remaining ⅛ teaspoon salt. Add remaining 1 cup sugar, very slowly (½ teaspoon at a time). Beat constantly. After all sugar is added, fold in remaining 1 teaspoon vanilla. Spread over batter and sprinkle with almonds.

Bake in slow oven, 325 degrees, for 25 minutes; then increase heat to 350 degrees and bake 30 minutes longer. Cool in pans. Before serving place one layer, meringue side down, on cake plate and spread with whipped cream flavored with rum or vanilla. Add fresh or frozen strawberries, sliced peaches, or raspberries. Place other layer meringue side up, and dot with whipped cream and fresh fruits. 6 servings.

South Carolina Peach Slump

Chef Manuel Filotis,
The William Hilton Inn, Hilton Head Island, South Carolina

6 cups sliced peaches	*½ cup peach syrup*
½ cup sugar	*Pie pastry*
1½ teaspoons ground cinnamon	

Combine first four ingredients in heavy casserole. Bring to simmer. Top with rolled-out pie pastry. Bake in 350-degree oven about 40 minutes. Serve with cream. 6 to 8 servings.

Chef Dickson prepared this dish especially for me. It was so new that he had not named it.

Dessert Soufflé with Fruit Sauce

Chef Bob Dickson
King & Prince Hotel, St. Simons Island, Georgia

5 egg yolks	*8 egg whites*
1¼ cups granulated sugar	*⅛ teaspoon cream of tartar*
½ teaspoon vanilla	*Confectioners' sugar*

Beat the egg yolks with 1 cup sugar until thick; add vanilla. In another bowl place egg whites, remaining ¼ cup sugar, and cream of tartar. Beat until firm and moist, but not dry. Fold egg yolks into whites; pour into buttered cast-iron skillet, place over heat about 1 minute, then slide into preheated 475-degree oven, and immediately reduce temperature to 375 degrees—about 25 to 30 minutes. Test as for cake. Sprinkle with confectioners' sugar. In the meantime prepare strawberry sauce:

1 tablespoon cornstarch   *¼ cup sugar*
2 (1-ounce) jiggers Cointreau
1 (10-ounce) package frozen
*   strawberries, drained*

Dissolve cornstarch in Cointreau. In blender blend half of the strawberries, bring to boil, stir in cornstarch, and cook mixture until thickened. Remove from heat, add remaining strawberries and sugar.

To serve: Cut and lift pieces of soufflé hot from pan or fold as French omelet. Serve with the sauce and ice cream or whipped cream. 6 to 8 servings.

Strawberry Whipped Cream Roll

Mrs. Jamie Malcolm, Monroe, Georgia

4 eggs, separated   *Confectioners' sugar*
1 cup granulated sugar   *2 cups whipped cream*
1 cup sifted flour   *1 (10-ounce) package frozen,*
⅛ teaspoon salt   *   drained berries or 2 cups*
1 teaspoon baking powder   *fresh*
1 teaspoon vanilla or almond
*   extract*

Cream egg yolks and granulated sugar; gradually add flour, salt, and baking powder mixed. Beat egg whites with vanilla until stiff; gently fold into egg-yolk mixture. Bake in shallow pan (18×11 inches) lined with oiled waxed paper, at 350 degrees for 8 minutes.

Turn out on damp cloth, sprinkled with confectioners' sugar. Trim hard edges and roll in cloth while warm. When cool, remove from cloth and unroll. Spread with whipped cream. Place berries on cream. Reroll and dust with confectioners' sugar. Chill; serve in slices with additional berries, if desired. 6 servings.

Hundreds of Tiffany lamps are in this charming place, which was once the basement under a general store in the 1900s. Interesting place and interesting food.

Pineapple Buttermilk Sherbet

Tiffany House, Savannah, Georgia

2 cups buttermilk	*1 teaspoon vanilla*
⅔ cup sugar	*1 egg white*
Dash salt	
1 cup undrained crushed	
pineapple	

Mix buttermilk, sugar, salt, pineapple, and vanilla and freeze to a mush. Whip egg white until stiff and fold into the well-beaten pineapple mixture. Return to freezer and freeze without stirring. 4 servings.

COOKIES

Cookies come in all sizes, shapes, and flavors. They are a child's delight, an aid to the hostess, and most of them are quite easy to make.

At home we had one sideboard drawer reserved for tea cakes, but we only were allowed to eat them when given permission. What music to my ears when I pleaded to Mama, "I'm hungry," and she replied, "Then, just run and get you a tea cake."

Cookies are great snacks with a glass of milk, they pack well for carried lunches, and can be just right for afternoon tea, outings, and as a light dessert for dinner's end.

Sugarplum Bonbons

1 cup butter or margarine, soft	*½ cup chopped almonds*
1½ cups sifted confectioners'	*2 cups quick rolled oats,*
sugar	*uncooked*
¼ cup cocoa	*Flaked or shredded coconut*
¼ teaspoon almond extract	

Beat butter and sugar together until creamy. Blend in cocoa and almond extract; mix thoroughly. Stir in almonds and oats. Chill dough until stiff, at least 2 or 3 hours.

Break off pieces of dough; shape to form thirty-six 1-inch balls. Roll in coconut. Refrigerate. 3 dozen.

Blondies

Mrs. L. L. Phillips, Soperton, Georgia

⅔ cup margarine
1 (1-pound) box light brown
   sugar
3 eggs
2¾ cups cake flour

½ teaspoon salt
2½ teaspoons baking powder
1 cup broken pecan meats
1 (6-ounce) package chocolate
   chips

Melt margarine. Remove from heat, stir in brown sugar. Let mixture partially cool. Add eggs to mixture one at a time, beating well. Sift flour; resift adding salt and baking powder. Add flour mixture to sugar mixture and combine. Stir in nuts and chocolate chips. Pour into greased 13×9×2 inch pan and bake at 325 degrees, for 25 to 30 minutes. Cool and cut into 16 squares.

Frosted Brownies

Debbie and Dale Roberts, Fitzgerald, Georgia (My great-nieces, who are now married and making wonderful homemakers)

½ cup margarine
3 tablespoons cocoa
2 eggs, beaten
1 cup sugar
¾ cup flour

½ teaspoon salt
½ teaspoon baking powder
½ cup chopped nuts
1 teaspoon vanilla
Frosting

Cream together the margarine and cocoa. Combine eggs and sugar; add to creamed mixture. Stir in other ingredients, except frosting. Bake in well-greased 8-inch square pan at 350 degrees for 25 minutes. Cut into 16 squares.

FROSTING

3 tablespoons milk	*3 tablespoons cocoa*
1 teaspoon butter	*Dash salt*
2 cups confectioners' sugar	*½ teaspoon vanilla*

Heat milk and butter. Combine sugar and cocoa. Add to milk. Stir in salt and vanilla. Spread over cooled cookies and cut in squares. Enough frosting for 16 brownies.

A very popular cookie, especially for holidays. They make a nice gift package, too.

Bourbon Balls

2 (12-ounces each) boxes vanilla wafers, finely crushed	*5 cups confectioners' sugar (sift if lumpy)*
2 cups cocoa	*1 teaspoon salt*
8 tablespoons light corn syrup	*6 cups chopped pecans or walnuts*
1 cup dark rum	
1 cup Bourbon	

Day before, combine wafers and cocoa. Stir in corn syrup, rum, Bourbon, 4 cups sugar, salt, and nuts. Roll into 1-inch balls. Roll balls in remaining sugar; let stand overnight. Next day, store in tightly closed container. 100 balls.

Charleston Squares

Mrs. Hermine Wolf, Atlanta, Georgia

1 cup flour	*2 tablespoons hot water*
1 teaspoon baking powder	*2 cups chopped dates*
½ teaspoon salt	*1 (12-ounce) package semi-sweet chocolate morsels*
2 eggs	
1 cup sugar	*1¼ cups chopped nuts*
1 tablespoon melted butter	

Sift together flour, baking powder, salt. Cream eggs and sugar, melted butter, and hot water; add dry ingredients and stir in dates, chocolate bits, and nuts. Bake in greased 8×10-inch pan at 350 degrees for 30 to 35 minutes. Cut into 20 squares.

Apricot Chews
Mrs. Dudley W. Garrett, Jr., Dunwoody, Georgia

½ cup finely cut dried apricots
½ cup golden or dark raisins
⅓ cup water
1 cup sifted regular or instant-blending all-purpose flour
1 teaspoon baking powder
¼ teaspoon soda
½ cup chopped walnuts
½ cup drained crushed pineapple
2 eggs
1 tablespoon lemon juice
1 cup granulated sugar
Confectioners' sugar

Cook apricots and raisins in water 8 to 10 minutes, or until tender. Drain well. Combine flour with baking powder and soda. Add walnuts, pineapple, and drained fruit to dry ingredients; stir to coat. Beat eggs with lemon juice in small mixing bowl just until foamy.

Gradually add sugar, beating just until blended. Fold in fruit-walnut mixture. Spread in well-greased 9-inch-square pan. Bake at 350 degrees for 35 to 40 minutes until golden brown.

Sprinkle with confectioners' sugar or granulated sugar. While warm, cut into bars. 24 bars.

Fruit-cake Cookies
Mrs. C. A. (Nelle) Estes, Ocilla, Georgia

½ cup butter
1 cup brown sugar
4 small eggs
2½ cups flour (save ½ cup for fruit)
½ pound candied cherries
½ pound candied pineapple
1½ pounds (6 cups) chopped nutmeats
2¼ cups white raisins
3 tablespoons milk
2 scant teaspoons soda
1 teaspoon ground cloves
1 teaspoon cinnamon
1 teaspoon nutmeg
1 (1-ounce) jigger whiskey or 2 tablespoons fruit juice

Cream butter and sugar; add eggs one at a time. Flour fruit, and combine all ingredients. Drop by teaspoonfuls on greased cookie sheet. Bake at 250 degrees about 35 minutes. Makes about 6 dozen.

Gingersnaps

Mrs. Wyatt Childs, Atlanta, Georgia

1 cup sugar	¼ teaspoon cloves
1 egg	2 teaspoons soda
¾ cup butter	4 tablespoons molasses
1 teaspoon ginger	2 cups flour
1 teaspoon cinnamon	

Combine all ingredients. Let stand in refrigerator at least an hour. (Sometimes it can be left a week.) Form into small balls about the size of a hazelnut. Roll in additional sugar, press lightly, and bake at 325 degrees until done—about 15 to 20 minutes. About 4 dozen cookies.

Lemon Yummies

Mrs. Harry Pippin, Barnesville, Georgia

1 cup shortening	1 tablespoon grated lemon rind
½ cup brown sugar	2 cups sifted flour
½ cup granulated sugar	¼ teaspoon baking soda
1 egg, well beaten	½ teaspoon salt
2 tablespoons lemon juice	½ cup chopped nutmeats

Cream the shortening and add the sugar gradually. Add the egg, lemon juice and rind, and mix well. Add the sifted flour, baking powder, salt, and nut meats. Mix thoroughly. Form into a roll about 2 inches in diameter, wrap in waxed paper, and chill in refrigerator. Cut into ¼-inch slices and bake on cookie sheets. Bake for 8 to 10 minutes at 400 degrees. About 4½ dozen cookies.

Male Cookies

Mrs. Ralph Roberts, Fitzgerald, Georgia
(The former Joyce Hartley—my eldest niece.)

¾ cup butter or margarine	1 cup chopped nuts
2 cups light brown sugar	1 teaspoon vanilla
2 eggs, beaten lightly	Dash salt
1 cup flour	

Cream together the butter and sugar. Add eggs and blend in flour. Add other ingredients. Bake in well-greased 9×9-inch pan at 300 degrees, 40 to 45 minutes. Cut into squares. 16 cookies.

Lizzies

Ms. Rosa Belle McDonald, Rufigio Plantation, Monroe, Louisiana

½ cup butter
1½ cups dark brown sugar
4 eggs
1 cup whiskey (Bourbon)
3 tablespoons sweet milk
5 cups flour
3 teaspoons soda
1 teaspoon each cloves, cinnamon, allspice, and nutmeg

2 pounds candied cherries (red and green)
2 pounds candied pineapple (red, green, and yellow)
1 pound dark raisins
1 pound white raisins
6 cups chopped pecans

Cream butter and sugar. Add eggs one at a time. Add whiskey and milk. Sift all dry ingredients (reserving ½ cup of flour for fruit) and blend with butter mixture. Cut up fruit and mix with ½ cup of flour before adding with nuts to mixture. Drop by teaspoonfuls on greased cookie sheet. Bake at 275 degrees for 12 minutes. Makes about 100.

Oatmeal Refrigerator Cookies

½ cup smooth or crunchy peanut butter
½ cup butter
2 cups firmly packed brown sugar
1 teaspoon vanilla

2 eggs
1¾ cups sifted flour
2 teaspoons soda
¾ teaspoon salt
1½ cups rolled oats
½ cup chopped nuts

Cream together peanut butter and butter. Add sugar gradually and cream together until light and fluffy. Add vanilla and eggs and beat well. Mix in flour sifted together with soda and salt. Then add rolled oats and nuts and shape dough into rolls about 2 inches in diameter. Wrap in waxed paper or plastic food wrap and chill in refrigerator. Slice about ⅛ inch thick, place on cookie sheet, and bake in moderate oven, 350 degrees, for about 15 minutes. 6 to 6½ dozen cookies.

Sweet Potato Cookies

Mrs. Harry Lutz, Albany, Georgia

1½ cups sugar	1 teaspoon cinnamon
1 cup shortening	½ teaspoon nutmeg
2 eggs, beaten	2 cups plain flour
2 cups mashed cooked sweet potatoes	1 teaspoon salt
	1 teaspoon cloves
1 teaspoon vanilla	½ cup broken nutmeats
4 teaspoons baking powder	2 teaspoons raisins, chopped

Cream sugar and shortening well. Add eggs and beat until smooth. Stir in mashed potatoes (no lumps) and the vanilla. Stir dry ingredients together and combine with nuts and raisins. Add to potato mixture. Drop by tiny spoonfuls on greased baking sheet. Bake at 375 degrees for 20 minutes. 6 or 7 dozen cookies.

A batch of these were usually to be found in a sideboard drawer in our dining room at home.

Old-fashioned Tea Cakes

½ cup butter or shortening	½ tablespoon vinegar
¾ cup sugar	2⅓ cups plain flour
1 egg	½ teaspoon salt
½ teaspoon soda	

Cream butter and sugar thoroughly. Add egg and beat well. Add soda, dissolved in vinegar.

Add flour, sifted with salt, gradually to make a stiff batter that can be rolled very thin. Cut with cookie cutter and bake in a moderate oven, 350 degrees, for 10 to 12 minutes. 3 dozen tea cakes.

Thumbprint Cookies

½ cup butter or margarine	1 cup sifted flour
¼ cup brown sugar	½ cup finely chopped nuts
1 egg, separated	Apple or currant jelly

Cream butter and sugar together until light and fluffy. Add egg yolk and beat well. Add flour and mix until well blended. Form into small balls about 1 inch in diameter.

Dip in slightly beaten egg white and roll in nuts. Place on cookie sheet about 3 inches apart. Bake in 350-degree oven for 10 minutes.

Remove from oven and with a teaspoon make a depression in center of each cookie. Return to oven and bake 5 minutes longer. When cookies are slightly cooled place a small amount of jelly in each depression.

Jelly will not melt, but will form a thin crust if placed when cookies are almost cool. Cookies will be more attractive if nuts are shaved instead of chopped as they will curl a little while baking. 18 to 20 cookies.

Toffee Treats

Ms. Jo Whitten, Macon, Georgia

1 cup butter or margarine
1 cup packed brown sugar
1 egg yolk
2 cups sifted all-purpose flour
1 teaspoon vanilla

1 (6-ounce) package
  semi-sweet chocolate pieces,
  melted
½ cup finely chopped nuts

Cream together butter, brown sugar, and egg yolk. Blend in flour and vanilla. Pat dough ½ inch thick on a greased jelly roll pan (17×14×1 inches). Cover with melted chocolate. Sprinkle nuts over top. Bake at 375 degrees from 15 to 20 minutes. Score while warm and cut when cool. 16 servings.

12

%%

BEVERAGES

A tasty beverage is refreshing. It may be a form of energy, it may complement our food, and many are suitable for social gatherings either large or small.

At times one may wish to add distilled spirits to a punch, but most beverages here are either milk, fruit, or tea based. There are so many from which to choose and so many preferences that the variety is unlimited.

I remember when we were small children and had our introduction to iced tea. (Ice was hard to come by during the summer if you lived in the country.) Mama served us all a glass of tea. No one really cared for it at that time, but my youngest of three brothers, Curtis, with grim determination, drained his glass to the last drop and in a quiet manner declared, "I am gonna learn to like that stuff." And he really did!

The following recipes have been used by many readers; a great many have been served in my own home. The Hartley egg nog is a Christmas must. On Christmas morning whoever gets up first lights the living room fire and I start the egg nog, which is served throughout the day. It has been served to hundreds of special party guests, too.

Spiced Cider Punch

Juice 5 lemons
1¼ pounds brown sugar
1 gallon sweet cider
1 quart hot tea
3 sticks cinnamon

1 tablespoon allspice
1 tablespoon whole cloves
2 pieces whole mace
½ teaspoon salt
5 oranges, sliced

Mix lemon, sugar, cider, and tea with the seasonings and boil 15 minutes. Add orange slices. Serve hot. About 40 half-cup servings.

Fruit Cup Punch

8 teaspoons tea leaves (or 8 tea bags)
2 cups boiling water
2 cups sugar
2 cups cold water
2 cups fresh lemon juice
1 pint strawberries, hulled and washed

1 large banana, sliced
½ fresh pineapple, cubed
2 oranges, peeled and sectioned
2 cups honeydew balls
1 (28-ounce) bottle ginger ale, chilled

Steep tea with boiling water 3 to 5 minutes; strain and add sugar, stirring until dissolved. Add cold water and lemon juice; chill. When ready to serve, pour tea mixture into a pretty punch bowl; add fruits and ginger ale. Serve in punch cups with wooden picks to spear fresh fruit. About 20 half-cup servings.

Ginger Coffee

1 cup crushed ice
½ pint vanilla ice cream, softened
1 teaspoon syrup from preserved ginger

⅛ teaspoon ground allspice
2 cups cold, double-strength coffee-with-chicory
Whipped cream
Preserved ginger

Preparing half the recipe at a time, in electric blender, combine ice, ice cream, syrup, allspice, and coffee-with-chicory; blend until smooth. Serve in tall glasses with whipped cream and ginger topping. 3 to 4 servings.

Orange Wassail

1 cup sugar
1 cup water
12 whole cloves
2 (2-inch) pieces stick
  cinnamon

3 quarts orange juice
1 quart cranberry juice cocktail
Baked Oranges

Combine sugar, water, and spices in saucepan; simmer 10 minutes. Remove cloves and cinnamon. Add orange juice and cranberry juice cocktail. Heat. Pour into heatproof punch bowl. Float Baked Oranges on punch. 34 half-cup servings.

Baked Oranges

Stud 3 oranges with cloves. Place in baking dish and bake in 325-degree oven for 3 hours.

Peach of a Shake

1 cup sliced fresh peaches
¼ cup unsweetened pineapple
  juice, chilled
¼ cup sugar

1 pint peach ice cream
¾ cup milk

The amounts given are for one blender load. Place peaches, pineapple juice, and sugar in blender. Blend at high speed until smooth. Add ice cream; blend until softened. Pour into chilled tall glasses. Add fresh peach slice for garnish. 2 servings.

Pineapple Lemonade

1 very large or 2 medium-size
  pineapples
1½ cups fresh lemon juice
All the lemon peels

2 quarts boiling water
2 cups sugar
1 cup diced fresh pineapple
1 dozen fresh strawberries

Wash and scrub pineapple with a brush. Peel pineapple and put peelings in a large bowl. From squeezed lemons, add lemon peels to pineapple peelings. Pour in boiling water, cover, steep 1 hour, and pour through a strainer to remove the peelings. Discard the peels. Add sugar and lemon juice to the pineapple water. Stir until sugar is dissolved. Add diced pineapple.

When ready to serve, place ice in a punch bowl. Pour in punch. Wash strawberries, cut in half, leaving the caps attached. Float over the surface of the punch. 2½ quarts. 20 half-cup servings.

Russian Tea

8 cups water	*3 oranges, squeezed*
1 tablespoon whole spice	*2 tablespoons tea leaves*
2 lemons, squeezed	*3 cups sugar*

Boil 4 cups water with spice 15 minutes. Boil other 4 cups with lemon and orange juice 15 minutes.

Put tea in water in which spice has been boiled. Let steep 2 or 3 minutes. Pour all together and strain. Add sugar. Serve hot. 8 servings.

Sparkling Tea Punch

4 cups strong hot tea	*1½ cups lime juice*
1½ cups sugar	*2 quarts sparkling water*
3 cups orange juice	*Orange and lime slices*

Combine tea and sugar and stir until sugar dissolves. Chill. Add fruit juices and pour over ice in punch bowl. Just before serving add sparkling water and float orange and lime slices on top. 35 half-cup servings.

Mr. Hansen Hillyer's Eye Opener

Savannah, Georgia

6 ounces light rum	*4 heaping teaspoons coconut*
2 ounces Cointreau	*malt*
1 tablespoon fresh lime juice	*1 cup cracked ice*

Put all ingredients in blender and add cracked ice; blend well, strain and serve. 4 ⅓-cup servings.

Watermelon Citrus Punch

3 quarts diced fresh watermelon
1⅓ cups fresh lemon juice
1⅓ cups fresh lime juice
2 cups fresh orange juice

1½ cups sugar
¼ teaspoon salt
Orange and lime slices

Put watermelon through a fine sieve. Add lemon, lime, and orange juices, sugar, and salt. Mix well to dissolve sugar thoroughly. Chill and serve in a punch bowl or watermelon bowl over ice. Garnish with sliced oranges and limes. 20 half-cup servings.

Champagne Punch

3 quarts fresh or frozen peach
  slices
1 fifth brandy
2 quarts strong tea

1 fifth light rum
1 quart soda water
2 quarts champagne

Let peaches stand overnight covered with brandy. When ready to serve, place a cake of ice in punch bowl and pour in tea, rum, soda water, and champagne over peaches and brandy. 40 three-ounce servings.

Hartley Egg Nog

6 eggs, separated
1 cup sugar
1½ cups Bourbon

¼ cup dark, heavy rum
1 quart heavy cream
Powdered nutmeg (optional)

Beat egg yolks until light: add two thirds of the sugar and beat until lemon-colored. Slowly add the Bourbon and rum, beating all the time.

Beat the egg whites (clean beater) and add remaining sugar, as if for meringue. Slowly pour liquor-egg mixture into the whites, folding gently. Whip the cream and fold into eggnog mixture. Serve in cups or mugs and add a sprinkling of nutmeg if desired.

If you are serving a crowd, it is best to make each batch separately for it should be mixed and served immediately. However, when serving large groups, we keep batches of beaten egg white, egg yolk-liquor mixture, and whipped cream in refrigerator ready for the next mixing. 12 one-cup servings.

Flaming Punch

3 oranges
Whole cloves
2 bottles dry red wine
1 fifth Bourbon
*1 tablespoon maple-blended
 syrup*

1 teaspoon nutmeg
1 teaspoon ground ginger
1 teaspoon cinnamon
1 teaspoon bitters

Stud the oranges well with whole cloves and roast at 350 degrees for about 20 minutes or until soft to the touch. Cut oranges into quarters, place in casserole or chafing dish.

Cover with wine, Bourbon, and maple-blended syrup. Add spices. Heat until steam begins to rise from mixture, but do not allow to boil.

Keep hot and flame just before serving. 30 half-cup servings.

Mocha Punch

1 cup freshly made coffee
2½ cups whipping cream
2 quarts chocolate ice cream
*¼ cup rum or 1 teaspoon
 almond extract*

¼ teaspoon salt
*Freshly grated nutmeg or grated
 sweet chocolate*

Prepare the coffee, chill well. Whip the cream until stiff. Reserve about a cup to garnish the tops.

Pour the chilled coffee into a large chilled bowl. Add 1 quart of the ice cream. Beat until the cream is partly melted. Add rum and salt. Fold in the remainder of the ice cream and the whipped cream. Pour the punch into tall glasses. Garnish the tops with the reserved cream. Sprinkle with nutmeg or sweet chocolate. 12 one-cup servings.

Creamy Hot Buttered Rum
Rod Carlyle, Atlanta, Georgia

½ cup brown sugar	1 cup heavy cream
½ cup melted butter	1 fifth light rum
Dash ground cloves	Hot water
3 dashes cinnamon	Freshly ground nutmeg

Combine brown sugar, butter, cloves, and cinnamon in saucepan. Place 1 teaspoon of the mixture in each cup. Add 2 tablespoons heavy cream to each cup along with 2 to 3 tablespoons light rum. Fill each cup with hot water and sprinkle with freshly ground nutmeg. Serve very hot. 24 half-cup servings.

A fine old southern beverage.

Syllabub

1 pint heavy cream	½ cup sugar
½ cup whole milk	½ cup dry sherry

Mix cream, milk, and sugar until sugar is well dissolved. Let stand 10 minutes, then add sherry. Whip with syllabub churn until foam is thick and heavy. An egg whip or nice clean willow switches or broom straws may be used instead of the syllabub churn.

Syllabub does not stand very well, and should be whipped and served immediately. Keep mixture cold for best success. 16 half-cup servings.

Brandied Citrus Wine Punch

Juice 4 lemons	1 fifth sauterne, chilled
2 cups fresh orange juice	1 (28-ounce) bottle sparkling
½ cup brandy	water, chilled
⅓ cup sugar	2 lemons, thinly sliced
1 fifth burgundy or claret, chilled	1 orange, cut into half slices

Combine lemon and orange juice with brandy and sugar; stir until sugar is dissolved. Pour citrus mixture over block of ice in punch bowl; add wines and sparkling water. Stir gently to blend. Garnish with lemon and orange slices; serve at once. About 40 half-cup servings.

Index